5,000 Years
of Korean Martial Arts

The Heritage of the Hermit Kingdom Warriors

R. Barry Harmon

R. Barry Harmon
Bay Area Kuk Sool Won
15230 Hwy 3
Webster, Tx. 77598
E-mail: kuksoolcl@yahoo.com

First published by Dog Ear Publishing
4010 W. 86th Street, Ste H
Indianapolis, IN 46268
www.dogearpublishing.net

dog ear PUBLISHING

ISBN: 978-159858-563-6

This book is printed on acid-free paper.

Printed in the United States of America

ACKNOWLEDGMENTS

I would like to express my heartfelt thanks to my parents, my wife, and to my mentor In Hyuk Suh, without whose help and support this book would not have come to pass; to Galadriel Nair, a friend whose help and expertise made it possible to take all my disassociated pieces of research and mold them into book form; to Master Oh, Yi Kuen who started me on the path of Kuk Sool, a true martial art in every aspect; to my brother-in-law, Lee, Hwa Nam, who allowed us to stay at his house for many months while I was gathering research for this book and to my brother-in-law, In Sun Seo from whom I learned many intricacies of Korean cultural family life.

I am additionally grateful to Ann Simanton for helping me prepare pictures for this book, and to the Boots family for giving me permission to use one of three remaining copies of Dr. John Boots' book on his collection of Korean traditional weapons. To Ken Hill for the front and back cover picture. For the help of many others too numerous to mention by name I offer my sincere appreciation.

NOTE TO READERS

Any mistakes in the research or information in this book is the total and complete responsibility of the writer. In no way should any contributors be held responsible for the writer's opinions or mistakes. For spelling of names and places I used the same spelling as the research material I obtained it from.

It is my greatest wish that readers of this book do not misunderstand the purpose of my writing. It may seem to some that I am attempting to denigrate Chinese and Japanese martial arts but nothing could be further from the truth. The history of Chinese and Japanese martial arts is well known and documented and needs no explanation. It is my goal to document the development and use of Korean martial arts and to place its history in proper perspective in relationship to Chinese and Japanese martial arts history. In doing so it may sometimes seem that I am one sided because I may not point out or elaborate on the Chinese or Japanese point of view.

Photos in this book were gathered from many historical places and material. Because of this the quality of the photo may not be very good in many pictures. I ask the readers understanding and indulgence with those photos of questionable quality.

Finally I hope this work will stimulate others to do more detailed and complete work on Korean martial art history.

DEDICATION

This book is dedicated to my family. My parents who never once tried to dissuade me from the pursuit of a martial art career; to my brother Hugh and my sisters Carol and Robin, who always seemed to know the importance of martial art in my life; to my beautiful wife Choon Ok Lee who supported me as a wife and partner; and my mentor, Grandmaster Suh, In Hyuk who taught me that I could accomplish anything if I put my mind to it, never give up, and pursue it with patience.

FOREWORD

After World War II and the Korean War, Asian martial arts started to be shown in America. These early demonstrations began a transformation within the American public that could not have been predicted. That transformation eventually flowed to me and ultimately had a profound impact on my life.

There was a time when I traveled from South Carolina to New York, some 13 hours one way, just to see Chinese martial art movies in Chinatown. I would drive up with a friend and watch several of these exciting films, then come straight back. My fascination with Asian martial art thought was overpowering. What was behind those piercing martial art eyes? I had to know!

A year after graduation from high school in 1969 I enlisted in the U.S. Air Force. Little did I suspect this would lead me to my life's work and love. After completing training as a security policeman, I volunteered for duty in Vietnam. Instead, I was sent to Korea. Unknown to me at the time, I was about to begin my life's journey into the Korean culture, its history, and martial arts.

I ended up at the U.S. Air Force base at Kunsan, South Korea. It was there that I was first introduced to the Korean traditional martial art of *Kuk Sool* by Master Oh, Yi Kuen. For two years I trained in this ancient art. It was at my black belt testing and promotion that I met Grandmaster Suh, In Hyuk for the first time. I had no idea what the future held for us. To me he was my instructor's teacher who taught only 4th degree black belts and higher which, I thought, put him way out of my reach.

After my discharge from the Air Force in 1974 I attempted to stay in Korea to study Kuk Sool but was unable to get a visa. I had no choice but to return home to South Carolina. Kuk Sool was not yet in the U.S., so I started a club. That was the only way I could keep in practice and not forget the techniques I had learned.

Upon receiving news that Grandmaster Suh had immigrated to the U.S. and was holding a seminar at Louisiana State University, I jumped on my Harley Davidson and roared out to Baton Rouge to meet him once again. He remembered me from Korea, and fortunately, with a letter of introduction from Master Oh, I was accepted as his second American student. I was later to become the first non-Korean to reach master level in Kuk Sool. I was given the Korean martial art name "Suh, Sung Sool" (*Sung Sool means: to achieve technical skill)* by Grandmaster Suh when he accepted me, and I began a martial art journey from the past that few will ever experience. Many years later I would receive a Korean Buddhist name "Ha, Il Moon" *(Il Moon means: first gate).*

My standing orders were to eat, sleep, and train. For five years I lived in Grandmaster Suh's school and followed those orders. At times it was very difficult and many people told me I was crazy and brainwashed, but I knew that it was a once-in-a-lifetime chance. I was determined to make the most of it, no matter how difficult.

My living in the school had to come to an end following my arranged marriage to Lee, Choon Ok, a Korean Kuk Sool instructor. Our wedding took place July 13, 1980, and we now have two beautiful daughters, Emerald Mi-Yong and Jada Mi-Ho.

In 1981 we opened our first Kuk Sool school in San Mateo, California, and we continue to train under Grandmaster Suh to this day. We have both taught and demonstrated Kuk Sool in many countries around the world, yet our martial art education goes on under the watchful eye of Grandmaster Suh.

With the encouragement of my mentor, I started college and earned my B.A. degree from San Francisco State University. Two years after that I received my acupuncture degree from the San Francisco College of Acupuncture and Oriental Medicine, providing me with a healing art traditionally obtained by high masters. The driving force for me to accomplish these studies was the fact that ancient martial artists were often scholars, and I wanted to follow the ancient tradition.

My interest in learning about martial arts expanded to the study of the historic roots of all martial arts traditions. To inspect the legacy of martial arts traditions more objectively, I decided to start with the history of Korean martial arts in depth. What better way to approach this than to go to its homeland? So I spent another two years in Korea collecting data and gathering research.

After my last sabbatical, I moved to Houston, Texas, in 1991, where I presently live with my family. I have dedicated my entire adult life to studying and practicing Korean martial arts. I have spent uncounted hours training my body and educating my mind. I truly believe that the martial arts, Kuk Sool in particular, have enriched and fulfilled my life in a way no other path could have.

As a small token of appreciation to my adopted culture that has given me ancient roots and the art that I love and admire, I humbly decided to write this book.

PREFACE

"... Simply to let the world know that our country always has been a land of hero-sages."

—Yi Kyu-bo (1168-1241)

Korea's most extensively lost history is that of her traditional martial arts. Because of the rigid neo-Confucian ideas of the last several hundred years, the attempted annihilation of Korean culture in the 20th century, and her own modern preoccupation with politics, the martial arts heritage of Korea that maintained her as an independent culture and country has been widely overlooked, forgotten, and misunderstood even by her own people. This unfortunate situation is partly due to the fact that very little of her martial art history is accessible or remains intact, either as artifacts or records. Information that is available is inclined to be biased, altered or blatantly false. Even the accuracy of her old records tended to be influenced by the powers of the times in which they were written.

The fact that Korea is still an independent country and culture, attests to the power of her traditional martial arts. The importance of this knowledge, closely guarded as secret throughout time, has often been overlooked or forgotten in the modern era. Powerful techniques were handed down through oral tradition from teacher to student for generations. Weaponry and weapon making were also passed on in this same manner. With almost nothing written to verify the oral tradition, we face an enormous problem today when investigating ancient Korean martial arts. However, we should also not overlook another important source of validation for the accuracy of Korea's oral history—-the rich oral tradition of all of Asia through which instruction in every art passed. While many Westerners give greatest credence to the printed word, Asian masters recognized that the highly trained memories of their many students were the safest repositories of knowledge. When we consider how defenseless the written word is in the hands of revisionists and censors, contrasted with the survival through to the present of ancient oral teachings, it seems wise to regard the reliability of oral history as seriously as do the great Asian teachers and cultures.

Writings on Korean history often miss the mark on martial arts. Some common examples include these statements found in contemporary martial art journals and books:

- The military training function of the famed Hwarang cult (predating the Japanese samurai) was only a "concept" which "did not become prominent until after World War II."
- "A great deal of Korea's culture, including much of its martial arts prowess, originated in China."
- "Koreans were indifferent swordsmen and used swords designed by the Chinese."
- "Few Koreans have had the heart for warfare."
- "If given the chance, Koreans ran."

These are just a few of the statements commonly offered as fact concerning Korean martial arts that are absolutely untrue and misleading.

In the last few decades we have seen history rewritten in many areas where new research and deeper reexamination have shown a need for revision of entrenched perspectives. In the field of martial art studies we find clarification is needed in many areas, particularly concerning the martial arts lineage of Korea. This is a country whose great heritage has been heavily obscured, repeatedly attacked, and competing political and philosophical interest have stripped Korea of features of its history which they have found counter-productive to their goals. Korea's martial arts tradition which threatened the influence of invading ideologies was hardest hit.

Many researchers, unaware of the extent to which recorded Korean history has been altered or destroyed, identify martial arts in Korea as essentially imported, even before the popularization of more current Japanese-based techniques. As a result, there is a conclusion fairly prevalent that there is little or no martial arts heritage indigenous to the country. This persists despite the fact that Korea shares the same reverence for the skills and accomplishments of its ancestors in every other field as do all Asian nations. In addition, the country's capacity for distinctiveness in every aspect of its culture is widely acknowledged. Many Korean martial art innovations have been exported and copied by her larger neighbors for centuries.

It is my hope that this book will make obvious the many facts still on record of Korea's tremendous martial arts spirit, giving readers insight into the existence of an intrinsically Korean martial tradition and its unique standing as a direct product of the Korean culture and its people. As a professional martial artist committed to the passing down of Korea's achievement in martial arts, I feel a responsibility to help bring it and its lifestyle out of the historical fog which has obscured its legitimacy. By sharing the sources and research I have gathered over many years, I believe it will become obvious that an unbroken lineage exists in Korean martial arts, that the Korean martial arts heritage is not derived or borrowed from its neighbors any more than the skills of these countries were based on imported knowledge, and that the Koreans actually were innovators in many areas of military development, including weapon-making, arms, armored warships, and the military lifestyle that was the forerunner of the *samurai* and *bushido* in Japan, to name only a few.

Furthermore, it is my goal to show that the Koreans were fighters as much as fortifiers, with a long roster of heroes who sought honor on the open battlefield and at sea, regardless of personal peril.

When investigating the origins of anything Korean, we are always at the mercy of the depleted and limited quantity of sources. The legacy of the Confucian-dominated Yi Dynasty's disinterest and even disdain of military arts, followed by the decades of Japanese colonial repression, had a devastating impact on Korean martial arts, pushing them to the brink of extinction. Historical records that were determined to be controversial were good candidates for rewriting, for careless storage where they would deteriorate, or for outright destruction.

While the records of nearby conquering nations abound with their own specific details on martial arts, Korea's records have what initially may appear as very peculiar gaps in this regard for a nation almost continually—and, until the 19th century, successfully—on the defensive. Despite the survival of documentation on arms from the prehistoric period forward, and of heroic legends about its armed struggles, Korean warriors have taken a back seat in modern times to those of other nations in terms of martial history. This was due in part to those hostile interpreters of history wanting to build up their own nation's image or tear down Korea's. If we go back to 12th century Koryo (as Korea was then known) we can find another potential source of censorship that explains the scarceness of documentation from early times. Records in Korea were then in the hands of the Confucians. Being strongly anti-military, they would not have been interested in preserving many of the military records of previous times, especially as these documents contained specific information regarding combat techniques or glorifying martial arts history. The specter of these biased sources, burned manuscripts and altered texts hangs over anything Korean that passed through times of invasion and occupation. It is one of the points that make research on Korean martial arts trying and difficult.

Indigenous Korean martial arts masters themselves have, by their traditional protectiveness of the art, contributed to the shortage of available information on ancient techniques and their evolution. Manuscripts of the ancient masters were, understandably, kept hidden in the days when their art embodied the great secrets of national defense and keys to personal advancement in the military and society. It was feared they might fall into the hands of invaders, evil-doers, competitors or just the inept.

Today, many martial artists continue to closely guard what has been passed down. This is frustrating for anyone seeking the significance of the Korean style and system of martial arts throughout history. Also, because of such secrecy, scholars often prefer to ignore claims that a Korea-born body of information truly exists since they have never seen it. When Korean martial arts masters further attribute to such "invisible" manuscripts a metaphysical depth, pragmatic scholars tend to discount their existence even more.

The fact that so much energy has been put forth by so many to keep certain aspects of indigenous Korean martial arts a closely guarded secret only validates the importance of this knowledge. Further, the fact that in the past so many have tried to destroy or steal this information gives a strong indication of its importance.

There is another very significant roadblock in the way of directly determining the original nature of Korean combat methods, philosophy, and way of life. The classical Asian character writing (now identified as Chinese but once universal throughout Asia) in which some still-surviving records were written, is very difficult to interpret. Most of the old references to Korean martial arts which have survived the trials and tribulations of Korean history cannot be translated correctly by most modern martial art masters or scholars. Not only are they written in a difficult poetical language with very subtle meanings but one must also be very skilled in the highest level of martial arts techniques in order to interpret them correctly. The only martial artist this author knows that can correctly translate the old poetry language is Kuk Sool Won Grandmaster Suh, In Hyuk.

Beyond doubt, the most devastating blow not only to the reputation of Korean martial arts but to its very existence was the invasion of the Japanese and their occupation of the country at the end of the 19th century and through decades of the 20th century. Isolated by choice from the rest of the world prior to the "Occupation," the Koreans had hidden their culture from Western nations who had no idea of what the Imperial Japanese had set out to obliterate. The invaders remodeled martial arts in Korea to suit their own objectives, which included indoctrinating Koreans with the impression that anything Korean was inferior to its corresponding art in Japan. Since Korean martial arts were supposed to be of lesser value, various types of Japanese martial arts were introduced and Koreans were only allowed to practice those. For several generations most Koreans lost the connection to their martial art heritage.

Under foreign occupation, inquiries made by visitors as to the origins of various techniques and histories were liable to be given highly biased or incorrect answers. If we examine Korean martial arts in the 20th century, for example, we quickly realize how the Japanese invasion of Korea impacted the survival of ancient references regarding the history of this art, considered highly subversive by occupying forces. The systematic attempt of the Japanese of that era to force Koreans to surrender their national identity along with their homeland was traumatic to Korean record keeping. Undoubtedly, it resulted in the loss of many Korean research materials related to indigenous fighting arts. It has been passed down orally that to resist the Japanese during their takeover, the Koreans would rally around ideas based in their history, most prominently the "*Hwarang* spirit." So we can easily imagine how invaders would consider very undesirable continued access for Koreans to any writings mentioning and supporting this martial spirit and Korea's "Art of the Warrior."

As part of the ongoing effort of the Japanese to erase Korean culture, the usage of the term "do" (way) entered the Korean lexicon to describe martial arts training. Its use became so common that today in the West, "do" is regarded as a Korean word to describe Korean martial arts. However, it is contrary to historical and cultural usage and does not reflect the way Koreans traditionally viewed martial arts or the place it held in their lives. (Hulbert's History of Korea, pg. ED98)

Ancient Korean martial arts training was never referred to as a "way" but by various names, usually with words meaning "technique," "skill" or "art." Pre-modern records do not contain word combinations like *moodo* ("martial way") and *kumdo* ("sword way"). Instead, pre-colonial Koreans would have used *moo-yea* ("martial art") or *moo-sool* ("martial skill"). *Kumdo* ("sword way") would have been *kum-sool* ("sword skill") and *yudo* ("fluid way") would have been *yu-sool* ("fluid skill"). The development of body and spirit required specific techniques in the Korean system, and would have been directly identified as such, not as a "way." The original *do* of *Hwarang-do* ("flower of youth group"), correspondingly, is a character meaning "group, circle or order" rather than another character meaning "way", which is the common method of translation today.

Another example of colonial influence may be seen by studying the development of *Tae Kwon Do*. Tae Kwon Do is widely believed to be a continuation of *Tae Kyun* and *Soo Bahk Ki*, but evidence to the contrary has been found since the name was first used in the late 1950s and early 1960s—-and after which *do* became identified with Korean fighting arts. Incorrect translations of the ancient text *Mooye Tobo Tong-ji (An Illustrated History of Korean Martial Arts)* referring to the term *do* is not uncommon and helps to propagate the incorrect history.

Self-serving translations have been commissioned by regimes with agendas opposed to the traditional Korean martial spirit and by individuals wishing to further their own personal interests. These have done a great disservice to Korean history by emphasizing outside influences and minimalizing indigenous culture. Understanding the colonial influence is important not as part of an argument over what style is older or better but to make clear the distinct differences of historical standing. The unique nature of the Korean fighting system and its impact on other martial arts becomes obvious only after intense research.

By logical inferences and deductions made from an abundance of evidence and clues, I hope to add to the strong case for the recognition of Korea's original martial art heritage and its vast contribution to her own culture. One of the more obvious indications that Korea had its own powerful and secret martial arts is the fact that it otherwise would have been annexed by an invading country centuries ago. Recognizing this provides us with a better understanding of the strength of Korea's cultural institutions to survive regardless of adversity and despite attempts by foreign militarists of the times to erase their achievements.

Even an inference can be made to support the integrity of a unique Korean martial arts tradition by examining the consistently different styles among the Koreans, Chinese, and Japanese in other cultural areas. For example, the preservation of identity can be seen in each country's language. In both language and performance of martial arts movements, the Korean preference is obvious for the curved and flowing joined with the straight and sudden. The Chinese language is fluid, almost flowery, much like their martial arts movement. The Japanese language is much more sharply defined in the way it is spoken which also reflects the type of movement in the Japanese martial arts.

In the modern era, with development of sophisticated weaponry, the need for martial arts to protect countries has all but vanished on battlefields. To many, an art like Korea's may seem like an anachronism. Others, fascinated at first with its form, may eventually experience its deeper layers which are still very relevant to people in today's world. For those who look beneath surface appearances, I have great expectations that the integrity and distinctiveness of Korean martial arts will become apparent in these pages.

There are those of us in search of
the Forgotten Knowledge,
while others search for
the Undiscovered Knowledge.
—R. Barry Harmon

CONTENTS

Acknowledgments iii

Note to Readers iv

Dedication v

Foreword vi

Preface viii

Chapter 1. The Genesis of Korea's Martial Arts Heritage 1
Chapter 2. The Three Kingdoms and the Rise of Martial Societies 18
Chapter 3. Unified Korea Integrates Martial Prowess 61
Chapter 4. Personal Power, Puppet Kings, and the Mongol Wars 79
Chapter 5. Confucianism, Foreign Intervention Impact "Land of the Morning Calm" 110
Chapter 6. Admiral Yi Sun-Sin: The "Admiral Nelson of Asia" 142
Chapter 7. Japanese, Manchurian Invasions Redefine Korean World View .167
Chapter 8. Beyond Tolerable Limits: The Rupture of 19th Century Korean Sovereignty 175
Chapter 9. New Perspectives on Korean Weaponry, Armor, and Fortresses 191

BIBLIOGRAPHY 228

1 The Genesis of Korea's Martial Arts Heritage

To begin defining the lineage of Korea's martial arts, we need to look back 5,000 years ago to the region where the Korean people have continuously lived since prehistory. For any cultural tradition to develop and survive over such a long period, certain elements are required. One of these is ethnic continuity—a way of life that endures, generation after generation, enabling people to pass down their ancient knowledge, skills, and traditions to those that follow. Maintaining this way of life in Korea for scores of centuries would not have been possible without the development and passing down of fighting techniques successfully used against invaders. This defensive capability would, of necessity, be guarded with secrecy, preserved for its efficacy, and revered by generations for its crucial role in sustaining and safeguarding a homeland.

Ancient warrior horseman with bow and arrow.

Among the reasons Koreans developed and preserved their own distinctive fighting style were Korea's well-known fierce nationalism and its far-from-passive convictions regarding its cultural preeminence among neighboring countries. With these considerations, there can be no question that an original and distinctive Korean martial art lineage exists, despite centuries of attempts to alter or destroy it.

Any culture subject to frequent attack has persisted in its homeland only because knowledge of defensive techniques has also endured. These techniques acquire their individuality in many ways, principally formed by habitat, climate, philosophy, and the offensive styles of its traditional aggressors. As internal and external threats were never far from the attention of Koreans, their fighting men would not have been likely to abandon a body of skills proven successful in meeting repeated challenges over many years. This is especially true considering the affinity of all Asian cultures for passing down the teachings and wisdom of their forefathers.

With Korea, its period of occupation in the 19th and 20th centuries by a foreign country—and several centuries of influence by an anti-military philosophy—represent small parcels of time under unusual circumstances. It's less than likely that Korea could have survived for five millennia, bordered by aggressive nations such as China and Japan, without a strong martial arts legacy to rely upon for national defense. In search of the origins of this legacy we look as much for signs of well-defended cultural persistence as we do for artifacts and documents. This search must extend to the farthest boundaries of the Korean people and the full extent of their range during various eras.

The Korea of today is of relatively new, politically defined dimensions. For thousands of years, neither its history nor the people who made it were confined to the borders demarcated on a contemporary map. Korean historian Kee-baik Lee noted that the entire region of what is now southern Manchuria, as well as the Korean peninsula, was the "arena in which Korean Bronze Age man played out his historical role." (Lee, 1984) Ancient records show that at the height of the Koguryo Kingdom's expansion in the 5th century, Korea extended beyond the Yalu River to the Liao and Sungari rivers far south.

The identification of all cultural artifacts and traditions on the north side of the Yalu River as Chinese has been a disservice done more than once to Korean history. (Similarly, for example, another people, the Tibetans, repeatedly have had to defend many aspects of their culture against Chinese claims that they were Chinese in origin.) For this reason, the changing maps of Korea's past need to be consulted as the accomplishments of its civilization under various empires are tracked. The ancient Koreans who shaped the culture of later societies are known to have inhabited for centuries the land now politically designated as Manchuria and northern China with its rivers such as the T'ung-chia, Tumen, and the more northerly waterways that feed what was once the homeland of the Korean people.

A legend concerning their first ruler illustrates the ancient extended boundaries of the original Koreans. It is the story of Tan-gun (also Wang-gum), the Lord of the Pak-Tal Tree. He is said to have been born of the breath of Whan-ung, the Spirit King, upon a bear, who had been transformed into the first woman as a reward for her faith and patience during a divine test. A son resulted, Tan-gun, who was found years later still under the pak-tal tree where he was breathed into existence, awaiting discovery by members of the Nine Wild Tribes, the Ku-i, whose land was demarcated as extending from present-day Korea through the territory immediately north. Historians say that these were the original inhabitants of all this land and that "Tan-gun" may also stand for a dynasty of chieftains, the first martial commanders of Korea. (Jeong-hak Kim, 1972)

The bear cult, at the core of the Tan-Gun legend, descended from the Paleolithic period and is still prevalent among the Ainu and some tribes in Siberia. The Stone slabs in the Wu family shrine are proof that the legend was not formed at the time of the Mongol invasion of Korea, as has been suggested by some Japanese scholars. The Wu family may have been part of the tribe belonging to the Korean people or of a tribe close to the Northeast Asian people. (Lee, 1993)

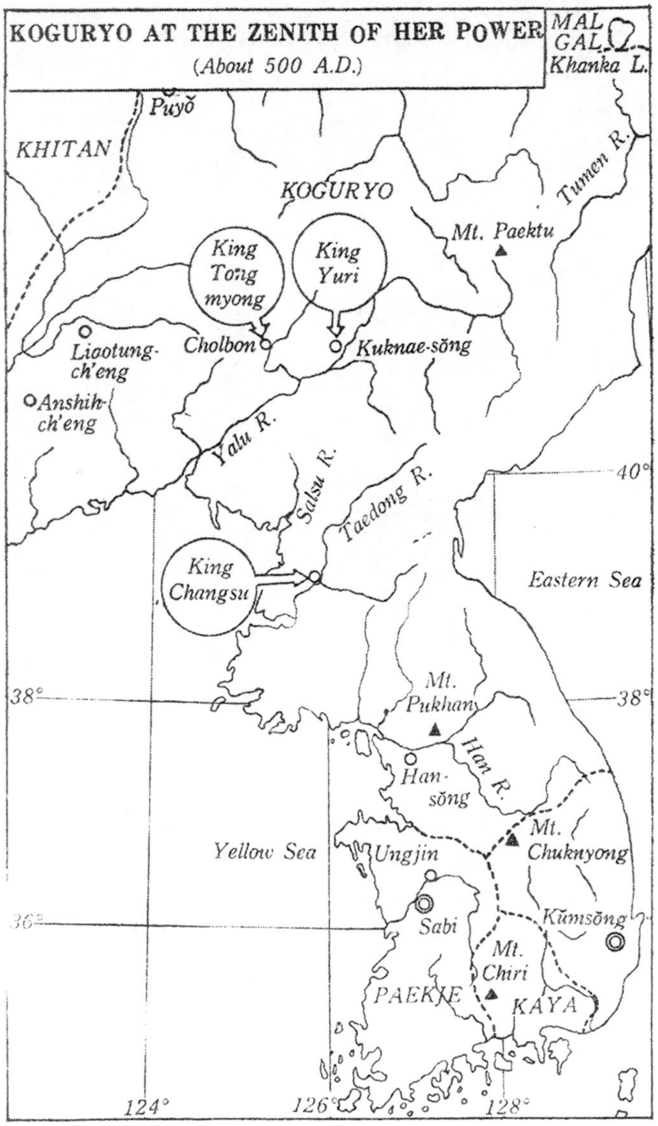

Koguryo at the height of her expansion when she occupied much of Manchuria and northern China.

Emperor Tangoon, Father of Korea

It was a long time ago. Hwan-in was God of Heaven and had many sons. The greatest of them all was Hwan-oong.

One day, Hwan-oong confided a secret to Hwan-in. "Father," he confessed, I want to go down to earth and become the king of men!"

"So be it, my son," his father agreed, and he began to look for a suitable place to send Hwan-oong.

He discovered a marvelous spot near Mount Taebaek in what we now call Korea. God of Heaven was satisfied with the place he found and called his son to his side.

"Hwan-oong," he said, "I bestow upon you these sacred symbols of royalty. Now you, too, are a king." He presented his son with a mirror, a sword and a bell. He assigned three thousand heavenly assistants to help with the work on earth.

King Hwan-oong went right to work. He called in the wind god, the rain god and the god of the clouds. He explained to them how to do their important work. Within a brief time, the new king brought peace and order to all the earth. Hwan-oong accomplished 360 great tasks that men could not do for themselves, one for every day of the lunar year.

A tiger and a bear lived outside Hwan-oong's city and one day they visited the king.

"We want to become people," pleaded the two. "If you change us into humans we'll do anything you ask."

King Hwan-oong thought a minute. He commanded servants to bring him mugwort and cloves of garlic.

"If you want to become human," the king directed, "You must eat bitter mugwort and hot garlic. You have to go into the cave by my palace and endure the darkness for 100 days without coming out even once."

The hot-tempered tiger didn't last very long. He dashed out of the cave in frustration after a week or two. But the bear managed to endure for 100 endless days. She turned into a beautiful maiden named Bear Woman.

Bear Woman wanted to marry and have children of her own.

Every day she trudged to a tall spirit tree near King Hwan-oong's altar and prayed for a husband and children.

King Hwan-oong fell in love with Bear Woman.

"Will you be my queen?" he asked her.

"Yes," she said, "Of course."

Soon a healthy and handsome prince was born to the royal couple. He was the image of his father and grew into a gallant and brave young man.

He succeeded his father to the throne, becoming Emperor Tangoon, father of Korea.

Tangoon established his capital at Pyongyang and named his country Chosun, Land of the Morning Calm.

Under the noble rule of Emperor Tangoon, Chosun enjoyed peace, and the people prospered beyond their dreams.

And that is how Korea came to be.

The First of Korea's Self-Defensive Societies

It is known that in the Neolithic period, ancestors of the people now called Koreans lived communally and were clan-centered. (Lee, 1984) The clan community village was an independent and self-sufficient entity. Reference is made to these ancient hunters in Korean legends such as the stories of the Six Villages of the King, Pak Hyokkose, bound together by blood lines. These were gleaned from records of the Shilla era.

Wherever there is an exclusive group, there is a corresponding exclusive territory staked out by that group from which it draws its vital sustenance. Sooner or later circumstances possibly including a shift in animal migration patterns or change in weather compels another group to broaden its hunting-gathering range. Inevitable contact between different groups causes various types of problems. When problems occurred, a payment for damages was prescribed, and in these Neolithic times when payment wasn't enough, conflict arose. This required the development of fighting techniques and various weaponry to defend territories.

From the Korean people's Neolithic period, archaeologists have found spearheads and arrowheads, as well as the bows that once propelled them. Both were used for hunting and in self-defense against animals and invading tribes. The presence of spears logically leads to the supposition that use of a staff pre-dated these stone types. This implies a stabbing motion had already been developed, the potentials of spearing techniques had been explored, both genesis techniques in the histories of all original martial arts cultures. These indigenous hunters did not wait around for visitors from the north, east, south or west to teach them how to survive food shortages or feuds. Like other groups later to coalesce into politically defined countries, they founded their own martial arts.

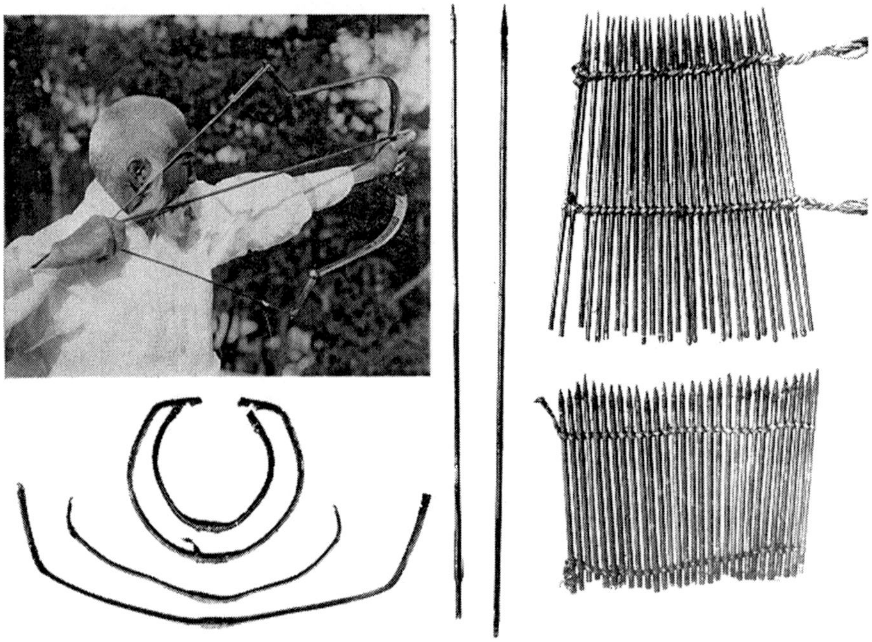

Pictured are several size ancient bows.
The arrows are wrapped together in a typical method
used for battlefield convenience.

Masters Harmon demonstrate two of many Kuk Sool archery postures.

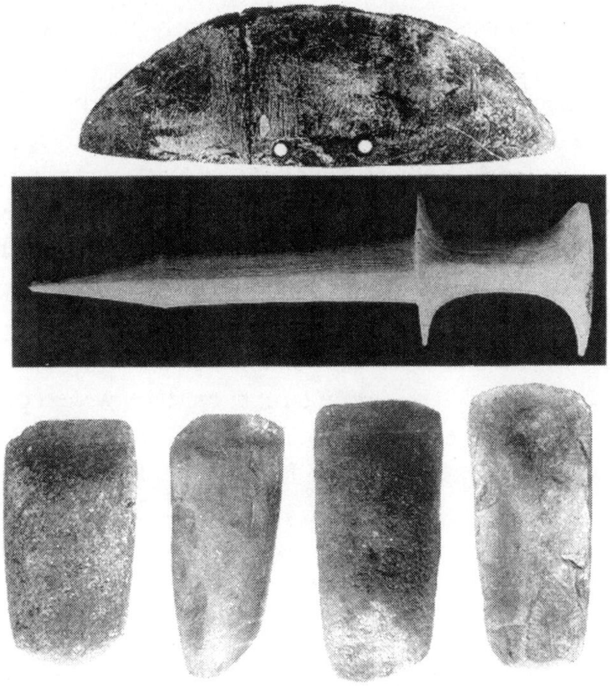

Some of the oldest weapons found are made of stone and bone.

Masters Harmon demonstrates the staff, one of the oldest weapons known that dates back to the beginning of humans using weapons.

Koreans have a term for the skills acquired by their early people: *sado moo sool* (clan or tribal martial skills). This, in itself, is indicative of the early prominence given to their fighting techniques. In a description of the people of Eastern Okcho, east of the great mountains of Kaema in Koguryo, it is seen how adept martial artists came into being. Their land, fair and fertile, facing the sea with its back to the mountains, was well suited to cultivation of grain, and they became good at tilling and planting. Simple and direct, strong and brave, they had few oxen and horses so became adept at fighting on foot, easily capable of wielding spears with accuracy. Perhaps Sado Moo Sool became well refined with tribes such as this. Today's Korean martial art of Kuk Sool Won still teaches the techniques that were once Sado Moo Sool so that it will be preserved for future Koreans and the world.

The people of Ye, a state continuous with Chinhan on the south (Lee, 1993), made spears so long they were sometimes carried by three men at once. They were capable foot soldiers and worshiped the tiger to provide strength. This is one of the first known references that show the Koreans have always related themselves to the Tiger spirit. The sandalwood bow of Lo-lang comes from their land.

The people of the Han, south of Tai-fang, were renowned for their personal courage and ruggedness. They pierced their bodies with large ropes or wooden poles to be joined together with others in certain community tasks. (Lee, 1984)

Grandmaster Suh shows empty hand martial art that preceded the use of weapons.

Reinforcing the continuity of a Korean martial arts tradition is the shared vision of both Korean martial artists of today and of Neolithic times as people identified with the natural world. Both drew strength from this outlook. Neolithic Koreans had animistic beliefs. They believed that, as humans have souls, so does every object in the natural world, and each is indivisible from its Creator. Even today Kuk Sool masters sometimes send their students into nature where they may feel strongly grounded to life in its many forms. In such a setting, their receptivity to spiritual sources is expected to be enhanced.

It is believed that early Neolithic clans formed distinct communities that developed representative governments by settling all matters in clan assemblages. Historians widely believe that a legacy of this custom can be seen in the Council of Nobles of the later Shilla Kingdom, indicating a descent of cultural traditions most certainly including those systems of defense and offense successful in preserving their government from hostile foreign influences.

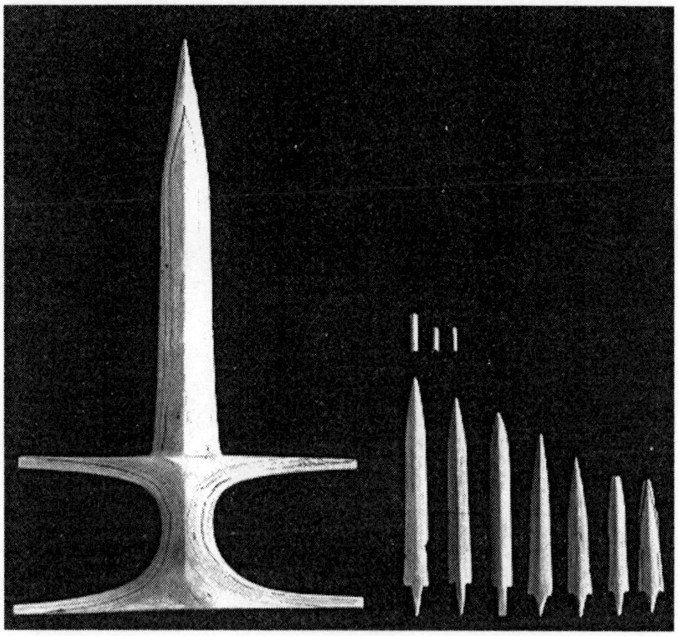

Jade daggers were property of the ruling class because only the elite could afford jade.

Bronze Age Weapons Unique to Old Korea

At about the eighth-ninth centuries B.C., a period of about four hundred years of cultural continuity began. It was identified by the use of bronze implements in a region that extended from the Sungari and Liao river basins in what is now called China and Manchuria, down through the Korean Peninsula. The bronze culture of this era was discovered to be a unitary and independent development of the people of the region. (Kim, 1972) Consider the implications of this analysis by historians. It logically follows that the Koreans, who have rarely been given credit for the invention and development of their own fighting system, did indeed develop their own weapons and fighting techniques. Conquest by warfare has been identified as a hallmark of Korea's Bronze Age. Weaponry of that era is regarded as having been independently developed by Koreans. Correspondingly, we know that ancient Koreans had the capacity to develop skills unique to the use of their weapons. Additionally, history indicates that their military arts were so effective that they sustained their culture and independence for 400 years before successfully evolving an even more efficient form.

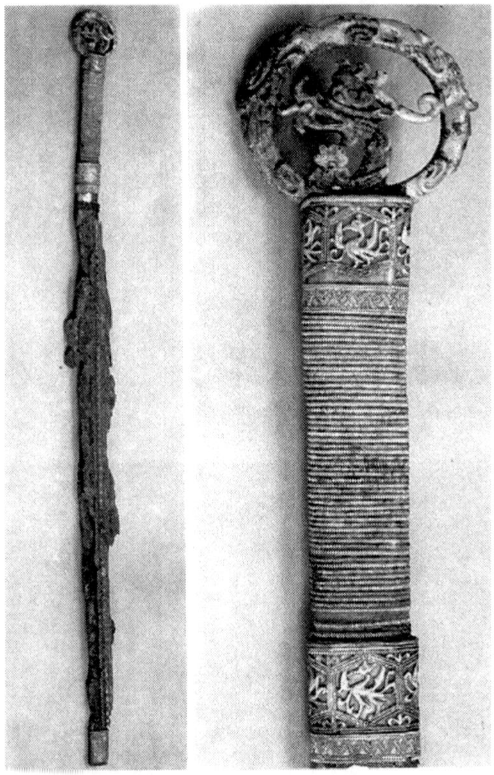

This sword with the hilt of a gilt-bronze single dragon pommel was found in the tomb of Paekche King Muryong (AD 501-523) which was discovered in the Kongju area.

Two typical bronze implements in use at this time were the mandolin-shaped dagger, decorated with geometric designs, and the multi-knobbed, coarse-lined mirror. Archaeologists characterized both as indigenous to this region. (Kim, 1972) As clans and conquerors multiplied and clashed, the development of indigenous types of weaponry and a corresponding fighting style were well on their way.

Historians connect the cultures of the Korean Bronze and Neolithic peoples through the repetition of geometric cross-hatching designs on their artifacts and also through similar styles of pottery. It is logical to assume historical continuity between Neolithic and Bronze Age Koreans in other important elements of their culture, including the martial arts. Anthropologists consider the ethnic stock of the Neolithic people as continuing unbroken to form one element of the later Korean race. In the course of a long process, these Neolithic people merged with each other, combining with the new ethnic groups of Korea's Bronze Age and eventually coming to constitute what we now think of as the Korean people. Gradually the Bronze Age people advanced their culture and became the arbiters of new societies as they developed in the area. (Kim, 1972)

Bronze Age artifact of Korean origin.

Bronze Age weapons were not widespread in ownership after their invention. They were considered precious articles, difficult to obtain, and were held by a privileged few whose possession symbolized authority. This gives us an indication that Korean society was beginning to be divided into classes. Stone tools were widely used in the Bronze Age. Bronze implements were reserved for weapons, sacrificial vessels, and ornaments. During this period there was a dual social structure in which status was developed and the seeds of political power sown in the peninsula. (Lee, 1993) Exclusive ownership of bronze weapons made their possessors part of a circle that was given special training in their use. Those that didn't own them had less refined fighting techniques. This inevitably created a class that was in control and that kept its martial art knowledge secret to maintain its authority.

The successors of the tribal chieftains of the Neolithic period carried on the traditions of leadership from their bases in walled towns, created to protect their increasingly plentiful harvest and spoils of war. These fortifications, representing a need to secure their expanding sense of territorial wealth, were the first strong forms of state structure to exist in Korea. Their influence is believed to have extended to the neighboring agricultural lands that surrounded the fortifications. There was only one way they could control the population in these expanding territories, and that was through power backed by varied and versatile martial art skills and weaponry.

Picturo of a partially restored fortification on Kanghwado Island, which was used many times over the centurles for national defense.

Eventually, fortified towns began to multiply and form the basis of small city-states. In the northern regions, several smaller states had developed their powers and societies to the point where their existence was known even in China. In the northern region, Puyo arose in the Sungari River basin. Yemaek developed along the middle reaches of the Yalu, along with Imdun in the Hamhung plain on the northeast coast. Chinbon arose in the vicinity of Hawanghae province and Chin, south of the Han River. The most advanced of these was Old Choson, which spread across the basins of the Liao (now in northern China) and the Taedong rivers where bronze artifacts have been abundant.

Old Choson originally included P'yong-yang, the capital city of the legendary Tan-gun. Its early leaders are believed to have borne the title *Tan'gun Wanggom*. Ultimately, Old Choson combined with other walled-town states between the Taedong and Liao rivers, until a single large confederation was formed and ruled by a king. The military prowess of this first confederated kingdom was so great that records show it was capable of mounting an attack on the North Chin state of Yen (China) on the other side of the Liao River. It is also recorded that Yen complained of the leaders of Old Chosen as being arrogant and cruel. This suggests that Old Chosen had developed formidable strength as an independent power in northeast Asia. (Kim, 1972)

Koreans Invent Exclusive Iron Weaponry

During the fourth century B.C. in Korea, two new metals, iron and bronze, rose to prominence in weapon making. The Taedong River region was the hub of this activity. Korean weapons and their use not only spread south from here, but also crossed the sea to Japan. There this form of Korean weaponry became central to the rise of the Yayoi culture. (Kim, 1972)

In this manner, history shows yet another of the major cultural influences Korea had on Japan, particularly in the area of martial arts. The movement of ironwork from Korea to Japan during this time is one of the earliest records we have that demonstrates the strong cultural impact of Korea on Japan. Clearly, Korean culture had a substantial influence on the early development of Japanese arms and art. The widely held belief that the cultural influence went exclusively from East to West is not supported by the historical evidence. There was also a Japanese importation of arts from Korea during that era, specifically in the Yayoi culture. The Plain Pottery Culture of southern Korea had a strong influence in the ceramics, stone artifacts, and burial systems in northern Kyushu in the Late and Final Jomon communities there. (Kim, 1972)

New forms of bronze daggers, spear points, and spears have also been retrieved from among fourth century B.C. artifacts found in the Taedong River region. A type of short and finely wrought bronze dagger (known as the *sehyong tonggom*), together with the bronze spear are unique in design to this area, and are not found among the artifacts of neighboring people. Due to the presence of horse trappings, axle caps, and other parts of horse-drawn vehicles, we know that delivery of these weapons to their targets could be affected by a mounted elite of soldiers. (Kim, 1972) The presence of Chinese coins among these artifacts is indicative of the ongoing activities of merchants through these North Asian lands. However, presence of commercial trade does not necessarily imply an exchange of military techniques. The exclusivity of weapons found only in what was then Korean territory shows a well-formed consciousness of independent ethnicity and cultural identity that undoubtedly embraced the accumulated treasure of its own martial arts.

The techniques for fighting with weapons such as swords and spears are as fundamental to a culture as the weapons themselves and their method of manufacture. Unfortunately, sword techniques cannot leave evidence of their existence in the same way as artifacts made of metal and clay. However, when we discover relics from Korea's far past, we know the martial arts techniques that went with them had to exist, as surely as dinosaur bones once had flesh. Numerous molds for casting bronze and iron have been found in the region of Old Choson, suggesting that this new metal culture was also not imported but indigenous. (Kim, 1972) One such example from Korea's Iron Age is the survival of the *ondol*. The Korean people of the Iron Age used this system of heating with an arrangement of flues under the floor, remainders of which can be seen in ruins today.

Various bronze weapons and ornaments from ancient times.

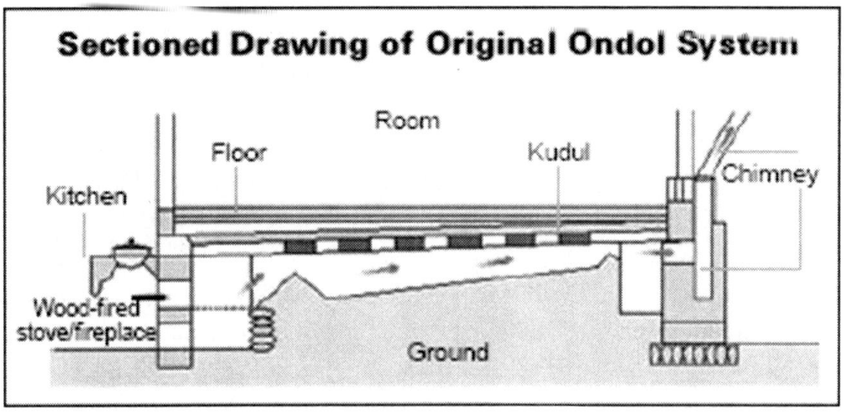

A drawing of the ondol system illustrates how the system works.

The ondol is still used in Korea, evidence that what continues to work for a culture is not abandoned, although written records of its more controversial traditions may be destroyed or rewritten by enemies.

This picture shows a wood burning furnace of the ondol system.

Choson Culture Survives Northern Invasion

As the powerful Chinese state of Yen advanced its influence southward down the Liaotung Peninsula at the end of the fourth century, Old Choson finally bent under its military might. Its gradual decline culminated in the annexation of Old Chosen as a commandery to the Yen territory. Renamed the Liao-tung Commandery, it subsequently was brought under the newly unified China, the Ch'in empire. About 106 B.C., Liu Pang, the founder of the Han dynasty, moved into the former Yen domain, investing Lu Wan as king. Lu Wan subsequently turned against the Han rulers and fled north.

This was a period of continuous political upheaval, creating many refugee groups that mostly fled east for sanctuary. One of these bands, numbering over a thousand, was organized into a fighting force by a leader named Wiman. King Chun of Old Choson engaged him to defend his northwestern border, but Wiman eventually gained enough power to turn against King Chun and drive him from his throne. He made himself king between 194 B.C. ad 180 B.C.

Because of the Yen invasion and the following continuous infiltration of Chinese political, military, economic power into the region of Old Choson, some historians once regarded what came to be known as the Wiman Choson as a remodeling of Korean culture in the Chinese style. The former view that Wiman Choson represented a colonial regime ruled by a migrant Chinese population has been challenged by scholars. Wiman himself is now interpreted not as a man of Yen, but of Old Choson. This is based on the fact that he is said in old records to have worn his hair in a different kind of topknot from the Chinese and to have been dressed in Choson style when he led his followers into Old Choson. Also, he continued to use "Choson" in the name of his kingdom. *Chosun* means "the land of the morning calm," and is, by the way, the name Japan historically has used for all of Korea, due to its early contacts with this large, influential territory.

Further strengthening speculation that Wiman Choson remained predominately a Korean culture was the survival of many men of Old Choson (notably the official *Igyesang* Sam) that occupied high positions under Wiman's rule. These are all clues strongly indicating that his kingdom had not become simply a Chinese colonial regime, regardless of the presence of migrant Chinese and their well-developed iron culture. Wiman Choson had the substance and influence to remain grounded on its former power structure and therefore the capacity to advance rapidly as a confederated kingdom. (Kim, 1972)

Wiman Choson is characterized by historians as having not only economic strength at this time but superior military power, subjugating its neighboring states to the north, east, and south. Chin-bon, lying between Chabiryong Pass and the Han River, and Imdun in the southern Hamgyong area were forced to submit to Wiman authority, thereby giving Wiman Choson control of a territory that stretched over several hundred miles. At this point, assessing its military superiority, Wiman Choson now barred Chin (located south of the Han River) and other smaller states near its borders from contacting the Han Chinese directly, forcing them to use Wiman Choson as an intermediary in their trade. This move, very profitable to Wiman, was not well received, however, by Han China. The Han were further concerned that Wiman would make a formidable alliance with the Hsiung-nu who were expanding into Manchuria from their homeland in Mongolia.

A major crisis arose when a Chinese envoy, who had earlier been rewarded for killing a Choson commander and fleeing back to China, was hunted down and killed in retaliation by an elite squad of Choson soldiers. This became the pretext for Emperor Wu of Han to finally launch an armed assault against Wiman Choson in 109 B.C. Wiman fought back hard against the invaders for a year, but then a circumstance occurred that Korean military commanders were to encounter at other times in the history of their country. Wiman Choson's resistance was undermined by the defections and enemy collaboration activities of a peace faction among its own people. This subversion culminated with the assassination of Wiman's grandson, King Ugo. A high official, Songgi, attempted to continue the struggle but with the fall of the Wiman capital Wanggom-song (at modern P'yongyang) in 108 B.C., Wiman Choson perished. (Kim, 1972)

The downfall of this first major military-political consolidation of the Koreans of this period was not due to military failing but due to political intrigue. Wiman Choson's ability to mount such stiff resistance presumably was enhanced by its ability to capitalize on its metal culture, rivaling that of the Han Chinese invaders. Clashes and differences in philosophy within the ruling class, however, opened the way for the decline of this once-influential kingdom.

Power Shifts and the Rise of the Three Kingdoms

In the year of its defeat, 108 B.C., Wiman Choson was carved up into three commanderies: Lo-lang (in Korean, Nangnang) in the Taedon River basin area of Old Choson; Chen-fan (Korean: Chinbon) from Chabi Pass south to the Han River; and Lin-t'un (Korean: Imdun) in the old Imdun area of southern Hamgyong province. The next year the so-called Four Chinese Commanderies were completed with the naming of Hsuan-t'u Commandery in the former territory of the Ye, spanning the middle reaches of the Yalu and the T'ung-chia River basin.

All of these entities invented by the Chinese were temporary. Opposition from the local populations forced Han China to make major adjustments in the boundaries of each of these four administrative units. Within 25 years, the Han abolished both Chen-fan and Lint'un, and attached them to the commanderies of Lo-lang and Hsuan-ts'u. Some of the more remote Korean districts are believed to have been abandoned. Then, less than a decade later in 75 B.C., Han moved Hsuan-t'u Commandery far to the west, out of the former Ye territory to a region in east-central Manchuria. This relocation is believed to be the result of the growing power of the rising Koguryo state. (Koguryo has also been called "Koryo," the origin of the latter-day name Korea.)

Meanwhile, in Lo-lang, unrest was gaining in momentum, and at the beginning of the Later Han dynasty a revolt occurred, led by Wang T'iao, a powerful member of the Lo-lang gentry. Although suppressed in 30 A.D. by Wang Tsun, the newly arrived governor, it had vast repercussions. Many people from Old Choson who had experienced the ordeal of rule after their territory became Lo-lang, left for refuge with the Korean Han societies in the region of the Chin state south of the Han River. Some of them moved down to southern Korea where they organized 54 minor tribal societies that existed in the area south of the Han River into a federation of Ma-han in the southwestern part of the peninsula.

At about the same period, two other federations, Chin-han and Byon-han, came into being in the southeastern section of Korea. Chin-han formed east of the Nakdong River and Byon-han on the opposite side. Together with Ma-han, these federations were called the Three Han. They gradually advanced northward to the southern part of Lo-lang, in a combined effort, eventually to absorb it.

In addition to the Three Han, there also existed two other societies of the Puyo tribe along the eastern coast: the Yemak or Ye and Okche (or Eastern Puyo). These two tribal groups put pressure on Lo-lang from the East, while a greater force of the Three Han was attacking it from the south. Soon, Chin-han and Byon-han merged to become the Kingdom of Silla in 57 B.C. Ma-han developed into the new Kingdom of Paekche in 18 B.C. About the same time, migrant Yemaek tribesmen and many other minor groups along the Yalu valley merged into a third kingdom, Koguryo, in 37 B.C.

At this point began the period of history known as the Three Kingdoms, signifying an escalation in the individuation of regional martial arts techniques. It was also the starting point of the written history of Korea.

2

The Three Kingdoms and the Rise of Martial Societies

Regardless of the cultural exchange and trading that occurred among merchants and artisans of bordering countries throughout Korea's history, it is certain that the martial arts were not part of this sharing. While traders may have welcomed free exchange of goods between regions, and artists may have incorporated ideas from other lands, rulers in the Korea of old had as their foremost concern retention of their land. To maintain their land holdings, fighting acumen was absolutely necessary. The martial skills behind the powerful leaders would have to have been kept as secret as the use of weaponry at any other time in history. Even though Chinese artifacts and others of various origins have been found in Korean cultures and vice versa—this is no indication that either their art or different ways of living were fundamentally infiltrated by foreign influences. It certainly does not prove that a trading of key martial art techniques—synonymous with national security—had occurred. This would amount to a compromising of territorial integrity that would defy tradition and constitute the grossest disloyalty and sedition.

One can imagine that the diversity of martial arts systems was greater when the impediments of natural boundaries and languages restricted travel and confined traditions within homelands. Rulers of the new kingdoms rising in the Korean river basins at the turn of the millennia were actively behind the martial way of life and learning. Their almost weekly activity was repelling the incursions of unfriendly and aggressive peoples such as the Chinese, the Hsei-pei, the Turkut, the Kitai, and the Mat-hat. To succeed at this, they most assuredly fostered the secret military systems handed down by their forefathers. According to legends and records, we can see how they elaborated on their way of life and the ethics of their armed elite as their societies became more sophisticated.

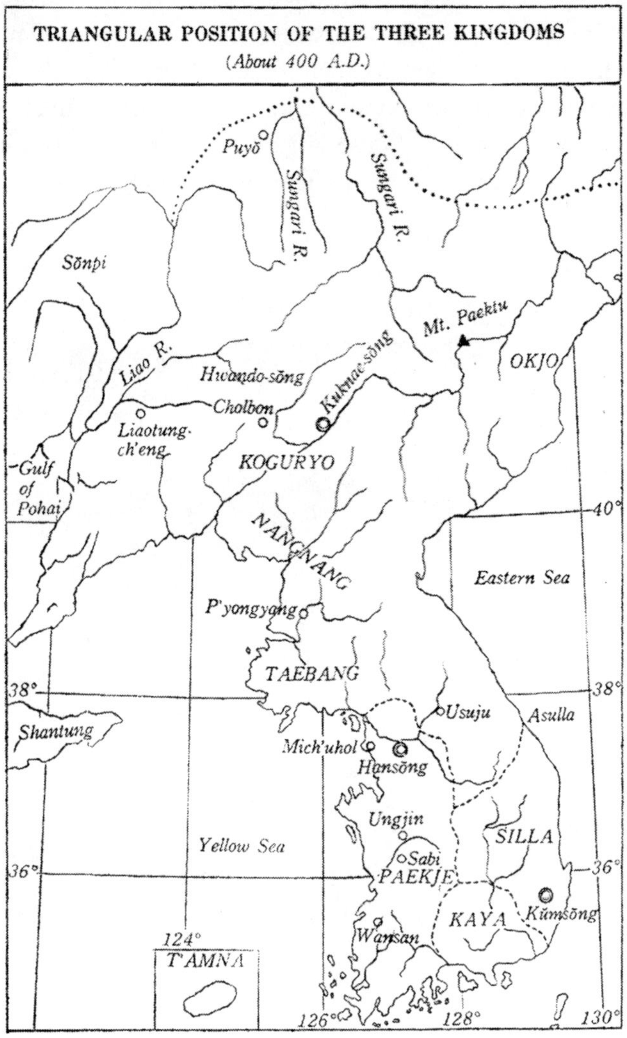

Detail map of Korean Kingdoms about 400 AD.

Puyo Koreans: Forerunners of Greater Koguryo

The Puyo people caused China's military considerable concern due to their competence in the martial arts. Puyo was an ethnically Korean kingdom that occupied the northern part of what is now Manchuria and a section of Mongolia. China was eager for friendly ties with Puyo, and the feeling was mutual as Puyo was wary of the nomadic peoples to its north and of Koguryo, building to its south. China formed marriage alliances with Puyo and promoted cordial diplomatic relations. Puyo supported Chinese interests by supplying provisions to the Wai army. The Chinese state of Chin helped restore the Puyo kingdom after its royal lineage had been interrupted at one point in its history.

With Chinese support, Puyo had sought first to expand and then to preserve its sovereign power. A catastrophe for its sovereignty occurred in 316 A.D. when the Chinese Chin kingdom was driven south by the nomadic tribes to its north and Puyo was in the way. In 346 Puyo's king, Hyon, and over 50,000 of his people were taken prisoner. Its ultimate fate became apparent 24 years later when the Puyo royal house was driven from its ancient home by the rise of the Malgal people in northeastern Manchuria. They were compelled to surrender to Koguryo, which absorbed Puyo.

King Tong·Myong, Founder of Koguryo

Artistic depiction of King Tong Myong, the founder of Koguryo

The Militarists of Koguryo

Koguryo, according to tradition, was founded by a Puyo prince, Chu-mong (King Tong-Myong), who located his capital in the central Yalu and T'ung-chia river basins.

Legends state that by the time Chu-mong (believed breathed into his mother's body by a divine father) was seven years old, he was as strong as a mature man. He made bows and arrows for himself and used them with such aptitude that he was called "Chu-mong, the Skillful Archer." (Kim, 1972) This early account of Korean archery prowess is one of the first of many indications that archery skills were enthusiastically practiced by early Koreans and were not foreign in origin, as is still believed in some quarters.

One well known story of Chu-mong's exodus to Koguryo begins with his seven brothers' jealousy for his spectacular and wily superiority as a hunter. He has been said to have overfed his brothers' ponies so their pursuit of game would be rather sluggish. His brothers' envy grew to the point where they were plotting to kill him. His mother heard of this, warned Chu-mong, and he fled southward with his councilors. "You can be successful any place you go," said his mother in farewell, "for your wisdom is deep and your bravery unmatched."

When he reached the Eum-ho River he found neither ford, boat nor bridge. It is said that he was inspired to strike the surface of the water with his bow, calling on the spirit of the river to aid him. Instantly, up from the depths of the river arose a shoal of fish and tortoises that laid their backs together and formed a bridge for his band to cross.

Historians believe this story is rooted in the huge salmon runs that once choked the Amur waterways. If Chu-mong encountered the crossing problem at the time of a salmon run, it suggests that the location of Puyo was, indeed, as far north as the Sungari or some other tributary of the Amur.

Leaving his brothers behind, and baffled, on the northern bank, Chu-mong trekked south to Chul-bon. The present town of Song-ch'un is where he founded Koguryo—the name likely derived from Ko, his family name, but also meaning "high," and Ku-ryu, a mountain in his native Puyo. Chu-mong enclosed what was to become his capital city in a heavy stockade and began his empire building—at first in a peaceful way by marrying the daughter of the local king.

At its peak, Koguryo stretched "a thousand *li*" beyond the Yalu River and southward to the banks of the Han, encompassing two races of people and several tribes.

A 5th century map showing the location of the 3 Kingdoms and Kaya on the Korean peninsula.

According to legends, territorial acquisitions were made through the very skilled use of swords, arrows, and spears. (Hulbert, 1905)

This land settled by Chu-mong and his Puyo people, previously had been inhabited during the fourth century B.C. by the Yemaeks. In an account written in the second century B.C., the Yemaek's ruler, the Ye (Lord) Namnyo, was said to have 280,000 subjects. The state that evolved there may have represented a joining of the people from Puyo with a considerable indigenous society. (Kim, 1972)

Prior to Chu-mong's arrival, the Ye Namnyo, resisting domination by Wiman Choson, called on the Han dynasty for assistance. The Han responded by establishing the Ts'ang-hai Commandery in the mid-Yalu region in about 128 B.C. but it was not officially manned until 107 B.C. About 30 years later the commandery retreated further west due to the resistance of the powerful Korean forces in this region. This is considered another sign that at this time Koguryo was evolving into a confederated kingdom.

These early records of the Koguryo kingdom confirm a long lineage of indigenous Korean martial arts. (Lee, 1984) They show the martial nature and skill of these early Koreans and their motivation to develop as effective a fighting body as possible.

The development of Koguryo was strongly affected by continuing conflict with the Chinese. The military character of its ruling elite was perennially reinforced in the course of its early, armed struggles. According to Historian Ki-baik Lee, "It would appear that even in times of peace this warrior aristocracy did not engage in any kind of productive activities but devoted itself entirely to training for combat." (Lee, 1984) In addition to routing their enemies, the Koguryo warriors had a considerable interest, it appears, in the spoils of war. Only through warfare could they compensate for the inadequate resources of their territory. Records show that the Chinese impression of the Koguryo was of people "vigorous, warlike, and fond of attacking their neighbors." (Lee, 1984)

This characterization undermines another modern misconception about ancient Koreans. Koreans of Koguryo worshipped the "tiger spirit," which illustrates their interest in offensive as well as defensive skills. This idea persisted for centuries. Koreans saw themselves as tiger-spirited people so much so that, at some point in Korean history, the Korean peninsula was painted in the shape of a tiger.

During the long decades of Japanese occupation in the 19th and 20th centuries, it was to the advantage of the Japanese to alter Korean history, misleading successive generations of the tradition-observing Koreans. They were "re-educated" to think of themselves as passive, as belonging to a people lacking in aggressive responsiveness, and, most significantly, coming from a tradition without a fighting spirit. It was during these occupation years that the traditional way of showing the shape of Korea as a tiger was dropped and a rabbit map depiction was instituted.

Koreans historically thought of themselves as tiger spirited and at some point in their history the shape of the Korean peninsula was drawn into a Tiger.

The rabbit map was created during the Japanese occupation of the 20th century because they wanted to portray the Koreans as a passive people.

Encouraging Koreans to think of themselves as a passive people served the interests of the Japanese but ran counter to historical truth. While at various periods it may have been in the best interests of Korea, politically and economically, to have rejected conflict, Koreans always retained an aggressive interest in holding onto what they had. Repeatedly, when circumstances were favorable, they were not averse to adding to their capital through the skillful exercise of their martial arts. The Koguryo kingdom is a preeminent example of this. The aptitude of Koguryo Koreans for the battlefield made them the envy of surrounding rulers. Records show that in 12 A.D., Wang Man, who in the next two decades was to interrupt the 400-year rule of the Han in China, appreciated the Koguryos' prowess to the extent that he asked them for (but was refused) military reinforcements in his fight against the Hsiung-nu.

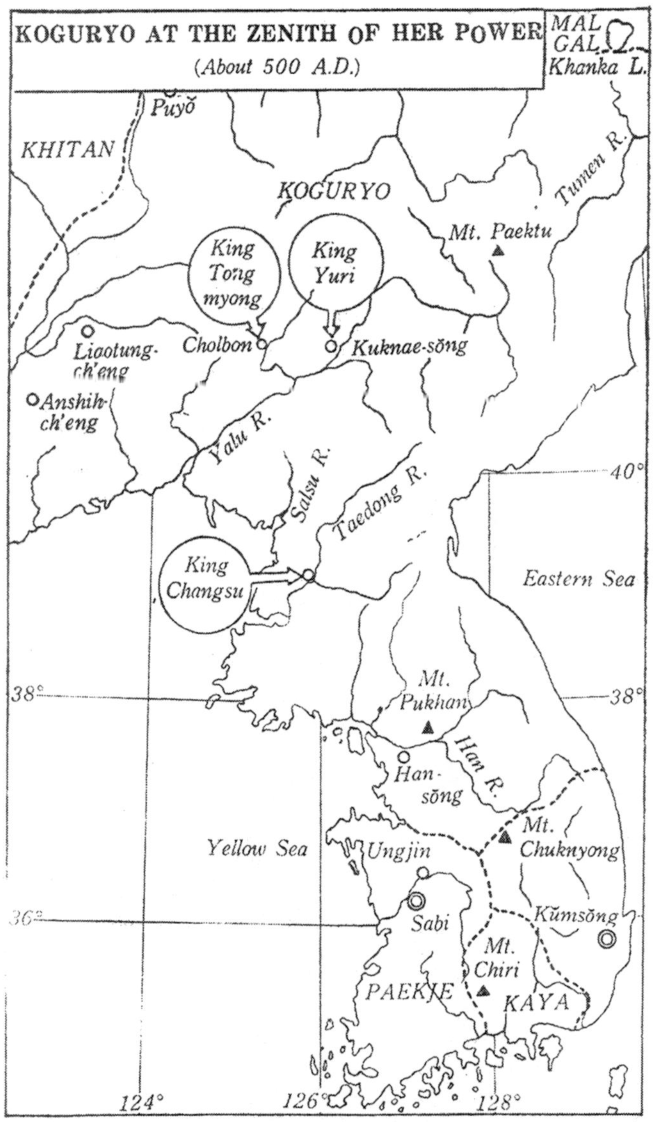

Koguryo at the zenith of her power.

There are a variety of clues from the Koguryo kingdom that attest to the well developed military capacities and traditions of the Koreans of that day, and also to their indigenous origins. Japan, at that time, was seeking Korean products and repeatedly sent political envoys (who initiated such trade then) to stimulate interest in business. This is borne out in the book *San Kuo Chih* (Vol. 30) in which it is again noted that the Japanese went to Korea even to purchase iron.

Weapons of the Koguryo Tiger Spirit

In fighting, the aggressive nature of Korean soldiers is seen in their weaponry and techniques of deployment. They used spears as long as three men. Frequently several men wielded the same spear together, which required considerable skill. They fought entirely on foot. Again, mention is made in ancient texts of their archery skills; their "celebrated *nang-nang* bows were of local Ye-guk origin, cut from pak-tal wood (a type of birch).

Consistently, ancient records also describe the tribal people who were absorbed into the Koguryo kingdom as warlike, reporting on their use of weapons, including spears. These reports include comment on such characteristics as aggressiveness and even vindictiveness. The people of the northern part of Koguryo were called "fierce" by historian Hulbert, "the Apaches of Korea." He applied the same description to the Heuk-su, adding that they were "expert archers, their bows being made of horn, and the arrows were 23 inches long."

These people of mountain and valley, town and fortified city, were to merge the fighting skills passed down for scores of generations into formation of the first great kingdom of what was to become part of latter-day Korea. Hulbert notes that a number of tribes contained accomplished archers, and also that the Mal-gal tribes of those ancient times were "skillful at mimicking the deer for the purpose of decoying it." We find this same observant nature applied to martial arts in the copying of animal movements useful for defense and offense in Korea (as well as throughout the world). The modern martial art system of Kuk Sool Won continues to use such animal techniques for offense and defense.

As the Koguryo kingdom developed, it is clear that military knowledge became assigned to an exclusive rank of its populace. The agricultural worker was not permitted to bear arms and fight in wars, serving instead in an ordinance capacity and transporting provisions. (Lee, 1993) Citizens who received the skills to carry out the designs of their king—and those who passed down that knowledge as teachers—coalesced into a class charged with nothing other than following a way of life that enhanced their abilities to fight and win.

The most ancient evidence of Korean martial arts that has been uncovered is on the walls of three tombs in China's Jillian province, near the town of Jian. On the ceiling of the royal Koguryo tomb of the Mu Yong Chong are paintings evidently of *subak*, translated as a punching and butting system. *Su* means "hand," *bak* to strike with the fist, to box or to punch.

As it rose in power, the Koguryo kingdom attracted numerous challenges from the Chinese that were met with persistent skill in defense by the Koguryo military. However, repeated incursions by new enemy tribal leagues, Chinese kingdoms, and the new Paekche kingdom in the south strained its resources. It was remarkable that Koguryo still survived after the earlier Yen state invaded it in 342 (capturing more than 50,000 people, in addition to the queen and queen mother), then after a later Paekche invasion, and further, after pressure from China during the reign of King Sosurim (371-384). The height of its military glory was initiated under Kwanggae-to-wang, also known as Kwanggaet'o and Kwang-gae-to (391-413), whose name means "the king who expanded the country's territory."

Grandmaster Suh trains empty hand techniques in the mountains of Korea using animal motions of the Crane, Snake, Tiger.

Grandmaster Suh trains empty hand techniques in the mountains of Korea using animal motions of the Snake, Dragon and Praying Mantis.

Grandmaster Suh trains empty hand techniques in the mountains of Korea using animal motions of the Tiger, Dragon.

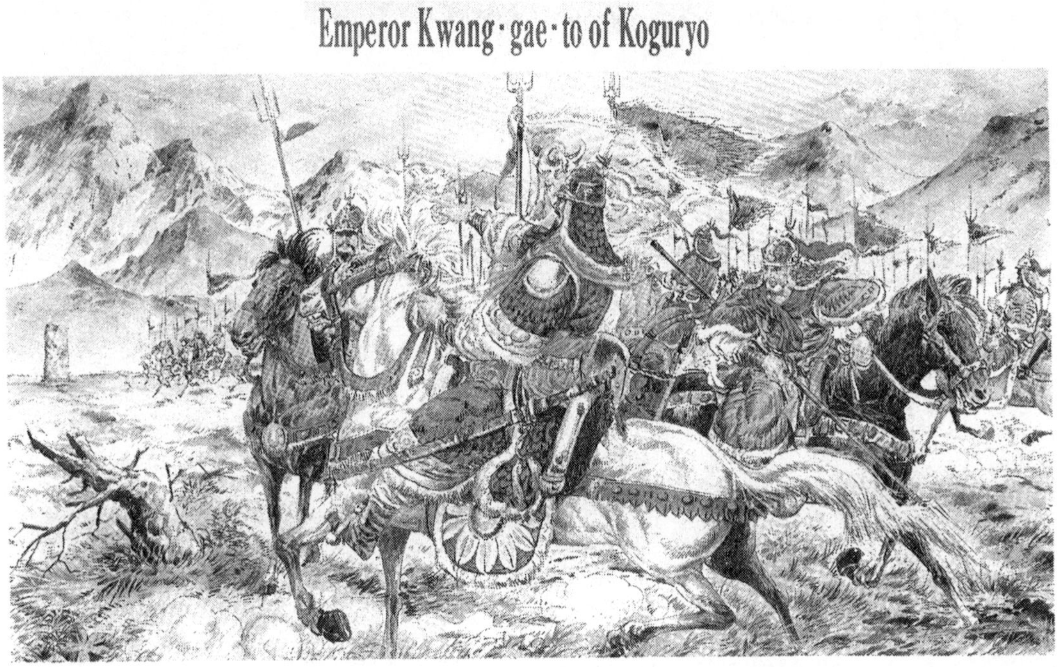

Artistic impression of Emperor Kwang Gae-to

KWANG-GAE-TO-WANG: EMPEROR OF ENDURANCE

Kwang-gae-to-wang was the first to adopt the Chinese custom of naming his period of rule. Assuming his slain father's throne at the age of 18 in 391, Emperor Kwang-gae-to-wang, within 60 days, led his army in an attack on Paekche. Impressively, he defeated a dozen enemy cities in two months. Six years later, he accepted the surrender of Paekche. Four years later he faced an invasion of Japanese pirates but pushed them back into the sea. Manchuria was the next target he punished for its incursions and by 411, huge areas of its southern territories had fallen to Kwang-gae-to-wang.

The emperor's endurance was legendary. He spent nearly all of the 11 years of his reign astride his warhorse, dying (by exhaustion, some say) when he was only 39. Conversely, his son, Chang-su died when he was 98, reigning throughout Korea's "Golden Age," longer than any king in Korean history.

A memorial in honor of Emperor Kwang-gae-to-wang stands to this day in what is now Manchuria, attesting to his prodigious feats. His military achievements were recorded in detail on a huge stone stele still rising over his tomb in Kungnae-song (at modern T'ung-kou, on the Manchurian side of the mid-Yalu river), at that time the capital of Koguryo. In the course of his reign of twenty-some years, he conquered a total of 64 fortress domains and 1,400 villages. His son, King Chang-su ("The Long-Lived"), reigned for 79 years and led Koguryo to its dominant status in the region.

Chinese Anticipate Koguryo Prowess with 'Mightiest Move'

Koguryo's military prowess was demonstrated by the bold assault it made across the Liao River against Liao-hsi in 598. The Chinese Sui emperor, Wen Ti, launched a counterattack but was turned back mid-course. Yang Ti, the next Sui emperor, proceeded in 612 to mount an invasion that was the largest ever recorded, said to number 1,130,000 men. This campaign, one of the "mightiest military movements in history," was a response to the resistance and military aggressiveness of the Korean people. (Hulbert, 1905) The Chinese force massed on the western bank of the Liao River was divided into 24 battalions, marching with an interval of forty *li* between each. The entire army stretched for 960 *li*, along the road. The emperor and his bodyguard came eighty *li* to the rear. (Hulbert, 1905) Said historian Ki-baik Lee, "Nothing can better prove the hardihood of the Koguryo soldiery than that, when they saw this well-neigh innumerable host approach, they dared to dispute the crossing of the river." (Hulbert, 1905)

General Ulji Mundok of Koguryo

Art impression of General UlJi Mundok who defeated a three hundred thousand man army of China.

General Ulji Mundok: Classic Scholar-Warrior

A classic exemplar of the famous Korean scholar-warrior, General Ulji Mundok penned a poem so strategically worded that it caused the downfall of a 305,000-man Chinese army in the early 600s.

After the Chinese exhausted themselves fruitlessly with a prolonged attack of Yondong Castle at the Koguryo border, General Ulji needed to bait the depleted Chinese into a fast, exhausting advance on their next target, Pyongyang, the capital. His means was a masterfully insolent poem (the finest surviving example of Three Kingdoms verse) sent to the Sui general, who was known for his rages. It worked well, provoking an immediate push by the weary Chinese through Koguryo territory with men too tired and hungry to mount an adequate defense against the fierce attack by Ulji Mundok's men. Only 2,700 Chinese soldiers (or perhaps even 1,000 less by some accounts) survived in a debacle, which ultimately resulted in the collapse of the Sui dynasty.

Koguryo's famed commander dealt Yang Ti a calamitous defeat at the Salsu River. It is said that only 2,700 of the 305,000 Sui soldiers who had crossed the Yalu survived to find their way back. Yang Ti was so determined to win against the Koguryo soldiers that he continued to send his armies against the country and, as a result of the consistently superior Koguryo forces he met, weakened his empire until the Sui Dynasty crumbled. (Lee, 1993)

Koguryo gave a message to the succeeding T'ang dynasty and the people of the northern tribes when it erected its famous 1,000-*li* wall across its northwestern frontier, straight across the peninsula from Eui-ju to the Japan Sea. Construction of the wall required 16 years.

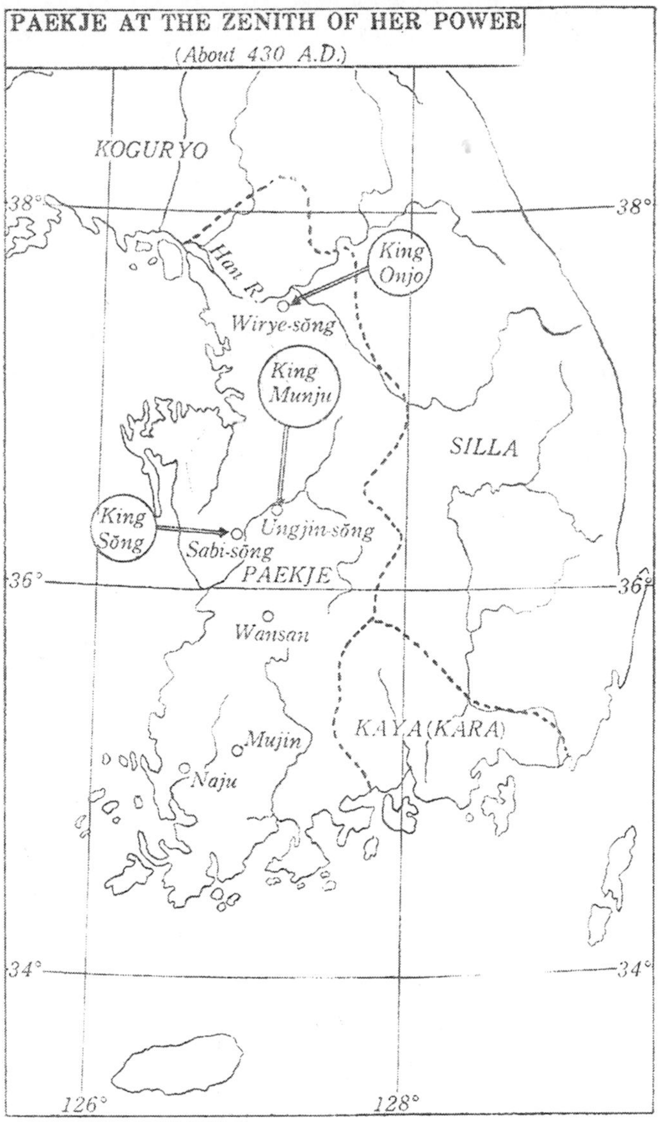

Paekche Kingdom occupied much of the Korean peninsula at her zenith as shown by this map.

The Power of the Paekche Kingdom

Many of the details of the founding of the Paekche kingdom are unknown. One of the northern Puyo tribes, migrating south, settled first at what is now Inch'on (then known as Mich'uhol). Later it relocated near the site of modern Seoul where it dominated all the tribes of the ancient Mokchi-guk area. Finally it spread its territory south to the present Kwangju, by that time becoming a strong tribal league ruling the Ma-han tribes.

King On-Cho, founder of the kingdom of Paekche and son of Chu-mong Ko, founder of the nation of Koguryo, was a canny general who repeatedly proved his cleverness in protecting his fledgling country by outmaneuvering enemy soldiers.

It probably was due to conflicts between the Chinese state of Wei and the southern Han tribes that forced the Ma-han tribes into a closer unity. Paekche took advantage of the situation to establish its leadership over them. By the reign of King Koi (234-285) Paekche emerged as a fully developed kingdom on a par with Koguryo. The rise of Paekche coincided with the acquisition of two Chinese colonies, Nangnang and Taebang, by Koguryo. At this point, Paekche and Koguryo faced one another across a common frontier. The result was war. Under the strong leadership of King Kunch'ogo (346-374) Paekche established control over the entire Ma-han area, and then marched north to attack Koguryo. Victorious, Paekche succeeded in extending its power north of the Han River into the present Hwanghae Province. King Kunch'ogo completed the foundation of the Paekche kingdom by securing trade relations with Japan and with the Eastern Chin dynasty, which at that time ruled south China.

As Koguryo became more threatening, Paekche concluded an alliance with Silla in 433 and, when invasion seemed unavoidable, King Kaero of Paekche dispatched a special envoy to the northern Chinese state of Wei to ask for help. However, in 475, Hansan, the capital of Paekche, fell to the Koguryo troops and King Kaero was killed. Paekche was forced to move its capital far to the south, to Ungjin (modern Kongju, South Ch'ungch'ong Province).

After the nation had recovered from its defeat, the capital was moved away from remote Ungjin to Sabi (modern Puyo), on the broad, navigable Kum River, giving Paekche direct access to China by sea. King Song-wang established ties with China and Japan, and Paekche became a conduit for the flow of culture north and east. Paekche craftsmen from many arts were sought by Japan and taught there. Ancient records indicate those probably included weapon makers.

King On-Cho Routs Malgals

Paekche was an infant nation when the fierce Malgal tribe attacked with 3,000 warriors in 11 B.C., laying siege to the capital of Kwangju. King On-Cho barricaded the gates and refused to answer the taunts of his enemy to send his small force outside the walled city. After the Malgal ran out of food and patience, and finally withdrew, King On-Cho chose his swiftest horsemen and swooped down upon the enemy, hewing down 500 of the invaders in a tremendous rout.

Artist drawing of King On-Cho the founder of Paekche.

Infuriated, the Malgal later sent more troops, attacking futilely again and again. Then the Nangnang people took their turn, and even the Mahan tribes from the southern tip of the Korean peninsula sought to pluck this ripe plum that was the new kingdom of Paekche. It was On-Cho's leadership and martial arts genius that secured the establishment of Paekche culture so that it could grow and develop for centuries.

Kun-Cho-Go: Powerful Prince of Paekche

By the reign of King Koi (234-285), Paekche had achieved military parity with Koguryo. Paekche faced its competitor across a common border and by 371, had attained military superiority. Its hallmark of victory to this end was marching on Koguryo with 30,000 troops, which attacked P'yongyang, killing Koguryo's King Kogugwon. Paekche's external power peaked under King Kun-cho-go, its tenth king. Even Koguryo, the most powerful state in the area now known as Manchuria and Korea, failed three times to win against King Kun-cho-go's forces. The Paekche crown prince, under his father's tactical guidance, pushed through an army of

30,000 to the Koguryo capital in November, 369 A.D., vastly increasing the stature of the Paekche kingdom.

King Kun-cho-go commissioned the first history of any Korean kingdom, 100 years ahead of the history of Silla and 250 years prior to Koguryo's first history. Because of the destruction of Korea's libraries by its enemies, all that survives of these precious volumes are the records noting their existence.

Artist impression of King Kun-Cho-Go in battle.

Paekche Swords, Bows Attained Fame

In a Japanese documentary about a 14th generation sword smith named Kuniira, the blueprints of a sword called "Seven Branch Sword," now a national treasure in Japan, were shown. It was stated that the sword and its blueprint were from the Kingdom of Paekche. This suggests that Japanese swords were influenced by Korean swords early on. In the Paekche kingdom we also find mention of bow and arrows as significant weaponry. King A-sin formed "a great school of archery" as a major mode of defense for his kingdom but its compulsory policy of attendance for those not talented with the bow resulted in a number of drop-outs. (Hulbert, 1905)

The military fortunes of Paekche waxed and waned as the country formed alliances with Silla against Koguryo and then armed against a betrayal by Silla. The latter move was unsuccessful. The Paekche king, Song-wang, was killed and his army routed. Silla then came to dominate the peninsula.

Emperor Park, Founder of Silla

Artistic impression of Emperor Park, the founder of Silla.

Emperor Park, Founder of Silla

About 2000 years ago, the six chiefs of the districts of the east coast of the Korean peninsula got together and decided they needed to have a king. They united their districts and founded a nation. Then they climbed a mountain to find a place for a capital city. As they looked south, they saw a strange pillar of smoke billowing out from a well at the foot of Mount Yang. A rainbow of blinding colors hid the well like a curtain, and a white horse was kneeling and bowing before it. As the chiefs approached, the horse took flight, disappearing into the heavens. "Look," shouted the chief. "Look! A huge, purple egg!" The flying horse had been bowing to the egg.

They broke open the egg carefully. Out crawled a baby boy.

As the chiefs washed the little boy in water from the magic well, they noticed that his body emitted light. Birds and wild animals were attracted by the light and gathered around the infant, singing and dancing gaily. That day the sun and the moon gleamed brighter than anyone could remember.

The elders decided the magical boy should become their king. "We shall name him Hyok-ko-se the chiefs agreed. The headmen also decided that Park should be Hyok-ko-se's last name. Park means "gourd," and the king had beeen found in a large, gourd like egg.

The same day that Hyok-ko-se was discovered, a dragon chicken rose from a well called Aryong in a village named Saryang. The dragon chicken gave birth to a beautiful baby girl.

"The magical girl would be a marvelous queen for Hyok-ko-se," suggested one chief. "I'll say, she's perfect," agreed another. The chiefs called the little girl Aryong, after the well from which the dragon chicken emerged.

The chiefs built a gorgeous palace for the new king and queen at the foot of Nam Mountain.

When Hyok-ko-se Park turned thirteen, he and Aryong were made king and queen. He assumed the throne in 57 B.C. He was the first king of "Sorabol" a nation which came to be called Silla. It was Silla which finally unified the peninsula under its banner in 668 A. D.

Martial Arts in the Silla Kingdom

The leading Korean source for the study of Silla's rise to prominence is the *Samguk Sagi*, compiled two centuries later but the oldest history in existence of the period. It chronicles Korea's past from its mythological beginnings to the 10th century, highlighting the reign of King Munmu of Silla from 660 to 681. During that period Silla accelerated from the position as weakest of the three peninsular kingdoms to one of sufficient strength to annex both neighbors. Silla then successfully turned back the T'ang Chinese to defend the newly unified territory's integrity. The *Samguk Sagi* clearly describes the defeat of T'ang naval attacks with ease by Silla southwestern coastal defenses, one in 671 and others led by Hsueh Jen-kuei in 675-676. The defeats were disastrous for the T'ang with destroyed fleets and considerable booty for Silla. (Jamieson, 1969)

It is a myth that weaponry and its skillful usage have not been documented as a major factor in Korean martial arts. With some searching among what is left of the ancient writings mentioning arms, we can find an abundance of relics. Many stories and legends show that Koreans have always been well armed, perhaps even more so at various times than Japan, which as mentioned, had to buy iron for its weapons from Korea. In the early days, Korean swords were imported for use in Japan and Korean forging techniques were highly admired. (Sugawara, 1988) (Pak, 1995)

From the *Samguk Yusa* (*Legends and History of the Three Kingdoms* written by the monk Iryon in the 13th century) is a story from the Silla Kingdom called "Youngjae and the Thieves," which illustrates that not only did Koreans routinely use a variety of weapons, but also their employment was artful.

This story tells of Youngjae, a humorous monk and a singer of the folk ballads called *hyang-ga* in the golden days of Silla. When he had reached the twilight of his earthly life, he decided to spend his remaining days quietly among nature, and so he started on a long journey to the forests of Mt. Chiri. When he reached the top of the steep mountain pass called Taehyollyong, a band of sixty thieves emerged from the forest, brandishing swords and spears and threatening to kill him.

Youngjae was calm and showed no sign of fear.

"Good morning, my forest gentlemen," he said. "You are wonderful dancers and I have never seen such a fine sword dance in my life."

"Sword dance!" said the bandit chief. "Can you say that, even as our great swords whirl above your head?"

But once the chief became aware of who his intended victim was, he let him keep his life in trade for a song.

"Mulkeja the Brave Soldier" is a story that has survived because of the Korean peoples' appreciation for their ancient martial arts history. It shows the code of honor existing, which always accompanies a martial arts tradition.

During the 17th year of King Naehae's reign (in 212 A.D.), the allied troops of eight states, including Poraguk (now Kosong) and Samulguk (now Saju) invaded the border towns of

Silla. The king ordered out a large army under the command of Crown Prince Nalum and General Ilpol to hurl back the enemy. After a fierce battle, all eight states surrendered to Silla.

During the battle, the brave soldier Mulkeja performed the greatest military feats, but the crown prince disliked him intensely and omitted his name from the list of those to be rewarded. Mulkeja's friends said, "Have you no resentment against the prince? Why don't you appeal to the king?"

"A loyal subject can never complain of his prince," Mulkeja replied, "and a patriotic soldier does not risk his life for reward, much less should he appeal to the throne in order to gain a reputation at the expense of others. I simply do my duty. Time will tell."

Three years later the kings of three states, headed by the prince of Kolp'o-guk (now Happo) attacked Kalhwa (or Kulbul, now Ulju). The king of Silla led his army in person and routed them. Mulkeja cut off the heads of more than a score of enemy soldiers, but the court never praised his valor. He in no way acknowledged the slight, focusing simply on his duty. In an explanation to his wife: "I have heard that the way of a loyal subject of a king is to risk his life in time of emergency, forgetting about personal safety and living only for king and country."

This code of behavior is characteristic of a highly developed martial arts tradition, which always includes a lifestyle and philosophy handed down by a long succession of masters. We see it well in place in Korea among the written records from the second century A.D.

Yet another example of sacrifice survives in the tale of an official named Pak Che-san from King Sil-sung's reign in 403. (Hulbert, 1905) The king had sent his two brothers on diplomatic missions to Koguryo and Japan but was worried that their safe return might be jeopardized by unstable relations with these two countries. Calling them back might arouse suspicion and precipitate a war. Pak Che-san, the magistrate of Sapna County, was nominated by the grieving king's courtiers as the wisest and most brave man to undertake the sensitive proposition of bringing them home. In accepting the mission, Pak made the following speech typifying the moral values of the time and the duty to the king, as recorded in the *Samguk Yusa*:

"When the King is grieved, his subjects are disgraced. If the King is in disgrace, his subjects must die. If the subjects do only what is easy and will not undertake what is most difficult, they are disloyal, and if they consider only saving their own lives, they are cowards. Though I am an unworthy subject, I will faithfully execute this mission, given me by royal command."

First, Pak journeyed to Koguryo where his diplomatic skills resulted in the return of Prince Pok-ho to Silla. The task awaiting him in Japan was more dangerous and he suspected it would cost him his life. His strategy was first to ask the king to imprison his family. The puzzled ruler acceded, whereupon Pak Che-san immediately left for Yul Harbor without changing his garments, in order to look like a fugitive. Even arriving in Japan dressed in this way, the ruler there suspected him until news came that his family had been imprisoned. He was then considered genuine, and even more so after he asserted that he wished to lead a Japanese force against Silla with Prince Mi-sa-heun, the Korean king's brother, playing traitor.

The Japanese king made them joint leaders of an invasion force. After they were under way and had landed at an island, Pak succeeded in spiriting Mi-sa-heun away in a little boat while he remained behind to divert attention from the escape. Mis-sa-heun begged him in tears to accompany him but he refused to jeopardize Mi-sa-heun's chances of escape, a selfless act of integrity identified with traditional martial arts philosophy. The ploy was successful, and by the time the Japanese discovered the deception, a heavy fog had settled on the sea, insuring his escape.

Death by torture would have been Pak's fate at the hands of the enraged Japanese, but his courageous response to their anger ended his life sooner. His words, which the Japanese admired, were that he would rather be a Silla pig or whipped like a schoolboy than to have become an honored collaborator of the Japanese. He was honored posthumously by his king who married the safely returned Mi-sa-heun to Pak's daughter. His widow withdrew to a vantage point at the pass of Ap-sul-yung where she died within a distant view of the islands of Japan.

Chae·sang Park, Loyal Silla Citizen

Artistic impression of the escape from Japan of Mi-sa-heun
that was arranged by Pak Che-san.

Stories such as this illustrate very well the brand of courage, devotion and loyalty upon which Korean martial arts are based. They helped define the Korean martial arts for centuries.

In the *Samguk Yusa* we also find many stories about spears used with superhuman powers, "dragon swords," great battle axes, etc., indicating that a variety of weaponry was used within the Korean culture.

As with its contemporary kingdoms of Koguryo and Paekche, Silla developed arts and military culture that was admired considerably by its Asian neighbors who continually sought trade and alliances. Records show the Japanese requested an early king of Silla to grant them a noble maiden of his kingdom to be their queen. Such was Silla's prestige. Emboldened after the king sent the daughter of a high official, the Japanese asked for an additional royal princess to be wed to their king. The Silla king said no, and war resulted. A Japanese force attacked the coast, rebuffed and approached the capital from another direction. The walled city thwarted their siege and at the point where the Japanese ran out of provisions, Silla opened its gates and the Koreans fell on the tired and hungry invaders.

Some years later the Japanese made a similar attempt but were outfoxed by the Silla strategists who augmented their smaller forces with soldier figures made from grass. Fearing the "reinforcements," the Japanese fled. (Hulbert, 1905)

One of many inventions of the innovative Sillans was to change the nature of warfare and the transportation of supplies. In 417 Nul-ji came to the throne of Silla and subsequently introduced the ox-drawn cart, increasing the volume of materials which could be moved and freeing manpower for less exhausting tasks. Nul-ji also was responsible for the introduction of Buddhism into his country.

Another "first" from Silla which gave it an advantage over its rivals was institution of a "pony express," a horse relay system called the *yong-ma* which was not only valuable in civilian life but which enabled battlefield news to travel faster. (Hulbert, 1905)

The Martial Culture of the Silla Hwarang

The elite martial arts society of the *Hwarang* started in the second and third quarters of the sixth century. It antedated not only the rise of the Sui (589-618) but also that of the Confucian T'ang (618-906), whose cultural influence on Silla did not imprint significantly until the late seventh century.

There has been some effort in the past to diminish the parallels between the martial arts culture of the originally Silla institution of Hwarang and the Japanese *Bushido* tradition. Bushido was exclusively interested in the martial arts life, whereas the Hwarang carefully selected its warrior members for their versatile artistic talents, as well, which included poetry, singing, and dancing. These arts were studied not just for art's sake but also for a better understanding of the beauty of order and harmony. Likewise, their touring of the famous mountains and rivers of their homeland was not simply for enjoyment but to increase their love of country. Their religious studies were not only for their spiritual edification but to make more effective their prayers for the country's peace and development. (Lee, 1993) This interest of the Korean people in developing what might be called today a well-rounded cultural education can be seen even in these ancient times. However, the fact that Hwarang schooled a greater range of talents and moral strength along with soldiery should in no way diminish what it provided for its elite fighting men: an integrated moral, spiritual, military, and cultural framework for devotion to country.

The Korean Catholic priest L'Abbe Laurent Eul Sou Youn further elaborated on the wide spectrum of Hwarang culture by declaring it to encompass the religious brotherhood of "Hwarang To." (Youn, 1939)

As with much of Korean military history—especially in regard to military societies—information about Hwarang has not been well preserved or disseminated. While songs and tales could not be obliterated, such inspiration as books and art depicting the Hwarang spirit would be the first material censored by foreign invaders. To discount the Hwarang influence on the development of Korean martial arts because documentation has not survived in bulk quantities would be a sizeable miscalculation of its lasting impact.

Some historians have consulted reference materials, which were not concerned with the Hwarang and so made no mention of this influential movement. The editor of historian Homer B. Hulbert's widely cited Korean history notes that, although King Chinhung's Hwarang was among the institutions fundamental to Silla's leadership of most of the peninsula in 668-677, it has received only limited attention from Western writers. This continued as the case even after the name Hwarang was revived as a symbol of patriotism in South Korea during the Korean War of 1950-1953. (Hulbert, 1905) (Yun, 1989)

The same editor takes Hulbert to task, not only for misreading the name of the Hwarang's founding king ("Pok-heung" instead of "Chin-heung" or "Chinhung") but also for his "failure to mention this key ingredient of Silla's public life." Hulbert did not refer to either King Chinhung or Hwarang "in view of his ultimate dependence on the Tongguk T'onggam," a Neo-Confusian work whose philosophy precluded an interest in Hwarang. Later, Hulbert did write of the movement in *The Korean Repository*, presenting "in a rather narrow way only one of a half-dozen facets" of the cult, according to his editor. (Hulbert, 1905)

Although the Hwarang concept is rightly regarded as being indigenous to Silla, through that country's later absorption of the other kingdoms, it spread and took root throughout Korea after unification of the three kingdoms. After World War II and the end of the Occupation, Koreans appropriately returned to referencing Hwarang as a military cult (which it was, according to the few surviving records describing it), as well as a "cult" of the performing arts, part of its incipient function.

The word Hwarang is alive in contemporary Korean culture with a multitude of applications, all relating to ideals of effort. Who the Hwarang were originally, and the scope of their activities is contended by historians, up to and including what the word actually means. Agreed upon is its root *hwa*, "flower." Some historians define its meaning somewhere in the neighborhood of "flower of manhood," or, in other words, an elite youth corps. Hulbert refers to the *Hwarang To*, translating this as "Circle of Knights of the Flower." He identified its purpose as the development of selected young men who would become leaders of the government and society as a whole. Not all members of a *to* (*do*), he said, were required to be of equally as high a rank as its leaders but all were of noble birth. "Circle of the Flower of Youth" is yet another interpretation. Woo-keun Han translates Hwarang as "flower knights," and calls them an institution at the core of Silla's military organization, a sort of military academy descended from the youth bands of tribal times. Its young men of aristocratic birth dedicated themselves, he says, to preparing to serve the state in war. In addition to their practical training, they were dispatched to visit famous mountains ("doubtless in connection with the belief in the spirits of such places," says Han, who characterizes their curriculum as an "aristocratic military academy.") They were taught ritual songs and dances meant to be a form of prayer for the welfare of the nation. They were charged with the development in themselves and in others of an appreciation of the arts, including poetry, music, dance, and the architecture and painting of temples, pagodas and Buddhist figures. They were encouraged to understand and enjoy the sights and wonders to be found throughout their own growing country.

Above all, they were dedicated to service as an elite military corps, and were entrusted with infusing the spirit of self-discipline, invincibility, and loyalty into the Sillan army, standing ready to sacrifice themselves in the front lines. The eagerness with which the Hwarang offered their lives as the currency with which victory was to be paid is exemplified in the deaths of the sons of Generals P'umil and Kim Hum'ch'un in the campaign of 660 against Paekche, recorded in the *Samguk Sagi*. The story of General P'umil's son, Kwanch-ang, includes this description:

In the fifth year of T'ang's Hsien-ch'ing period (660), the king set out his armies to invade Paekche in concert with the T'ang generals, and made Kwanch'ang a lieutenant general. When the opposing armies came face to face on the plains of Hwangasan,

[Kwanch'ang's] Father P'umil said: "You're young but you have the will and spirit. Today is the day to establish merit and fame, to obtain wealth and position, and you must be valiant, must you not?" Kwanch'ang answered "Aye!" then jumped on his horse and with outstretched spear, rammed head-on into the enemy columns. He killed several men while galloping through, but heavily outnumbered, was captured by the bandits and brought alive before Kyebaek, the Paekche commander-in-chief. When Kyebaek had his helmet taken off, he was moved to see the youthfulness of one so valorous and could not bear to have him killed. He sighed and said, "There are many extraordinarily brave soldiers in Silla, but if this is an example of their youth, what must their mature warriors be!" He then let [Kwanch'ang] return alive.

[On his return] Kwanch'ang said, "It is the deepest of humiliations that I was unable to behead the general and snatch their standard while among the bandits. I must succeed the next time." He scooped some well water with his hands, drank, then rushed into the bandit columns, battling with fury, But he was snared by Kyebaek who cut off his head and sent it back, lashed to his saddle. P'umil lifted the head and said, while wiping the blood with his sleeve, "My son looks just as if he were alive. He was able to die for our king...there's no regret." The Great King bestowed the rank of kupch'an [on Kwanch'ang] and buried him with full honors. Thirty bolts of T'ang pongee silk, thirty bolts of 1600-thread cloth, and one hundred sok of grain were presented to his family as funeral expense offerings.

The special character of the Hwarang can be traced to a traditional communal institution dating back to the Three Kingdom's formative period and the Koguryo institution of *Kyong-dang*, thought to be devised as a means to reinforce local units. Like the Hwarang, the Kyong-dang carried on an earlier tradition of communal bodies of unmarried males, and the youths devoted themselves to cultivating moral values and practicing the military arts. (Lee, 1984)

King Chin-hung of Silla

Artist impression of King Chin-hung. King Chin-hung was crowned in the year 540 at the age of 17. He was the 24th king of Silla.

King Chinhung: Initiator of the Hwarang Tradition

During the first half of his reign King Chinhung was believed to have originated the great Hwarang warrior tradition, implanting a nationalistic form of idealism, which survives to this day. King Chinhung led his armies against Paekche and Koguryo, seized vast lands from the lower Korean peninsula to the Yellow Sea, and laid the groundwork for the first unification of Korea a century later. He is believed to have built the largest Buddhist temple ever constructed in Asia. The stone monuments he erected throughout his huge territory during the 37 years of his reign have been invaluable in the study of ancient Korean history and language.

His "Hwarang spirit" of intense loyalty to friends and country directly motivated almost every great figure involved in Silla's rise to power, and also incorporated religious and aesthetic philosophies into the model lifestyle it promoted.

A society similar to the Hwarang may also have existed in another form during the reign of King Pophung in 525. It seems agreed, from accounts in both the *Samguk Yusa* and the *Samguk Sagi* (*History of the Three Kingdoms*)—the latter written by soldier-statesman Kim Pusik (1075-1152)—that as a concept, they were immediately preceded by a group headed by two women, Chunjong and Nammo. These women were singled out for their beauty, grace, and moral virtues by King Chinhung (r. 540-576). Both acquired separate camps of followers who were taught filial and fraternal piety, loyalty, and sincerity. At some point however, Chunjong, turned on Nammo because of jealousy killing her. Chunjong was put to death, the group disbanded and its followers dispersed

Persevering with the ideal he had in mind for young people, the king still favored the development of a cultural cadre of exemplars of youth and artistic attainment. He introduced the institution of Hwarang, consisting of the finest physical specimens of males from families of high moral status. Both the previous groups and the young men's cults fostered strong religious and leadership development. It has been speculated that members of the original society headed by young women had the abilities of shamans to cast spells and cast out spirits.

The credo underlying this society was a combination of the traditional way of life of the tribal communities with the new spiritual disciplines of Buddhism. Historians such as Lee feel it is plausible that in a society marked by strict social stratification, the Buddhist teaching of reincarnation was especially appealing to the aristocracy. With a rebirth based on the quality of a previous life, it may have been welcomed as a doctrine giving recognition to the privileged and could have been accepted as a system of thought well suited to the needs of a centralized aristocratic state headed by a king.

The conviction that the Buddha Maitreya or "Buddha of the Future" had experienced several incarnations on Silla soil in the form of famed Hwarang warriors is another reflection of the belief in Buddhism as the protector of the state. Soldiers were exhorted not only to fight bravely in battle, to safeguard the state and its ruler, but to defend the "way of the Buddha," lending a sense of holy mission to combat. (Lee, 1984)

Quite often Buddhist monks were members as well as instructors of the Hwarang. The monk Won'gwang Popsa was the author of the famous *Sesok Ogye*, or *Five Commandments*, which became the basic rule of life for the Hwarang. These were: 1) to serve the king with loyalty, 2) to serve one's parents with filial piety, 3) to be faithful to one's friends, 4) not to retreat in battle, and 5) not to kill indiscriminately.

Women's Position in Old Korea

That the first two Hwarangs selected were female is an indication of women's status in Old Korea. Three of Silla's monarchs were queens. Even at the end of the 1800's, it was the queen, not the king, who Japanese swordsmen attacked and killed.

Old customs such as marrying for love seem to have survived until the end of the Koryo dynasty. Not until the introduction of Confucianism did conventions of Chinese origin infiltrate the culture, disempowering them with the institution of match-making and blaming them for societal weaknesses with the infamous "Seven Sins" of married women.

Still, under the Confucian system, women's feet were not bound as in China, and women maintained control of household management. A man could divorce, but was not allowed to legally remarry as long as his former wife lived. A typical Yi dynasty woman differed considerably from her counterpart in the West. She was educated for independence, moral strength, and endurance. Every yangban clan had to restart at one time or another with a strong mother and her children who were spared from the purges often killing off all male members of a clan. A woman always carried a small ornamental knife with which to kill herself should she ever be threatened with rape.

Abuse of female spouses was rarely encountered as such a man and his own family would be expelled from his village if he were found guilty. (Yun, 1989)

Won-gwang is one of the greatest monks in Korean history.

Silla Monk Writes Conduct Code for Hwarang

The Hwarang youth were taught "the five cardinal principles of human relations": kindness, justice, courtesy, intelligence, and faith; the six arts: etiquette, music, archery, horsemanship, writing, and mathematics; the three scholarly occupations: royal tutor, instructor and teacher; and the six ways to serve the government: "holy minister, good minister, loyal minister, wise minister, virtuous minister, and honest minister." They were engaged in the study of both political and military administration, the nomination of non-Hwarang men for office, and the supervision of the work of those who received appointment.

A youth named Sol-Wonnang was made an early head of the order with the title of Kukson. There is a stone monument at Myongju (now Kang-nung) which was erected in his memory. (Ha, 1969)

While their talents in the arts were initially emphasized, it is certain they were educated in mountaineering and in martial arts, since the Hwarang is known to have produced generals and soldiers and played a vital part in the unification of Korea. The existing records verify their military training in the use of chariots and archery.

Korean society of those times was divided into "bone-ranks," castes determined by ancestry. The chin gol ("true bone") rank provided generals and the highest civil servants. Most of the Hwarang came from this, and as historian James Gale has noted, they were a band of adolescents of high purpose, "who could not avoid being both religious and at least quasi-military, sometimes very military, because that was the nature and need of the society in which they lived." Considering their pivotal role in the unprecedented process of unifying the three Korean kingdoms, it is certain that "very military" is more applicable.

Most of the great military leaders of Silla belonged to the Hwarang, prominent among them being Kim Yu-sin (also known as Yu-shin-Kim), architect of the victories that led to the unification. Another was Kim Ch'un-ch'u (also known as Chun-chu-Kim), later King Muyol, whose political leadership both before and after he attained the throne was also key to unification. (Han, 1974) The younger men who followed a particular Hwarang were identified as members of his *to* (circle, group or order). These youths, like their leader, were of noble birth, but they were apparently not required to be of equally high rank.

Many stories of Hwarang heroism survive, including those of Sa Ta-ham, Kim Yu-sin and Kwanch-ang.

Two Friends Named Kim Lead Silla to Greatness

Kim Yu-sin was Silla's most famous general and greatest military strategist. He and his close friend, statesman Kim Chun-chu (later King Mul-yol) teamed to lead the Silla nation to pre-eminence over Paekche and Koguryo. Kim Yu-sin was a member of the royal family of Kaya, a tiny kingdom annexed by Silla. He was called the "Seven Star General" because seven star-crests were seen on his back as a baby. From his childhood he stood out for his abilities,

Yu·Shin Kim and Chun·chu Kim

Artist impression of Kim, Yu Shin and Kim, Chun-chu, the Silla general and future King who was ultimately responsible for uniting the three kingdoms under Silla rule.

and at the age of eighteen was said to have mastered the art of swordsmanship and to have become a Hwarang.

Both Kim Yu-sin and Kim Chun-chu were involved in the diplomacy and strategies to first make China and Koguryo allies against Paekche, and then to inspire former Paekche and Koguryo solder's loyalties against China, ousting it from Silla. This accomplishment underlines the sense of identity as a Korean people that was already in place even among former enemies when threatened by the Chinese. Brought together by Silla as one blood, one language, and one culture, the Koreans stepped united from ancient to medieval history.

At one point when the forces of T'ang and Silla had settled down before the gates of Paekche, the two commanders planned a coordinated attack. Right at this time a fierce-looking bird circled around the head of General Su. A fortune-teller said it was an omen of his sure death in the coming battle. The general trembled from head to foot and was about to order his men to turn back. But Kim Yu-sin unsheathed his long sword, struck the swooping bird dead, and laid it at the general's feet saying, "A small grotesque bird cannot interfere with our great expedition against a bad king." King Uija of Paekche, and his crown prince subsequently fled to Ungjim and ultimately he and his sons were taken prisoner by General Su and removed to the T'ang capital, Changan. (Ha, 1972)

Another story that illustrates the intensity, spirit, and martial training of the Korean soldier concerns General Kim Yu-sin and his group arriving late for an appointed meeting at the T'ang encampment. Ting-fang was about to have the Silla governor Kim Munyong decapitated at the camp gate because Yu-sin and the others missed the appointed schedule. Yu-sin said to his horde, "The Great General did not witness the campaign at Hwangsan, yet is treating our missing the appointed schedule as a crime. I cannot accept this shame while guiltless. We must first fight a decisive battle with T'ang and then crush Paekche." He stood at the camp gate gripping a battle-axe, his hair bristling with anger, and the jeweled sword at his waist leapt instinctively from its scabbard. Ting-fang's General of the Right Tung Pao-liang stepped on Ting-fang's foot and said, "The troops of Silla are going to revolt," whereupon Ting-fang absolved Munyong of any crime. (Jamieson, 1969)

Yu-sin has another act of bravery recounted about his warrior spirit in an attack on Koguryo's Nangbi Fortress in 629. The Koguryoans sent out a massively destructive counterforce that virtually broke the morale of his men to the point that none would fight on. Yu-sin was a commander of the Central Banner at that time. He came forward to his father in the battle, stripped off his helmet and announced, "They've defeated us. But my life has been guided by loyalty and filial devotion, and I must be courageous in the face of battle. We hear the saying, 'Shake a coat by its collar and all the fur will fall smooth. Lift up a net's head rope and the whole net will open.' Can't I be the collar or head rope now?"

Then he mounted his horse, drew his sword, and leapt over a trench into the enemy ranks, beheading the general. He came back holding the head up high, and when his army saw this, they struck out in attack to take advantage of his victory. Over 5,000 enemy men were killed and beheaded, and a thousand were taken alive. (Lee, 1993)

Evolution of the Hwarang

In the early eighth century Kim Tae-mun wrote a book entitled *Hwarang Segi* (*Records of Hwarang*), which described the lives of about two hundred Hwarang. This, according to Han, presumably was the source of many of the Hwarang tales that survive, although the book itself, like so many, has disappeared.

Silla's King Chinhung was well known for his exemplary character. The kingdom of Paekche had proposed to Silla that the two kingdoms launch a joint attack on Koguryo. King Chinhung flatly refused, saying "The rise and fall of kingdoms depends on heaven. If Koguryo has not provoked the wrath of heaven, how can I dare to attack her?" Word of his response reached the king of Koguryo who was deeply moved and subsequently strengthened his ties with Silla. This caused the exasperated king of Paekche to vent his anger by attacking Silla.

After the consolidation of Korea, the versatile Hwarang, when not participating in the wars of the old kingdoms, returned to the role of sophisticated performers of the arts. Following the Silla period, however, the Hwarang in the central and northwestern parts of the county became known as *Sollang* and *Kukson*. These names are believed to be related to the location of the subsequent Koryo dynasty (918-1392), while the word *Hwarang* survived longer in the southern and eastern parts where the original Hwarang lived during the Silla period. (Gale, 1972)

Ultimately, the institution of Hwarang splintered, the entertainment aspect predominated, and popularization resulted in the misapplication of a term originally connotating dignity and renown to the Korean people. It wasn't until the 20th century when the word resurfaced during the Korean War that it regained more appropriate usage, later becoming more widely and specifically applied in the context of Korean martial arts and sports.

In the *Samguk Yusa*, powerful stories of miracles, soldier monks, and morals define the golden era of the martial tradition of Korea. One of these stories concerns the monk Hyesuk, a follower in his youth of Hoserange, one of the most renowned Hwarang of Silla. It contains several of the dominant elements that motivated Korean warriors of the time, illuminating the seriousness with which they viewed the moral obligations of the Hwarang and describing the caliber of spiritual adepts who distinguished the upper levels of the society.

After Hyesuk's master, through circumstances told in another story, was barred from the order, Hyesuk retired to a mountain villa. There he led the life of a religious recluse for twenty years.

One day Kugam, a noble Hwarang warrior, was riding in the mountains near Hyesuk's home. Hyesuk ran out to meet him and held his horse's head.

"Welcome, master," he said. "Permit me to follow you in the hunt. I can keep up with your steed on my flying feet." [Author's note: A parallel exists to "flying feet" among the "leaping lamas" of Tibet, spiritual adepts whose powers included the ability to accelerate their travel across vast distances.]

"Fine!" said Kugam. "Come along, then."

They raced over the hills, and Kugam killed many birds and animals with bow and arrows. Finally they sat down to cook the meat, falling into conversation.

"I have some meat more delicious than this," Hyesuk said. "May I serve it to you?"

"Good, bring it," said Kugam. "I have a fine appetite today."

Hyesuk reached for his own thigh with a sharp knife and cut a piece of his own flesh to set before the astonished Kugam.

"Please help yourself," he said.

"What are you doing?" Kugam exclaimed with horror.

Said Hyesuk, "I thought you were a kind-hearted gentleman and merciful to your fellow creatures, so I followed you in admiration of your high virtues. But now I see that you are a cruel and selfish man who likes to kill living creatures, doing harm to others in order to fill your stomach. This is not the way of benevolence and you do not belong to our order."

Hyesuk then stood and left Kugam.

"Ah, the sad day," said Kugam, blushing with shame. "But what is this? I have eaten my fill, and yet the table is still spread with the same dishes and appears untouched."

Kugam returned and told his strange story to King Chinp-yong, who marveled at the events and sent an official to bring the uncommon monk to his court. When the official arrived at Hyesuk's home, he found him, he thought, lying in bed with a woman. He cursed him for his shameless breach of Buddhist law. However, only a short time after leaving Hyesuk, he met him on the road, coming from the opposite direction.

"Hello, good monk," he said. "Where have you been?"

"I have been at a rich man's house in the city," he said. "I officiated at a memorial service and offered prayers for the departed soul for seven days. Now I am returning to my home in the mountains."

The official returned to court and reported his puzzling experience to the king who sent a messenger to the house Hyesuk had mentioned. Indeed, they said, the monk had been there when he said he was. [Author's note: Appearing in two places at once is an ability credited to spiritual adepts across Asia.]

Shortly thereafter, Hyesuk died and the village people buried him on a hill east of E-hyon (Ear Pass). But while his friends were still at the gravesite, a traveler arrived from the other side of E-hyon. He stated that he had just met Hyesuk over the hill. When asked where he was going, Hyesuk had said, "I have lived too long in this mountain village and now I am going on a sightseeing trip."

Then the traveler said that the monk mounted a cloud and soared into the sky about half a mile from where he had said goodbye. Amazed, the villagers dug into the grave into which they had just placed Hyesuk's body and found in it only one of the monk's old shoes.

Today there remains a temple called Hyesuk-sa north of Ankang-hyon, where the mysterious monk lived. Visitors can see his image in bas-relief on one of its walls. This tribute to a Hwarang has survived to remind Koreans for centuries of the profound depths of their martial arts heritage.

From the Samguk Saki: *Heroes Eager to Die for Their Country*

Simna and Sona of Sasan: Since Sasan's border was continuous with Paekche's, there was not a month that went by without plundering and attacks back and forth. Whenever the soldier Simna went out to fight, however, the strongest columns could not stop him. During the Inp'yong period (634-646), troops were sent out from Paeksong Commandery to seize Paekche border towns. When Paekche responded with a swift thrust by crack troops, all officers and men except Simna retreated in scattered confusion. Holding out alone, Simna drew his sword and, cursing madly, eyes ablaze with fury, lopped off the heads of several scores of men. The bandits were so frightened that they pulled back their troops, not daring to confront him. They referred to Simna as the "Flying General of Silla." It was also said among them that "While Simna still lives, one does not approach Paeksong."

Sona, his son, was also famous for his prowess, and had his father's spirit. Once Paekche was defeated, he was transferred to Adal Walled Town. One day in 675, the town's Protector, Hanson, instructed all of the people to go out to plant hemp on a certain day. No one was to disobey the command. A Malgal spy learned of this and returned to report to his chieftain. Then, on the designated day, when all the people had left the fortress and were in the fields, the Malgal troops slipped by and rushed into the walled town, pillaging and stripping the whole area. The aged and young who had been left behind were in total confusion and could do nothing when Sona came toward the bandits, brandishing his sword and shouting loudly, "Don't you know that Sona, the son of Simna is in Silla? I have no fear of death or thought for my life so why don't those of you who want a fight come and get it?" Then he rushed at the bandits, full of fury. They fired at him; not daring to wait until he came close but Sona fired back with so many arrows the exchange looked as thick as a swarm of bees. From sunrise to sunset he engaged the bandits, taking so many arrows he looked like a porcupine. Finally, he toppled over dead.

Sona's wife was the daughter of a good family belonging to the Karim Commandery. When the people of the Commandery heard of his death and went to mourn him, his wife wept and answered them with, "My husband always said, 'The heroic one must die in battle. How could I die while lying on my bed mat attended by my family?' He always talked like this and now he has died the way he wished."

When the king heard this, he sobbed, and with tears wetting his garment, said, "Both father and son showed bravery for their country. One can certainly say of them, 'Their devotion has saved our generation.'" He was posthumously awarded the chapch'an rank.

Chu'udo, The Saryang, and His Brothers: Ch'udo left home to join the priesthood during King T'aejong's time when Paekche advanced on Choch'on Walled Town. T'aejong moved his army out to fight the invaders but was unable to achieve a decisive victory. Knowing this, Chu'udo was concerned that he was useless to his country as he had not yet been able to acquire the highest level of practice ("one who can regain his essence by purifying knowledge and techniques") or to "implement [religious] methods and practices for others' benefits," the second level of achievement. He felt he was "merely" an ascetic monk "doing nobody any good. It would be better to go with the armies and be killed to repay our country."

Shedding his clerical garb, he obtained a military uniform and joined the Three Thousand Banner, setting out with the armies towards the enemy. When banners and drums of the opposing sides met head on, he grasped a lance and sword and rushed into the columns where he battled ferociously, killing several enemy bandits before he died.

Ch'udo's brothers were also heroes. His eldest, Pugwa, was a Banner Chief and ranked first in battle merit when he was killed. His younger brother, P'ipsil, made Second Overseer in Noble Banner, explained his family's philosophy of self-sacrifice to his wife when he left for his final engagement:

"My two elder brothers have died in the King's service, acquiring permanent fame. I'm not worthy of comparison with them, yet could I be afraid of death only to survive in humiliation? I leave you alive today but it is as if parting at death. Live well and do not be grieved."

When the columns clashed, he went out and struck alone, dying only after he had beheaded twenty or thirty men. When the Great King T'aejong heard this, he tearfully lamented, "Ch'udo's sacrifice of his life roused the hearts of his younger brothers, so that both Pugwa and P'ipsil could show gallantry in duty, paying no heed to their own bodies. Is it not magnificent!?" They were presented the sach'an rank posthumously.

Kim Yongyun, Saryang Soldier: Yongyun was from a family which served the court from generation to generation. His grandfather, a Hwarang who had fought alongside Yongyun's father, Pan'gul, said to him at the battle on the plain at Hwagsan where they both faced death at the hands of Paekche general Kyebaek's troops: "Loyalty is the officer's highest ideal as is filial devotion the son's, and should one give his life in the face of danger, he would be perfect in both of these." Pan'gul acknowledged his words, then immediately went into enemy ranks where he fought with all his strength and was killed. Yongyun eventually became Infantry and Cavalry Overseer in the Yellow Collar Sworn Banner. Just prior to setting out, he said, "I'll make sure that my clansmen and friends will hear nothing ill of me from this campaign."

In a battle near Kajam Walled Town, his co-commanders were assessing their next move in a conflict in which an enemy with superior numbers was cornered. Common wisdom dictates never to press a cornered enemy. His peers advised, "Our best move would be to pull off to the side, wait until they're thoroughly wearied and then strike. In that way we'll snare them without even bloodying our swords." All the commanders agreed with this and pulled back for a period. All but Yongyun. He refused to retreat and wanted to fight.

One of his followers spoke out and said, "How can it be that all the commanders are so anxious to save their skins; they hold their lives so precious that they agree with what was just said and are going to wait for a convenient opening! But, sire, you cannot make a direct advance alone!"

Yongyun countered: "We not only are warned by the Canon of Ritual of facing the columns without bravery, but it is the natural duty of a soldier to advance and never retreat. A hero makes his own decisions when faced with a problem. Why follow the crowd?"

He then rushed into the enemy columns, grappled furiously and died. He thus made the ultimate contribution to a family tradition of heroism. When the king learned of his act, he was moved with grief and tearfully said, "Only such a father could produce such a son. We rejoice in such gallantry and sense of duty." Rich titles and awards were posthumously given to him.

Yolgi, in the First Year of King Munmu: Yolgi (surname not recorded) was Infantry and Cavalry Overseer on a mission of King Munmu's to send military previsions to P'yongyang. Blizzards and freezing cold were encountered on the way and great numbers of men and horses froze to death. Koguryo soldiers were waiting to attack, knowing that the opposing troops were exhausted. Sending a message to P'yongyang was imperative for the king's men but how, under these conditions? Yolgi came forward and said, "This nameless one is dull and feeble but I want to be among those who go!" Given permission and brandishing swords, they dashed on horseback, armed also with bows, passed the Koguryo soldiers who were unable to block them. Within two days they had delivered the command to General Su. The men of T'ang were relieved and overjoyed at the news of the provisions and sent a return message which again took Yolgi only two days to bring. Yolgi was rewarded with kupch'an rank, the highest his commander, Yu-sin, could give but he was so impressed with Yolgi's achievement that, when he reported to the king, he requested the honor be upgraded to sach'an. The king then asked, "Isn't sach'an level a bit excessive?" to which Yu-sin, bowing twice, replied, "Titles and emolument are official tools for the repayment of merit. How can it be considered excessive?" The King agreed and awarded the higher honor.

P'lpu of Saryang, Son of Chondae: At a time when Paekche, Koguryo, and the Malgal had formed varying alliances, were "as close as lips and teeth," and were scheming to invade Silla, King T'aejong sought those of "loyal and valorous timber who could calmly govern." P'ilpu was picked to be District Commandant of the area below Ch'ilchung Walled Town. In 660 Paekche was brought to its knees by King T'aejong and the T'ang armies. Retaliating, Koguryo sent troops to lay siege to the walled town. But when P'ilpu held firm and fought for more than twenty days, it became obvious to the enemy that the Silla men were fighting "with all their hearts, with no regard for themselves." They were about to pull back from the walled town when a traitor, Pisap, secretly sent a man to report that the town had run out of provisions and that if they attacked, the fortress would fall. P'ilpu learned of the betrayal, drew his sword, and lopped off Pisap's head, casting it over the walls in the direction of the enemy. He said to his officers, "The loyal subject and righteous warrior do not bend even unto death. Give it all your strength, for the survival of the fortress rests on this battle." Then, when he waved his fist and gave a shout, even the injured rose and struggled to be first to the walls to fight again.

However, the exhausted heroes could not last long; soon more than half lay dead or injured. The enemy set fires as soon as a breeze blew up, then attacked and stormed through the walls. P'ilpu, with his officers, met the enemy and fired at them point blank. Flying arrows showered on P'ilpu, piercing his body and limbs. Blood streaming to his heels, he fell to the ground dead. When his king learned of this, he wailed in pain. The rank of kupch'an was posthumously conferred. (Jamieson, 1969)

Military Organization of the Three Kingdoms

As the kingdoms developed into centralized aristocratic states, and military units came to be organized on a national level, kings became the commanders-in-chief of their nation's military forces. Frequently the monarchs of the Three Kingdoms led their soldiers in person and fought alongside them in battle. (Lee, 1984) This is indicative of the inseparable value of martial arts training to leadership in those days and reflects the expectations of the people that their leaders be personally powerful, fit, courageous, and highly competent in the arts of defense and offense. A leader likely to go down in battle or shirk his personal duty to fight with his men was unthinkable. Accordingly, the soldiers of that time looked upon their military service as an honor and privilege, rather than as a burdensome duty or danger to be avoided.

Little information survives on the organization of units in the new military structure. It is known that in Silla, six divisions called *chong* or garrisons were established, one in each of the provincial administrations. Each was commanded by generals of "true-bone" status and was composed of men who lived in the capital, drawing on the elite lineage's centered there.

Supplementing these core forces were companies of very young men, often in their mid-teens, like the Hwarang. In Koguryo, like the Hwarang of Silla, the Kyongdang carried on an earlier tradition of communal groups of unmarried males. The youthful members of the Kyongdang also devoted themselves to cultivating moral values and practicing the military arts. (Lee, 1984)

Each of the Three Kingdoms organized military forces at the district or local level where the units of civil administration also served as the basic units of the local military order. In each of the fortresses that served as the centers of district administration, military units of fixed strength were garrisoned, and it is thought that the Kyongdang was instituted as a means to reinforce these local units. The songju, the "castle lord," was the commander of a district's military contingents, and the provincial governors in charge of a number of fortified district centers also doubled as military commanders. To the commanders for their victories in battle—or to the aristocratic holders of government office—large grants of land and numerous prisoners of war were added to their holdings.

Unification of Korea

The growing reputation of Silla in the sixth century had been attracting more and more alliances from neighbors. The kingdom of Ka-rak had existed side-by-side with Silla on terms of mutual friendship for 482 years, but in 527 her king gave up his sovereign power and merged his kingdom with Silla, retaining governorship of Ka-rak under appointment by the king of Silla. This move forestalled the chance of Ka-rak's becoming disputed territory between the rival powers of the peninsula.

Ruk U, Kaya's Master Mu sician

Kaya's Master Musician Ruk U invented the 12 string Kaya harp called the Kayagum which is still used in Korean traditional music today.

Ruk U, Kaya's Master Musician:

King Ka-sil of the Kaya kingdom invented the Kayagum harp, but Ruk U is the composer who made the Kaya harp sing like the angels. The 12-string Kaya harp probably descended from other stringed instruments. Ruk U created 12 famous compositions for the Kaya harp. The title of each was borrowed from place names of his day.

When the Kaya kingdom fell, Ruk U moved to Silla, where the King was happy to welcome him. Three students studied voice, dancing and the harp under him, and they made rapid progress. One day, however, they got together and decided to simplify Ruk U's compositions, which they felt were too complicated. Ruk U was furious when he found out, but finally agreed to listen to the new versions. Ruk U was so impressed by what he heard that he told his students they had honored him, rather than slighted him, and had them go play for the king.

Because of the genius of Ruk U, the voice of the gods has sparked from the strings of the Kaya harp to the hearts of the Korean people for over a thousand years.

Even the Japanese, separated by the sea, were concerned about Silla's rising pre-eminence. In 560 the Ha tribe, from the northern Japanese island of I-so, sent their chief to swear allegiance to Silla. (Hulbert, 1969) Japan also continued in its fascination with the dominant Korean culture around this time. Artists of both the kingdoms of Koguryo (Tamjing) and Paekche (Prince Arja) were invited to Japan. Their talent was so acclaimed that such outstanding works as the murals at the Horyuji temple and the portrait of Shotoku Taishi, both in Nara, traditionally have been attributed to them. (Hulbert, 1969) In 661, many Japanese were interested in rallying to the cause of Paekche. Prince P'ung, a son of Paekche King Uija, and a younger brother of the puppet Crown Prince, was able to enlist some 5,000 Japanese soldiers to accompany them back from a recruiting trip to face the repressive Chinese.

Adding to the revitalization of Silla was Buddhism, which was rapidly gaining converts. Monasteries had been erected, and in 551 the king authorized publication of the teachings of the eight laws of Buddhism against (1) the slaughter of animals, (2) theft, (3) licentiousness, (4) lying, (5) drunkenness, (6) ambition, in terms of wanting what someone else had, (7) the eating of garlic, and (8) levity, in the sense of improper flippancy or frivolousness.

Paekche had lost a large tract of territory, perhaps as much as half its kingdom, to Silla, starting with the war in 555. With Silla's superior forces, at a time when the other two most powerful Korean kingdoms were weakened, it expanded its territory, placing the economically significant Han and Naktong River basins under its control. Possession of the Han River basin also separated Paekche from Koguryo with the stationing of a powerful force there. When Koguryo sent General Ondal to this area in an attempt to regain the territory at the beginning of the reign of King Yongyang (590-618), defeat again further weakened Koguryo. (Han, 1974)

Not to be brought down easily, Koguryo had held against six T'ang attempts to subdue it. The last and most extensive was repulsed by Koguryo's "iron man," Yon Kae So-mun (or Kaesomum), prime minister of Koguryo until his death in 666. In the 7th century, when the threat by enemies of the Three Kingdoms had never been, greater, Yon Kae So-mun became Lord of Koguryo. The Sui dynasty and the Korean kingdom of Silla had formed an east-west alliance against Koguryo. In defense, Koguryo made treaties with the north-south powers of Tolgwol, Japan, and Paekche. An epic clash loomed. The crisis came at the Sal River, where the Koguryo hero, Ulji Mundok, crushed a massive Chinese force.

Artist impression of Yon-gae-so-mun who is known as the iron man of Koguryo.

Yon Kae So-mun was a small boy at the time but news of the stunning victory electrified him. He was inspired to grow up to be a fearless, strong and tough fighter, but was possessed with a violent personality, no patience for detail and ruthless ambitions. Able to command the loyalty of his fellow soldiers, he eventually formed a plot to gain control of all Koguryo. He invited his king, Yongnyu and his ministers to a feast, had his soldiers murder the guests in what has been described as a "wholesale slaughter," (Lee, 1984) and appointed himself the Mangniji, a lord with full powers over the government and army. This is comparable with the Shogun position of the Japanese culture but was centuries before the Japanese Shogun was created. With this, Yon Kae So-mun issued commands near and far, taking all state affairs under his absolute control. He was extremely stern and commanding, keeping five knives on his person at all times. No one ever dared raise his or her head to look at him. Whenever he mounted or dismounted his horse, he would have a nobleman general crouch on the ground as a stepping-stone. When he left the palace, columns were sent to mark the way and a runner sent ahead to shout loudly, whereupon everybody would scatter and even throw themselves into pits and gullies so as to not look directly at him.

Many subsequent military clashes with China were rebuffed by this indomitable leader, forcing China to abandon its campaigns. He set Koguryo on a collision course with both T'ang and Silla, demanding that Silla yield up the Han river basin and spurning T'ang requests that Koguryo halt its military operations against Silla. Kae So-mun's defiance prompted a large-scale T'ang invasion.

Crossing the Liao River, Emperor T'ai Tsung brought down the Liao-tung fortress and a number of others but suffered a massive defeat at Koguryo's An-shih fortress at what is now Ying-ch'eng-tzu and was compelled to turn back. The soldiers at this fortress withstood a siege of more than sixty days, during which the T'ang army massed as many as six or seven assaults in a single day. But the stubborn defenders, commanded by Yang Man-ch'un, hurled back each fresh attack.

Koguryo's victories over both the Sui and T'ang invasion armies have special significance in the resistance of the Korean people to foreign aggression. (Lee, 1984) The conquest of Koguryo was identified as part of a Chinese plan to dominate the whole of East Asia. Had Koguryo's soldiers lacked either skill or will and had been beaten back, Paekche and Silla likely would have fallen as well under Chinese dominion. But Koguryo held firm, serving as a breakwater against which the repeated Chinese invasions foundered. Had Koguryo not possessed weapons of equal or superior design and quality, and a martial arts training heritage equal to the finest, Korea might be part of China today. Koguryo was equal to its adversary, if not better.

It was the weakening of Koguryo as a result of rivalry among Kae So-mun's sons and the defection of the eldest son to the Chinese side, not military weakness that caused the kingdom to be defeated in 668. (Hulbert, 1969; Lee, 1984)

In 624 Paekche regained some territory lost to Silla, and in the succeeding two decades, both Koguryo and Paekche made repeated attacks on the territory of Silla in retaliation for Silla's earlier aggression in the Han valley. Koguryo and Paekche formed an alliance in 643, but another alliance seven years later between Silla and China was far more significant to the outcome of Silla supremacy on the peninsula. The decision by the Chinese emperor to cast his weight behind the perceived winner sealed the destiny of Korea as a united country for the first time. (Han, 1974)

The high status of Korean martial prowess in eastern Asia at this time, and the degree of respect Koreans drew, is evident in the military and diplomatic stances they felt free to take in regard to Chinese overtures. Both Koguryo and Paekche confidently refused to follow T'ang suggestions that they conciliate with Silla. Further, Koguryo wounded the Chinese emperor's pride with impunity by reinforcing its hold on Liao-tung, which was entrenched as a Chinese outpost, and by maintaining at least one major fortress west of the Liao. When a Silla emissary asked the Chinese emperor for aid against Koguryo, the emperor, already determined to avoid confrontation with the soldiers of Koguryo, facetiously proposed three outrageous plans to discourage Sillan interest in active Chinese participation: (1) Incite the Malgal tribes to harass Koguryo's northern borders, drawing attention from an anticipated Koguryo confrontation with Silla; (2) take from the Chinese a large number of red flags to march against Koguryo, giving the impression of having Chinese allies; or (3) if Silla were to temporarily depose the first woman on a Korean throne, its Queen Tong-man, a man could more ably plan Sillan wars. As the historian Hulbert said of that period, "China was willing to do anything but meet the hardy soldiers of Koguryo in the field."

In all the struggles leading to unification, the forces of the three regions fought with distinction, despite their subsequent losses, as is widely documented. Frequently, the reasons for a defeat had political overtones, followed in-fighting or a change in government, or were the result of misalignments with Chinese emperors. Both the Koguryo and Paekche soldiers have been noted consistently as superior martial adepts. Resistance to the Chinese colonialism of T'ang by Paekche occurred even before the fall of Koguryo. A rebel army said to number 30,000 under Hukch'i Sangji won many victories, capturing about 200 forts.

General Kye-Paek of Paekje

Artist impression of General Kye-baek, the most brilliant general in Paekche history.

General Kye-baek: Fighting Zeal Personified

The story of General Kye-baek of Paekche became legendary as an illustration of Korean courage and fighting zeal. In 660 A.D., with an army of 50,000 supported by a Chinese army of 130,000, Silla's Kim Yu-sin attacked the kingdom of Paekche while political in-fighting weakened it. Cornered, General Kye-baek felt compelled to save his family members from dishonor and slavery by ending their lives himself. With that tragedy fresh in mind and knowing he would soon be meeting his own death on the battlefield, he then assembled 5,000 Paekche soldiers who swore to die rather than retreat. He led them to the Plain of Hwangsan for the final battle. The Paekche force crashed into the Silla army like an avalanche, capturing one of their leaders, Kwang-chang.

Enraged, the Silla warriors roared back to battle, but were repulsed four times by Paekche troops. The last encounter, however, totally decimated the resources of the Paekche. When the dust of battle cleared, General Kye-baek lay dead and only a handful of his wounded soldiers survived.

The nation of Paekche, exhausted by internal conflicts and war, virtually died with Kye-baek. His tragic and fearless determination to defend his country to the end and spare his family from slavery is identified by modern Koreans as an example of the national spirit and unity.

Wives Join Paekche's Doomed Army

Another Paekche army under the noble Poksin and a monk named Toch'im took Churyo fortress and besieged Sabi, the capital. In 660, Toch'im founded, along with Prince Pok-sin, the Uibyong, the "Righteous Army" of patriotic volunteers. It was begun with a handful of men and swelled as the great mass of the people of Paekche found this force to be the expression of their self-sacrificing loyalty. Wives and children were said to be equally devoted to the cause, and they fought with remarkable effectiveness until internal dissent caused the army's collapse. It is possible that this is one of the first documented times that women were official fighters for a nation.

Twenty thousand Silla and Chinese troops were cut off and surrounded before Silla, allied with T'ang, retook the Paekche Churyo fortress in 663. Behind these military maneuvers were political intrigues that resulted in Toch'im's murder by Poksin who was in turn assassinated by Prince P'ung. "King" P'ung disappeared shortly thereafter. The Paekche leader of another force, Chiusin, fled to Koguryo. The T'ang allies of Silla took over Paekche and installed Paekche Prince Yung as puppet head of their government. Among the vast royal families of Paekche and Koguryo, there often were to be found opportunists willing to be used by the Chinese as leaders in name only.

Fate put Silla in position as the final victor, although near the end of the Three Kingdom period, even Silla's future was cloudy. The alliance with the Chinese T'ang against Paekche turned against Silla. Former Silla territory in Koguryo was not returned. Silla was ready for active resistance to Chinese domination soon after the fall of Koguryo, first supporting rebellions in Chinese-controlled territory. In 671, Silla's King Munmu started advancing directly against Chinese rule, invading Paekche territory and taking Sabi. Emperor Kao-tsung sent invasion forces to Silla but the Silla warriors drove them back and out of their headquarters at P'y-ongyang. They fled all the way to the Liaotung peninsula. Silla then controlled most of the Korean peninsula; however, Emperor Kao-tsung tried political maneuvers to overturn its stability. In 677 he then appointed the former Koguryo king, Pojang, who had been demoted to a military governor of Liaotung district, and a Paekche prince, Yung, military governor of Ungjim, to mobilize against Silla. They were turned back. Ultimately, in 735, the Chinese gave up claims to the former Paekche and Koguryo territories and granted formally that all territory south of the Taedong River belonged to the independent Kingdom of Silla.

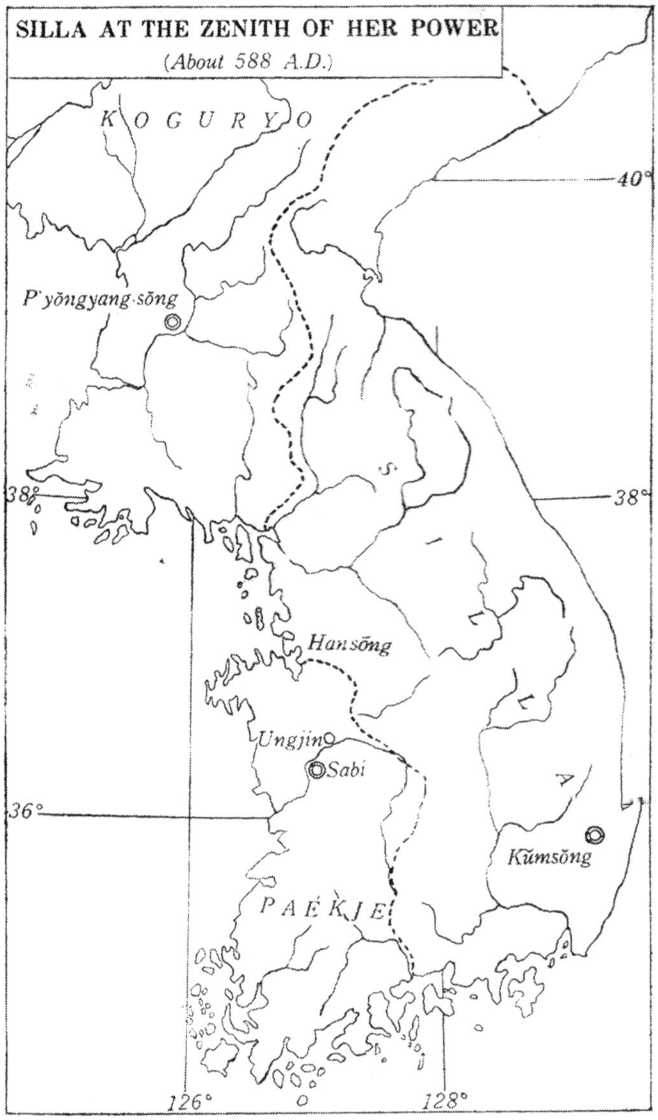

This map shows Silla at the zenith of her power just before the unification of the 3 kingdoms.

Rulers of Silla promoted further interest in Chinese culture and Buddhism, adapting only the most appealing and complimentary aspects into their society and ignoring the remainder. Korean aristocrats still remained as staff and general officers in the military, unlike in China. The young men of this aristocracy devoted themselves almost exclusively to military training during this era of frequent conflict—also a significant difference from Chinese practice. (Han, 1974)

This strong adherence to tradition while experimenting with the new is a hallmark of Korean culture. It seems highly unlikely, therefore, that the great Korean teachers of the Three

Kingdoms martial arts schools would have any interest in tossing aside the practices of the revered adepts of their lineages in favor of predominately Chinese techniques. No doubt intermittent alliances with various Chinese kings resulted in some exchange of ideas in the martial arts, but there would be no motivation for abandoning the highly effective Korean combat skills and the complementary Korean martial arts way of life, particularly when there was no pressure to do so, as there definitely was in later years.

That the Chinese borrowed at this time from Koreans is a matter of record: In the Chinese battle with Koguryo forces for the renowned fortress of Liao-tung, the Chinese were materially aided by Paekche-designed armor which Paekche had sent as a gift to the Chinese Emperor. (Hulbert, 1962) As history moved on and records were lost it is most certain this armor by Paekche came to be known as Chinese not Korean. Many mistakes of this type have occurred throughout Korean history. How many weapons, armor, literature and other items that were Korean in origin, transmitted to China or Japan, and thought to have originated in those countries has history recorded incorrectly?

That the Chinese admired the Koreans was also noted. When the Chinese conducted a siege of An-si fortress, two incidents in surviving records credit Korean troops. Through his skill and the absence of adequate Chinese defenses, one Korean soldier managed to wound the Chinese emperor in the eye, an encounter not mentioned in Chinese histories. The Koguryo forces were able to delay the siege until late autumn when approaching cold weather compelled the emperor to consider withdrawing. He was filled with admiration for the pluck and bravery of the little garrison of An-si and before breaking camp, sent a message to the commander of the fort, praising his faithfulness to his sovereign and presenting him with one hundred pieces of silk. He then withdrew 70,000 soldiers to begin the long march back to China for the second time after attempting the takeover of Koguryo.

When loyalty to teacher and secret strategies, identification with heroes of the past, and pride in the mastery of their own art predominated so markedly, it is a certainty that Koreans continued to pass down with the greatest respect their own hard-won and effective martial arts skills.

Japanese Adoption of Korean Cultural Innovations

When students of martial arts history talk about who borrowed what from whom there are several points of reference in historical records that clearly indicate the interest of the Japanese in replicating many aspects of Korean culture. In the sixth and seventh centuries, powerful Japanese clans sent their sons to Paekche for on-the-job training as bureaucrats. Paekche dispatched to Japan technicians in metal processing, saddle making, cloth weaving, dress making and irrigation; divination, calendar-making, Asian (Chinese) scriptural interpretation, temple architecture, and tile-making. In addition, many members of the royal families, including royal princes, went to Japan from Paekche, returning to Paekche to accede the throne.

While the culture of Paekche was being transmitted from northern Kyushu to Yamato, Silla culture, particularly the arts of black smithy and Silla Buddhist temple construction, also was being introduced, via the southeastern section of the Korean peninsula, to the Sanin coastline of Japan. As well as copying the advanced institutions of Buddhism from Silla (reflected in the design of Koryuji Temple), Japan adopted Koguryo architecture, following its earlier contact with Paekche Buddhist temple culture (seen in its Hokoji Temple). The Silla hyo system as both administrative and military units was incorporated into Japan. The educational system of Japan's reform government was an imitation of Silla's education system, and it was, in fact, to Silla that Japan looked for models for education, sending its students exclusively to Silla during the Taika period.

After Silla erected an observatory during the reign of Queen Sondok (632-645), the first Japanese observatory was patterned after it in the fourth year of Emperor Tenu (676). (Kim, 1989)

Silla Buddhism itself made a considerable contribution to the development of major Buddhist schools throughout East Asia with its diverse schools. Korean Buddhism was the state religion for 865 years (527-1392) and from it came the great scholars Wonhyo (617-686) and Uisang (625-702). These men influenced Fa-tsang (613-696), who systematized the Chinese "Flower Garland" school. Oral legends credit the monk, great martial artist, and teacher Wonch'uk (613-696) with exerting a profound influence on early Tibetan Buddhism. He is believed to be the originator of the ecumenical tradition characteristic of East Asian Mahayana Buddhism as he sought to harmonize the doctrinal differences of various schools. Musang (680-762), the Silla monk of the Meditation school active in the Szechwan region, was the first Ch'an master known to the Tibetans.

Koguryo monks also made contributions to Chinese and Japanese Buddhism. Sungnang played a major role in China as a master of the Three Treatise School, and Hyegwan founded the same school in Japan. Kwalluk and Hyech'ong went to Japan as experts from Koguryo on the Three Treatise School, and Tojang founded the Tattvasiddhi (Jojitsu) school in Japan. The Disciplinary school in Paekche enjoyed international status after its founder Kyomik of Paekche returned from India to codify the fruits of his studies there. In 588, three Japanese nuns studied the rules of discipline in Korea for three years, returning to their homeland to open the first Disciplinary school in Japan. In Paekche in 599, a decree was issued to prohibit the killing of living beings. Domestic birds were set free and hunting and fishing equipment were burned. (Lee, 1993)

These and other examples demonstrate that Korea was an innovative country and suggest that its martial arts were unique and indigenous, despite the purge and loss of explicit documentation.

3

Unified Korea Integrates Martial Prowess

The Koreans were one of the first people to form a nation from diverse states. This strength in unity began in the year 700 A.D., and the unification forged by Silla initiated the welding. By the opening of the tenth century, Paekche, Silla, and Koguryo were so firmly joined that no sectional differences would seriously threaten their disruption for eight centuries. In 996 this unity was reflected in Korea's first coining of money in the form of iron disks. (Hulbert, 1962)

Two bloodless changes of dynasty would occur but not a single successful revolution, in the ordinary sense of the word, disrupted Korean unity. There would be three great, and several small, invasions, but none of these left any lasting rent, either racially or linguistically. Nationalism drove the martial sciences and fueled its traditions as a way of life.

Subjugated Koguryos Resist Chinese

Strictly speaking, Silla did not succeed in unifying all of the territory occupied by the Three Kingdoms. Koguryo's share of Manchuria remained outside the influence of Silla. Unified Silla and Parhae were still maintaining north-south hostility, but ultimately it was the land and people of a unified Silla that coalesced the culture of Korea that was to come. This is considered the principal factor for emphasis on the historical importance of the consolidation of Silla, together with the similarity in ancient and modern boundaries. (Lee, 1984)

After the fall of Koguryo, thousands of its citizens were taken captive to what is now Cha-yang where a base was set up to control the eastern tribes. Resistance by the Malgal, Khitan, and others was certainly anticipated, and in 696 a Khitan chief named Li Chinchung led his people in revolt. At the same time, Taejo-yong, a former general of Koguryo, drew together an army made up of Malgals and Koguryo soldiers, and mounted a migration out of Chinese-controlled territory. They settled eventually near Kirin in northern Manchuria. There they founded a state which was initially called Chin but in 713 was renamed Parhae. Taejo-yong became King Ko in 698.

Despite the large proportion of Malgal tribesmen in the new kingdom, the ruling class was comprised of Koguryo people who clearly regarded their state as a transplanted Koguryo. This is evident in the text of an official communication conveyed by a Parhae envoy to Japan, in which Parhae still regarded itself as "Koryo-guk"—Koryo or Koguryo territory. (Han, 1974)

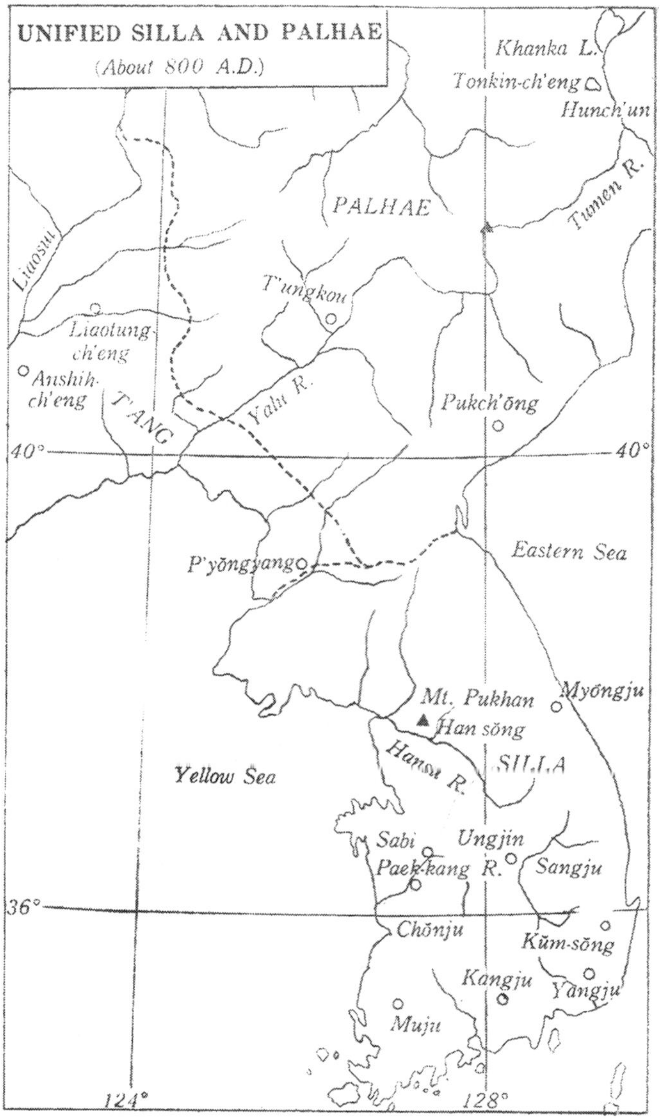

This map shows the territory that Palhae occupied before it eventually fell.

Envoys dispatched from Parhae to foreign states for the most part had the surname *Ko* (belonging to the Koguryo royal house). Archeological remnants pointing to the cultural transference between Koguryo and Parhae include the *ondol* (the previously noted Korean system of heating by means of flues laid under the floor). Ondols were discovered at the site of the palace of Parhae in the inner citadel of the capital at Sanggyong, and the stone burial chamber structure of Parhae tombs with a horizontal entrance shaft. Buddhist statuary and roofing end-tile decoration between the two states also bears witness to the crossing-over of cultures.

The former Koguryo people, indefatigable, were to begin a rise in both territorial extent and cultural achievement which would peak in the time of King Son (818-830), when they would occupy a vast area reaching to the Russian Maritime Territory to the east, K'ai-yuan in south-central Manchuria to the west, the South Hamgyong region in the Korean peninsula to the south, and the Amur River to the north.

Unified Silla Reorganizes Military

The resurrection of Koguryo as Parhae was not welcomed by T'ang China or Silla, which expressed its concern by building a long wall along its northern border. This wall stretched completely across the northern part of the Korean peninsula from the East Sea to the West Sea.

Unified Silla also reorganized its military. With the Silla unification, the *yukchong*, or six garrisons thought to have been structured according to earlier tribal traditions, went out of existence. The nine *sodang* ("oath bannermen") divisions of King Sinmun's reign (681-692) formed a national army that was stationed in the capital. At first it was voluntary, but it developed into nine divisions, each with uniforms colored distinctively green, purple, white, scarlet, yellow, black, cobalt, red, and blue. A special characteristic of the *sodang* was that they drew their recruits not only from native Sillans but from the former inhabitants of Koguryo and Paekche, and from Malgal tribesmen as well.

In 733, the T'ang emperor asked Silla for military help in conquering Parhae, sending a 604 man military mission for the negotiations. The joint force was unsuccessful. Parhae grew in stature and established relations with the nomadic tribes of the north in China and Japan. By the late eighth century, Chinese chroniclers were referring to Parhae as "Haedong Songguk," the prosperous country of the east. Finally, when the T'ang dynasty fell, the Khitan conquered Parhae, dominating much of Manchuria and north China. When Parhae fell in 926, its culture faded from what is now Manchuria due to the fact that the standard-bearers of the culture, the ruling elite of Koguryo ethnic stock, fled to the new Korean state of Koryo. Parhae's indigenous Malgal people shared little of the distinguishing marks of the Parhae culture and were incapable of perpetuating it. (Even today there are villages in the northern part of China that speak Korean as their second language because of their link to these earlier kingdoms.) The Malgals founded their own Jerchin state, drove out the Khitan, and emerged as masters of all Manchuria and of the northern half of China. Parhae was the last state through which the Korean people represented themselves in the Manchurian area.

In debates about the historical origins of various martial arts, one needs to consider the relatively short time frame in which modern martial arts have been identified with particular areas. In the case of Korean martial arts, it is beyond debate that for a thousand years, Koreans were at home, physically and culturally, in lands throughout Manchuria and far into what is now China. With that in mind, it is even within the realm of possibility that many of those

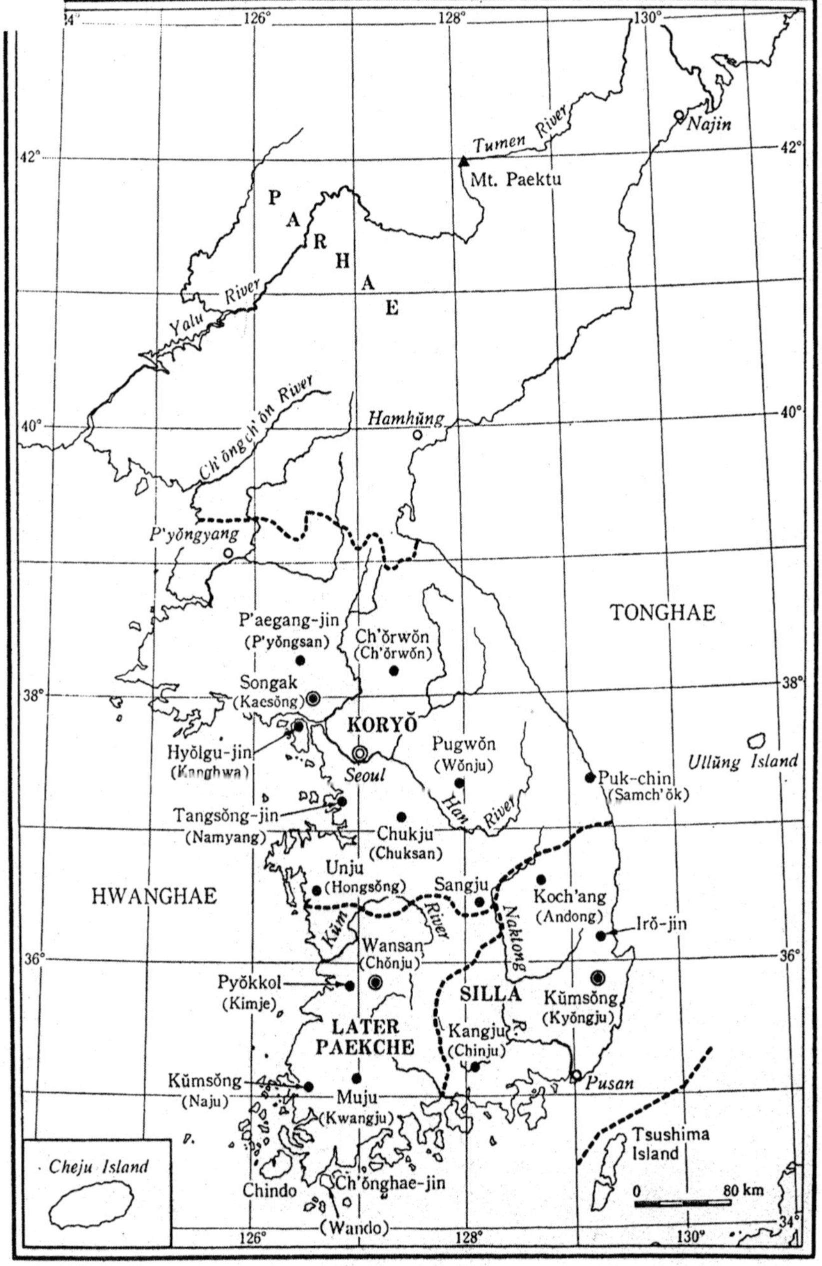

KOREA IN THE LATER THREE KINGDOMS PERIOD
(LATE 9th—EARLY 10th CENTURIES)

This map shows the boundaries of the Later Three Kingdoms.

martial arts techniques widely identified as northern Chinese may well be Korean in origin. To insist that martial traditions flowed in only one direction, China to Korea, without documentation, makes those who favor this theory appear biased in favor of the now-dominant Chinese culture.

As many of the ruling class of Parhae came south, they joined the newly founded Koryo dynasty, which supplanted Silla territory at this time. After the Manchurian part of the Parhae lands was lost, the territory south of the Yalu-Tumen boundary remained Korean. Silla ruled the rest of the peninsula and its culture overlaid the basically similar cultures of the other two kingdoms, though local variations remained. Cultural landmarks of the times are plentiful and include the world's oldest extant example of woodblock printing, a Korean achievement found in a copy of the *Dharani Sutra*, dated sometime prior to 751 A.D.

Records from this era also mark the accomplishments of astronomer-astrologer Kim Am who was also commander of the P'aegang Garrison. He was so well versed in military science that he taught his troops a "six-column battle formation" that was proven highly effective.

During the reign of King Hyegong (765-780) comes another story pointing to the early Korean use of steel armor, a device some have mistakenly speculated was not Korean. While the core of the story may seem fantastic to those not inclined to believe in the supernatural, the specific reference to this particular armor would not have been a necessary detail unless it was known to have come from that time. The legend relates to the sudden appearance during a great wind of a dignified general mounted on a horse and followed by forty honor guards clad in armor. They emerged from the sky and descended into the vortex of the mighty wind issuing from the great Kim Yu-sin's tomb. Inside the tomb, a dialogue was heard between the spirit of the king and the general from the sky who was imploring the dead ruler to release him from his duty of protecting his country. The ungratefulness of his subjects was infuriating the mighty general's spirit. The spirit king denied his request with a moral lesson for Korea's living soldiers, "If you and I do not guard this country with our immortal strength, what will become of our poor people? I command you to continue to display your patriotic spirit with loyal mind for the welfare of the state." (Ha, 1972) This story sent a clear message down through the military ranks for centuries that even ingratitude was no just cause for suspending one's duty to safeguard the homeland. It reflects the deeply ingrained military zeal of Koreans.

In some circles there is a misguided belief that Korean offensive and defensive techniques and weapons were Chinese imports, especially its weaponry. Again, this time in records from the ninth century, we find a reference to more weapons imbedded deeply in the tradition of the Korean people. The battle axe and halberd were designated as symbols of a Koryo Grand General's power and were presented by the king in dispatching the Commissioners of Men and Horses, the *Changmasa*, to their commands, one in the northeast and one in the northwest frontier districts. A weapon of their Chinese foes would hardly be selected for this honor. The halberd, called *chung-yong-waldo* or "heavenly dragon moon knife," would not have been singled out for this ceremony had it not, along with the battle axe, been very significant to Korean warfare.

These are just a couple of types of moon knife used throughout Korean history.

An earlier reference from the seventh century after the battle for Ongsan Walled Town, merits were weighed, with the sword being conferred on the ranks of *kakkan* and *ich'an* who served as commanders and the halberd on *chapch'an*, *p'ajinch'an,* and *taeach'an,* who also served as commanders. (Jamieson, 1969) Mistaken opinion has often said that Korea didn't even have the halberd; a few claim it didn't have *any* traditional weaponry. In view of Korea's 5,000-year history, it staggers the imagination to deny innovation and pride in the arts of warfare in a land of arch-nationalists.

The Gentry Rises to Power

King Hyegong (765-780) inherited the first signs of rebellion from the authoritarian power of the throne since King Kyongdok's time. The latter detected the winds of change and tried a program of political reform built around the Chinese model. His program failed to gain support. In 768, Kim Tae-gong formulated a plot against the throne, which grew into a power struggle with the *kakkan*, Silla's highest ranking officials. In 774, a high-born member of the aristocracy seized power and reduced the king to a figurehead. The king was finally killed, ending Silla's golden years with the beginning of a long period of internecine strife and decline. Members of the aristocracy had joined forces to break the authoritarian power of the throne, but it was just this unquestioned power that kept rival factions from destroying the gains of Silla's warrior society.

Formation of the Private Armies

A shift of power to the nobles resulted in an increase of individual wealth with the return of the former "stipend village" system but it destroyed the country's solidarity. Now, ambitious nobles seeking to protect their vast economic resources innovated personal military forces, armed their slaves, and recruited the landless peasants who roamed the Silla countryside. These Korean private armies were among the first of their kind in the world. Now it became political leverage and armed might, rather than blood lineage that became decisive in determining succession to the throne.

Under these circumstances, whoever could collect and train the better army might emerge victorious in the struggle for the kingship but he could no longer represent the aristocracy as a whole. Only his own partisans who had raised him to the throne could keep him there, resulting in a precarious monarchy. Each new king became the target of revenge of the factions he had defeated. Twenty kings occupied the throne during the approximately 150 years of the later period of Silla, which ended in 935. (Lee, 1984)

Chang Po-go, Warrior Master of the Yellow Sea

Chang Po-go was apparently the scion of a gentry's family from Wando who became a renowned pirate hunter. He traveled to China as a young adventurer, and there his Korean martial skills were so prized by the Chinese that he rose rapidly in the service of T'ang. After some time it came to his attention that his Korean countrymen were frequently captured by sea marauders and sold into slavery in China. Outraged, he returned to Silla and appealed to King Hungdok (826-836) to establish a garrison on Wando with him in command.

Chang Po-go had already built a personal armed force around other members of his family, similar to many other powerful families who for several generations had exercised such control, far from the scrutiny of central authority. These gentry houses typically were in the midst of a population center, protected with fortifications famous throughout Asia. Their owners became known as 'castle lords' (*songju*) or 'generals' (*changgun*), since they commanded their own private soldiery recruited from the locals. From both the "true bone" aristocracy and those of "head-rank six," these included many aristocrats from the capital city. They had been forced to retreat for political reasons to the Silla countryside where they re-formed power structures. Some were also the local elite, headmen's families expanding their original power bases. Castle lords of both types eventually usurped the power of the prefecture and county magistrates sent from the capital, and eroded the economic foundation of the central government with their independent taxes and demands for service.

With a force of 10,000 men, Chang Po-go patrolled Silla's coastal water, crushed the Chinese pirates, and controlled a lucrative trade with both China and Japan. His ambitions to become a major political influence in the capital lead to his downfall and his "navy" ultimately was relocated to another part of the country.

Peasant Revolt

Other castle lords were less colorful but luckier and continued to undermine the authority of the central government of Silla over the countryside. The government's response was to create its own "army" of aggressive tax collectors. The castle lords continued to embellish their lifestyles with their own tax levies. The result was doubly negative for the peasants, many of whom were forced to abandon their land and roam the countryside, further destabilizing the old social order.

The first peasant revolt erupted in the Sangju area in 889, and many others followed. Two rebel leaders finally appeared, Kungye and Kyonhwon, who were strong enough to create new state entities in the areas they controlled. They challenged Silla's dominance and claimed that the states they founded were restorations of Koguryo and Paekche. The almost half-century of disputes spawned by these challenges became known as the Later Three Kingdoms period.

One of these leaders, Kyonhwon or Chin Hwon, was of poor peasant stock from Sangju who rose in the ranks of the Silla army due to his martial abilities. The catalyst for his ascent to leadership was Queen Chinsong (888-898) who appears, according to the *Samguk Yusa,* to have represented the declining capacities of the Silla rulers. Her misrule and inattention led to widespread oppression of her people. Kyonhwon, "the tiger-spirited general," gathered together a mass of supporters, led a revolt, and occupied the old southwestern Paekche territory. He proclaimed himself "Commander-in-Chief of the Armed Forces of Southwest Silla and Founding Prince of Hannam [south of the Han River]," establishing his capital at Wansan (modern Chonju). A course of despotic and intractable rule followed.

Kyonhwon's advanced ambitions were thwarted by the rival rebel, Kungye, a Silla prince ousted from the capital during a power struggle. He first became a monk, and then shifted toward more full time confrontation with Silla as a soldier in the armies of other rebels. Finally he assembled his own large force and made himself head of the state of Later Koguryo, ultimately renaming it Majin, then T'aebong. Bitter at the loss of what he rightfully considered his, the Silla throne, he renamed Silla "Nation of the Damned" and is said to have killed all those from Silla who entered his territory. He became an imaginative despot, claiming to be the returned Buddha (the Buddha Maitreya), and designated two of his sons Bodhisattvas (potential Buddha's who gave up heaven to aid suffering humans). The net result of his behavior was his assassination, after finally being chased out of his capital by a disgruntled citizenry.

Wang-kon, one of Kungye's young lieutenants, was destined to become the founder of a dynasty. His life is detailed in records that style him as fore square in the tradition of the Silla

Hwarang. His story has the classic Hwarang elements of tutoring by an accomplished monk with the emphasis on soldiering as an art, and guidance in spiritual matters to access supernatural powers.

His father, Wang-yung, "a large-minded and ambitious man," according to old records, lived in the town of Song-ak. As he was building his house a monk, To-sun, predicted that a great man would be born inside. The monk handed his father a letter to be given to the yet unborn child when he was able to read it. On the night Wang-kon was born in 878 A.D. a luminous cloud hung over his home, making the house as bright as day. The child was described as having a very high forehead and a square chin. When he reached his 17th year, monk To-sun reappeared and became his tutor, instructing him especially in the art of war. He showed him also how to obtain aid from the heavenly powers and how to make sacrifices to the spirits of mountain and stream. To-sun also prophesied that after 160 years, circumstances would require the changing of the capital city of Koryo, which in fact, was begun sometime after the assent to the throne by King Suk-jong in 1095.

Eventually he came to serve Kung-ye who made him governor of Song-do for his outstanding service. (Hulbert, 1962) However, times changed and Wang-kon turned on Kung-ye, overthrowing his government in 918 and founding the Koryo dynasty, with the capital at his hometown of Kaesong.

Swordsmanship of the Ninth Century

In the *Samguk Yusa* there is a continuity of evidence as to the relevance of the sword in Korean warfare, a point one might hardly consider worth emphasizing, given the history of Korean warfare. Nevertheless, since there are still some who downplay the prominence of the sword in Korea, its chronicles involving this weapon are revealing.

One story in which Korean swordsmanship is memorialized concerns General Yom-jang's mastery of intrigue and swordplay. Yom-jang discovered that a disgruntled commander of a naval base, Kungp'a, was plotting an armed rebellion against his king, Sinmu (836—he reigned for only about a year). Yom-jang received permission from his king to go and bring back the traitor's head by himself.

Using his wits, he concocted a story to tell Kungp'a, claiming he had fallen from King Sinmu's favor and wanted asylum with Kungp'a to escape death. Kungp'a took him into an inner room to question him in private. Finding Yom-jang's tale convincing, he toasted his new-found ally with too many cups of drink, and when he was intoxicated, Yom-jang suddenly drew the long sword sheathed at the rebel's waist and cut off his head with a single stroke. When Kungp'a officers and men were informed of the feat, they prostrated themselves before Yom-jang in fear and astonishment. The general returned triumphantly to Kyongju with Kungp'a's head advertising the success of his mission and the skill of his arm. Highly pleased, the king gave Yom-jang a large reward and promoted him to a high official rank.

This tale was preserved to illustrate both the guile and the powerful sword-wielding abilities of heroes in those times. Yom-jang had the intelligence to obtain access to his victim under high guard, to immediately take advantage of his distracted state, and, although he was at least somewhat drunk, employ his resources with powerful effectiveness. It also tells us that military men were always expected to be wearing a sword.

The Korean use of the sword to underscore dominance and victory also appears in the story of Wang-kon (or Wang-gon; later King T'aejo). In the name of Kungye, he seized almost the whole of the territory included in the present provinces of Kyung-geui and Ch'ung-ch'ung. In 901 he proclaimed himself king, emphasizing his dominance by slashing with a sword the portrait of the king of Silla which hung in a monastery.

In another story there is a reference made to the dance of the Spirit of the Northern Peaks. This dance was called the *Ok-do-ryong* ("ok" meaning "jade") because it was performed with a jade sword and a jade ring. A weapon that was not central to preservation in the consciousness of Koreans would not be employed in such imagery, nor would it be described as jade, with the deep significance that stone has to Koreans.

The dragon is a very common image on Korean traditional weapons.
This picture was taken by the author at the war museum in Seoul.

In *Poems by Zen Masters,* compiled by Jaihium J. Kim, a monk appears as the epitome of a commander with a sword representing the worldly concerns he is leaving behind. In "To General Chong," he says, "You swell in a golden helmet, long sword worn by your side." This is a detail that would likely have been mentioned only if it were typical and pervasive in a soldier culture.

Korean Proverbs by Bruce K. Grant includes the ancient saying, "Like slicing water with a sword," to show that marital squabbles should leave no lasting scar on a relationship, despite how much force is used in their delivery—similar to a sword passing through water. To use the sword as a metaphor for analyzing the institution of marriage shows how deeply the sword was imbedded in Korean culture.

Koryo Martial Society Before Bushido

Koryo society was intensely focused on martial life. Emerging from a matrix of military conflict in which it destroyed its powerful Later Paekche foe, it continuously went to war with the Khitan in the north. To most efficiently utilize its famed fighting men, it refined its military organization, built around the military strength of the Kaesong region. Led by Wang Kon (known posthumously and historically as King T'aejo), a Kaesong native who founded the Koryo dynasty in 918, this was the central body to conduct the unification of the Later Three Kingdoms. The weaponry and tactics of the Korean military had to be at least equal to their opponents, if not superior.

The forces of the central government under T'aejo became the nucleus of King Songjong's military, likely around 995. They became known as the "Two Guards and Six Divisions." "Divisions" refers to the Division of the Left and Right, Divine Tiger Division, Elite Striking Division, Internal Security Division (exercising political power in the capital), Thousand Bull Division (used for state ceremonies) and the Capital Guards Division (military presence at the palace and city gates, and at the government buildings). The first three divisions were charged not only with defense of the capital but guarding the frontiers.

The two Guards units, the Soaring Falcon Guards and Dragon-Tiger Guards, were formed later as the king's personal bodyguards, and they ranked above the Six Divisions. Each unit was composed of regiments of 1,000 soldiers each. These regiments were classified as infantry, cavalry, prison guards, army ceremonial, naval ceremonial, and gate guard regiments, totaling 45 regiments.

The evocative names of these Korean divisions surprise some people who associate colorfully symbolic designations in the military solely with the Chinese. Korean military duty was enhanced liberally with interesting appellations for many aspects from weapons to fighting units.

Rank and file Korean fighters initially were professional military men from families traditionally military. Their names were separately recorded in a military census roster as military householders. The state granted them compensation for service in the form of "soldier's land" (*kuninjon*) and assigned two "supporting households" to cultivate each of their plots, the income of which provided for the soldier's livelihood and equipment expenses. The granting land for service through the Stipend Land Law indicated the high esteem in which military service was held. It was similar to some of the systems that evolved later in Japan. It considerably predates the *bushido* system in Japan.

This land and its "support households" were inheritable *if* the soldier had a son or grandson to carry on his obligations when he retired from active service. Otherwise, the land had to be returned and exchanged for a modest pension land allocation, which also went to families of officials and deceased soldiers, including war widows with no means of livelihood.

Once again we see the importance of martial arts skill to the Korean culture. Skill and knowledge meant power, translated tangibly into extensive land and servants otherwise inaccessible to the average family. We can see that the secrecy and elitism surrounding martial arts was not only a matter of national security but such training could be the basis of great power and wealth. Keeping land in the family required the rearing of sons in the military tradition; the more males in an extended family who fought, the more land and servants the family acquired and controlled.

When the number of soldiers fell below strength, the Koryo military recruitment system normally sought out young and vigorous men from among the *paekchong* peasantry. However, sufficient numbers of paekchong weren't always available and *ch'onmin* or lowborn soldiers were recruited instead. This ultimately led to the decline in the social status of the soldier. (Lee, 1984)

Sunset of a Thousand-Year-Old Kingdom

From the *Samguk Yusa* comes a poignant tale of the fate of the Hwarang spirit in Silla and an illustration of high moral ground in Koreans of the tenth century. It features King Kim Pu (927-935), better known by his posthumous title of King Kyongsun, and reintroduces the villainous Chin Hwon (King Kyonhwon), the Tiger-Spirited general of Later Paekje.

In the year 926, King Kyong'ae of Silla received word that Kyonhwon was marching on his capital city of Kyongju. He sent word to his ally, King T'aejo, but before reinforcements could arrive, the king's castle was stormed by Kyonhwon and his troops. The king, his queen and court had been celebrating at the time and all persons enjoying the revelry suddenly fled the banquet hall in terror to hide.

Kyonhwon ordered his men to plunder both public and private treasures freely, to find the king, and force him to fall on his own sword. Then, with his men, they violated the queen, court ladies, and king's concubines, returning home with hundreds of aristocrats, pretty women, and precious jewels.

Before Kyonhwon left, he chose Kim Pu, a distant cousin of King Kyong'ae to rule under him. Although Kim Pu wore the coronation regalia for his throning ceremony, after Kyonhwon left, he changed his dragon robe for mourning clothes and his royal crown for a hat of hemp. He next ordered that the body of King Kyong'ae lie in state in the West Palace where Kim Pu wailed loudly with his courtiers.

Soon King T'aejo (Wang-gon or Wang Kon), the king of neighboring Koryo, heard of the brutal raid and, although a competing kingdom of Silla's, sent his condolences and deep sympathy. The following year T'aejo, with fifty horsemen, visited Kyongju. King Kyongsun and his court went to the outskirts of the city to greet him and invited him to a welcoming banquet.

After formalities, King Kyongsun shed tears as he told his noble visitor of Kyonhwon's savage raid. He also bemoaned the falling fortunes of Silla. In tears himself, the king of Koryo comforted his royal host and extended his visit for ten days before returning home. During his stay in Kyongju, records state his soldiers behaved like gentlemen, not one violating military discipline or committing lawless acts. The people of Silla compared Kyonhwon to a man-eating tiger and T'aejo to an affectionate father. On the day of the mid-autumn moon festival, the king of Koryo sent an envoy to the Silla court with an embroidered brocade robe and a saddle for the king, along with gifts for all the nobles and generals.

King Kyongsun had few illusions about where his ancient land was heading. By October of 935, most of the territory of Silla was occupied by rebels and there were more uprisings daily. The countryside teemed with bandits, famine was taking many victims, and decay had seeped into the military. Circumstances had disarmed the royal troops; it was said that they had lost the martial Hwarang spirit.

Despairing, the king conferred with his highest officials, putting the matter to them: "Should we surrender to King T'aejo and cede to this kind-hearted neighboring monarch our sovereignty over Silla or should we continue to fight the fierce war-dogs at home, then prepare for a final battle for supremacy with T'aejo, which it seems to me would mean the total destruction of Silla?"

Opinions were divided, the crown prince wishing to fight to the end. Said he, "The rise or fall of a nation depends on the will of Heaven. We must rally all loyal subjects and patriotic soldiers to defend the fatherland with all our strength and be of one mind with our people till the last minute. Why should we give up without a fight? How can we so easily surrender our thousand-year-old country to a neighbor?"

The king replied in disagreement. "Silla is now helpless and we cannot hold out any longer. If we are neither strong nor weak, we will be caught in the middle. It is unbearable to see thousands of good people suffering tragic deaths in a losing war. Rather we must lose face and surrender peacefully to save the people from great catastrophe."

He then ordered his minister to present his official letter of voluntary surrender to the King of Koryo. "All is over," he said.

The crown prince, weeping bitterly, chose to leave the court and retreat to the Diamond Mountains where, dressed in hemp and feeding on grass roots, he rallied the loyal sons of the Hwarang to fight King T'aejo.

The king's youngest son became a monk and resided at the Popsu and Haein temples the rest of his life.

The process of the king's surrender of his court and country was done with the utmost dignity, and was received with respect and honor by the King of Koryo who pledged his eldest daughter in marriage to the surrendered monarch. His first minister of state was sent to Kongju with orders to conduct King Kyonsun and his entourage to Kaesong with an honor guard. King Kyongsun set out for Kaesong accompanied by his court and carts laden with royal treasures, stretching over ten miles of highway lined with throngs of spectators.

Instead of having to watch his country sink under a weight of death and destruction, King Kyongsun witnessed an alliance of two honorable royal houses that saved his people. His title as king was reconfirmed by King T'aejo, and he was promoted to the highest position in the

Koryo court, ranking even above the crown prince. Further, he was given the old Silla territory as his fief. (Ha, 1972) In order to avoid the peasant revolts, which featured in the fall of Silla, taxes on farmers were deeply cut. Farmers were also exempted from taxation for a period of three years, which stimulated agricultural production.

This story acknowledges and honors the Hwarang spirit on two levels. It underscores the centuries-old dependence on the Hwarang to motivate soldiers in disastrous times. It also points to its influence when hope for victory is gone and an honorable compromise can be made between leaders who both subscribe to its ideals.

King T'aejo Commandments to His Son

At the age of 65, King T'aejo became deathly ill. Before he died, he drew up a list of 10 rules for Prince Mu (King Hyejong), his son and heir, to follow. They reflect the perceptions of the successful warrior-king as how best to maintain the strength of the kingdom to which he gave his life. The first was to defend Buddhism as the state religion. Another was to establish an annual Buddhist festival. However, no more monasteries should be built in order to keep the power of the priests within bounds. He advised selecting as heir the son most fit to rule, not merely the elder, according to custom, and banishing bad advisers while listening to the good. He foresaw the Khitan people as eternal enemies and urged not befriending them. In the same vein, he ruled out intermarriage with people of the south as they were perpetual trouble. Pyongyang was to be honored as the ancient capital. Last so they would be remembered most easily were advisories to look after the interests of the army and always to be ready for emergencies. He believed in maintaining peak performance in soldierly skills and urged his son to treat the military in such a way as to insure its perfect loyalty.

Koryo Squelches the Khitan

The first decades of the eleventh century watched the Khitans and Koryo seesaw for power. They each made and put aside alliances with the Chinese and Jurchen tribes. The third great Khitan invasion in 1018 was all but annihilated by a massive attack by Koryo at what is now Kusong. Scarcely a few thousand of the 100,000-man Khitan force survived. The rout resulted in a peace settlement and peaceful relations between them thereafter.

Seoul: A Martial Monk's Prophecy Capital

In 1095, the king of Koryo was succeeded by his son who, after a year, was driven from his throne by his uncle, King Suk-jong. His reign stands out principally because it was he who founded a second capital at Han-yang, now Seoul. While we don't know precisely in what year the monk To-sun predicted that Koryo would do well to move its capital 160 years hence, the preliminary arrangements made by King Suk-jong came at a time relatively close to To-sun's prophecy. It was not until the year 1104 that a palace was actually constructed there.

Koryo's "Great Wall"

Koryo's problems with the Khitan remained, despite their apparently decisive defeat of these people. One response to their threat was Korea's "Great Wall." It was built by King Tuk-jong between 1033 and 1044 from Kon-gung-na Fortress near Eui-ju at the mouth of the Yalu eastward to the Japan Sea at Yong-heung (modern Yonp'o). It was intended to discourage not only the Khitan but also the Jurchen. Nearly a thousand *li* long, it would seem an almost incredible feat except that the details of its construction are so meticulously recorded. It was as wide as it was tall, and defied regular but futile Khitan attempts to thwart is construction.

Another famous wall was built by King Tuk-jong's younger brother, Hyong, his successor. It spanned from Song-ryung Pass in the west to the borders of the Yu-jin tribe in the northeast. (Hulbert, 1962)

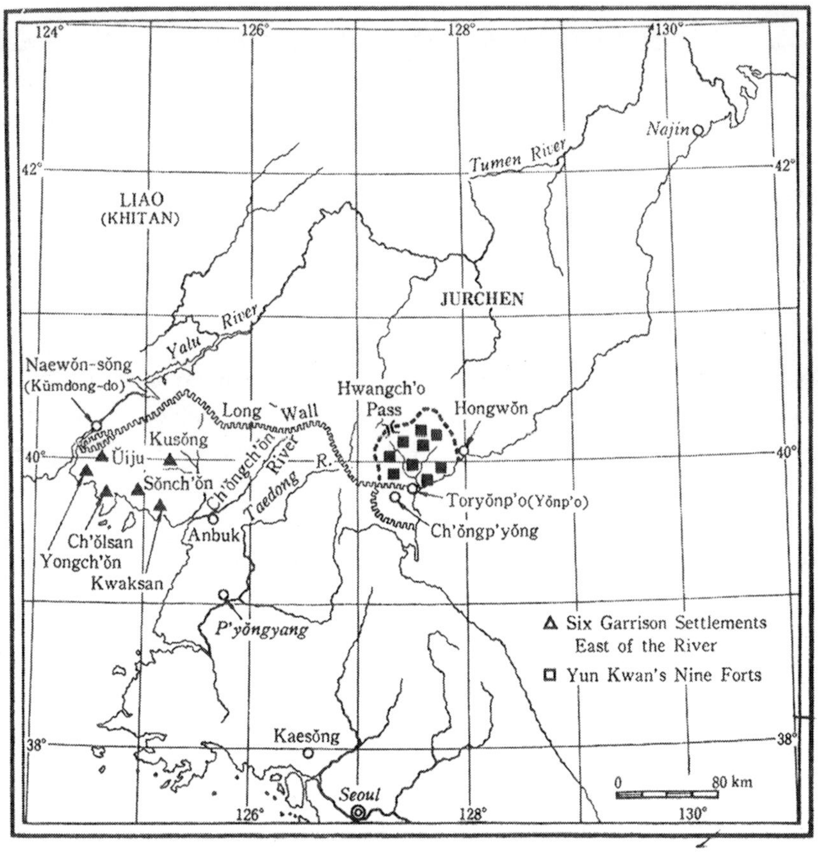

KORYŎ'S NORTHERN FRONTIER REGION
(LATE 10th TO EARLY 12th CENTURIES)

An undertaking to build such a wall could only be accomplished by a very organized and powerful nation.

In 1107 the army of Koryo was radically reorganized to better mobilize the country's defenses. Petty officials (civil and military) and merchants formed the cavalry. Farmers formed the bulk of the army—the infantry—and a third unit was composed of Buddhist monks. The Subdue Demons Corps of warrior-monks was mobilized against the Jurchen invasions. The monasteries welcomed this role in order to protect their growing wealth. They had already been training their monks as soldiers and this was another way they could protect their influence. (Lee, 1984) The monks were enlisted into the *Hang-magun.*

An army of 170,000 was raised by Koryo and dispatched to Jurchen territory, killing 9,000, capturing 5,000, and destroying 130 villages. The territory proved harder to hold than to win. Later, Jurchen leader Wu Yu-tzu made the cession of the newly fortified northwest territory the price of peace. The Koryo court gave in, lending the Jurchen vigor to turn against the Khitan monarchy of Liao. Successful, Wu titled himself emperor of the Chin dynasty and by 1117, controlled most of southern Manchuria. The Chin empire expanded to include the entire northern half of China

Despite hostilities, the Jurchen had long looked to Korea for their culture, and considered Koryo their parent country. Akuta, who unified Jurchen in 1113, had named his empire Kim (pronounced "Chin" in China) as he traced his ancestry to a Kim from Kyongju. Thus, his ancestry was "Korean," from the same fighting stock as his southern foes. (Yun, 1989)

Koryo supplied the Jurchen with grain, cloth, iron, agricultural implements, and iron weapons, which they exchanged for horses and furs. (Lee, 1984) Here is seen the adoption of Korean weapons by the Jurchen who were to carry them throughout the very northern part of what was Korea into Manchuria. This is evidence that Korean weaponry did flow to the mainland, contrary to popular belief.

Eventually all the Jurchen tribes were united under the leadership of Ukkonae, chieftain of the Wan-yen tribe in northern Manchuria. As they consolidated and realized their own power, the relationship of the Jurchen and the Koryo people became more antagonistic. Military clashes were frequent, but since the Koryo standing army had deteriorated and consisted mostly of infantry, it was only a matter of time before the mounted Jerchens dominated. Because of this threat, King Sukchong created a new defense organization called the Extraordinary Military Corps that existed apart from the Six Divisions, the regular army. It was made up of a cavalry corps, an infantry, and a so-called *Hangmagun* ("Subdue Demons Corps") made up of Buddhist monks. (Lee, 1984)

Echoes of Buddhism in Contemporary Martial Arts Lore

The promotion of Buddhism was considered by the dynastic enterprises of this period as vital to their success. This included support of temples, festivals, the special replication of scriptures, and the proliferation of honors granted to monks, including new titles such as The Royal Preceptor (*Wang sa* or "King's Teacher") and the National Preceptor (*Kuk-Sa*). These were considered the greatest honors that monks could achieve. Ancient titles such as *Kuk-Sa*, handed down directly from the days of ancient Koryo, are still used today in the indigenous Korean martial art of Kuk Sool Won.

The uniform colors represent the Royal colors and the twin dragon symbol represents the king's mandate.

A unique aspect of the Buddhist martial arts in Korean history was that, although the monks certainly acquired and used their fighting skills in defending the interests of their monasteries, their patriotic duty to defend their nation as well was clearly and repeatedly recorded.

A comparison of the martial monks of Korea and China sometimes is made, particularly in reference to the famous Shaolin temple. While the Shaolin temple has caught the imagination of latter-day Western society, there are those who maintain that the aura surrounding it as a venerable martial arts training ground is exaggerated, if not essentially a fantasy. While martial arts adepts may have taken refuge from antagonistic government authorities at Shaolin, their training most likely preceded their arrival.

Many of the great generals of the Three Kingdoms are recorded as having trained in Korean Buddhist monasteries, and as it has been noted, more than a thousand years ago. Korean monks were routinely schooled there in traditional defensive and offensive techniques.

Korea's Yangban Class Is Founded

When the court of Koryo was in formal session, the King sat facing south. Civil officials lined up according to rank on the east, hence the name *tongban* or eastern file; they were also called *munban* or literary group. The military officials lined up according to rank of the west, hence their designation *soban* or western file; they were also called *muban* or military group. Collectively, they came to be known as *yangban* and this term took on the meaning of aristocracy, 'upper classes'. The term *yangban* is still used today, but chiefly as a term of reference meaning simply "gentleman." The yangban as a system was established in the 14th year of the reign of Songjong (982-997). (Henthorn, 1963) It is important to note that martial artists of the past held such high positions in the government and society. That position deteriorated during the Yi dynasty and disappeared during the nineteenth and twentieth century Japanese occupation. However, from such historical records we can know that skilled martial artists were considered of a high status, a far cry from their perception by the public at the gangster level following W.W. II.

Personal Power, Puppet Kings, and the Mongol Wars

The first decades of 11th century Korea were characterized by military frustration with the politics of the court. Yun Kwan's troops were primed for success as they crossed the pass at modern Chongp'yong and occupied the Hamhung plain as far north as Hongwon, a region inhabited up to that time by Jurchen tribesmen. The Nine Forts were appropriately garrisoned for defense under the normal circumstances of direct attack by the relentless Jurchen attacks. They could not withstand, however, the wavering appeals of the Koryo diplomats to the Jurchen, along with the jealousy at the Koryo court over Yun Kwan's brilliant leadership. Once again, what appeared as a Korean military defeat with the return of the region of the Nine Forts to the Jurchen, actually was the result of political intrigue.

The next decades were rife with frustration and unease for the Koryo military as the kingdom fell in step with politics on the continent. Ukkonae, whose brother A-ku-ta had united the Jurchen tribes, was succeeded by his brother who founded the state of Chin (1115) from which contemporary China takes its name. The Khitan Liao dynasty was annexed to Chin in 1215, and two years later the Sung emperor and his father were captured when the Sung capital was raised. As Chin gained in strength, it put increasing pressure on Koryo, finally demanding that Koryo enter into a suzerain-subject relationship.

Despite the fact that many in Koryo considered this an insult, Koryo's King Yi Cha-gyom acquiesced. Maintaining peaceful relations with Chin was essential to the continuance of his own political dominance. Koryo's Kaesong port at Yesong was flourishing with international trade as the country exported to Chin and all over the world its famous celadon porcelain, gold, silver, copper, ginseng, pine nuts, paper, brushes, inks and fans, among other goods.

Koryo's Military Revolts

For decades privilege in Koryo society was tilted towards the noble class to a degree that the majority of military officers found intolerable. They ranked below civil officials politically and economically, and even the posts and ranks that ordinarily were their due often fell to civilians. Famous military leaders, who actually were of the aristocracy rather than from traditional military clans, included the renowned Kang Kam-ch'an (948-1031) of the Khitan campaigns, Yun Kwan (?-1111), and Kim Pu-sil (1074-1151).

The declining fortunes of the professional soldiers spurred their discontent. Although the law clearly stipulated that military men were to have their livelihoods assured through government grants of land, in reality few such allocations had been made. Those land grants that had materialized ultimately were confiscated and reassigned to paying off official stipends.

Koryo's declining interest in military readiness was reflected in increased discrimination and exploitation at the hands of civilian officials. Soldiers frequently were mobilized for enforced and unpaid labor in peacetime, reducing their status to little more than menial laborers. Many deserted. The aristocratic literati and the eunuchs worked to strengthen their powers by making the military as weak as possible while abusing them individually. (Henthorn, 1963)

As early as 1014, a *coup d'etat*, initially successful, was staged by military officers including Ch'oe Chil and Kim Hun of the Khitan wars. However, it was the neglect and abuses of the military by King Uijong (1146-1170) that inspired the military revolt of 1170. An aesthetic who scorned the warrior class, he was enchanted by such peaceful arts as gardening, building a number of pavilions with names like "Tranquility," "Joyful Pleasure," and "Beauty Attained." Around these he fashioned lily ponds and mock hillsides for his enjoyment.

King Uijong's contempt for the military was blatantly exhibited by such practices as requiring distinguished commanders to serve as lowly military escorts. During this period other insults were recorded. Without suffering any consequences, Kim Ton-jung, the son of Kim Pu-sik, maliciously pulled and set fire with a candle the beard of Chong Chung-bue, a military officer. It was the outrageous behavior of another court favorite, Han Noe that severed the loyalties of the soldiers to this regime. Han Noe's striking General Yi Pak-ung in the face triggered the revolt of 1170 in the 24th year of Uijong's reign. Commanders Chong Chung-bu, Yi Ui-bang, Yi Ko, and others assigned to escort the king on a royal procession to the Pohyon-won temple outside of Kaesong sounded the rebels' sneering cry: "Death to all who wear the civil official headdress!" Peasant and slave revolts were triggered across the country.

Improvement of status was a common cause that unified foot soldiers and officers, and ensured the immediate success of the revolt. The military removed Uijong and installed his younger brother, Myongjong (1170-1197), as regent. Major offenders such as Kim Ton-jung and Han Noe, and countless other civil officials, were executed.

Three years later, Kim Po-dang attempted to restore Uijong to the throne. Captured and faced with death, he tried to justify his efforts by declaring "The civil bureaucrats all joined in plotting with me!" True or not, this only served to inspire another purge of the remaining civil officials who had escaped death earlier. Subsequent attempts by Cho Wi-ch'ong and others to depose the military junta in Kaesong by force were thwarted.

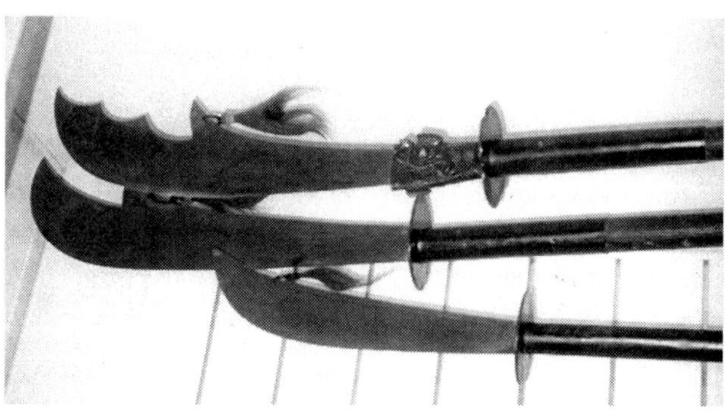

Moon knives such as these were often used for official executions.

IRON MACE ENDS ASSASSINATION ATTEMPT

General Yi Ko shared power unhappily with two other revolutionary generals. He tried to recruit his friends to help eliminate one of his co-rulers and promised them high honors if successful. Convinced, a number went with him with swords hidden in their sleeves to a feast where the unsuspecting generals would appear. General Ch'oa Wun, however, became suspicious and communicated his fears to General Yi Ui-bang who coaxed General Yi Ko to accompany him out to an ante-room. There, Ui-bang killed General Yi Ko with an iron mace to his head. Yi Ko's followers were also seized and killed. (Hulbert, 1962)

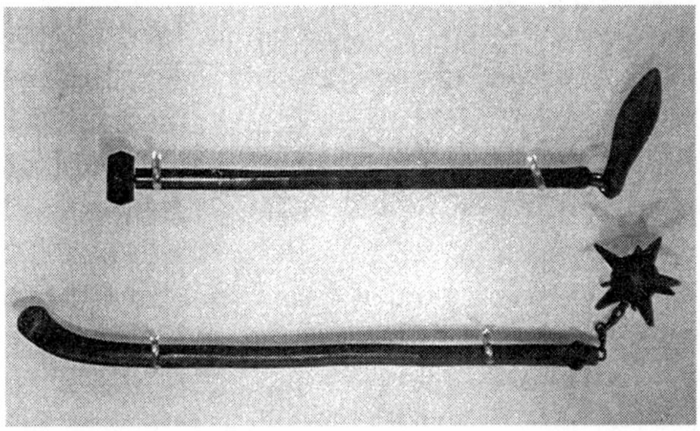

These are two of the many types of Korean Iron Maces.

Koryo's Military Individualism Pre-Dates Japan's Samurai

Koryo's military finally turned the tide of bureaucratic oppression and began to dominate every aspect of life. It first took control of the *Chungbang*, the supreme military council, using it to manage state affairs. Soldiers monopolized government positions from the most prestigious to the lowest office. They used their power and influence to expand their private land holdings and take control of the country's economic resources.

Vast wealth soon became common among members of the military hierarchy. This resulted in the creation of expansive private domains and personal house armies *(kabyong)*. Military men in a reordering of society similar to, but preceding, the *samurai* era in Japan hired other military men to command private forces of armed family retainers and household slaves. Peasant rebels and slaves felt empowered to turn society on its ear. Unlike the situation under the old nobility, the new military leaders came from any class, including merchants and sons of slaves. Through their own wiles, muscles, and acquired martial arts skills, they acquired formerly unheard of status.

Household retainers *(mun`gaek),* like their counterparts in feudal Europe, served their powerful lords with fidelity, but in Koryo, with the backing of their masters as patrons, they could gain *entree* to the bureaucracy. Koryo now experienced a radical shift in values from prestige based on exalted lineage to influence based on raw power. (Lee, 1984) Power through influence by way of marriage connections to the royal house was virtually obsolete. Desirable alliances became characterized by who was related to the leading military strong-men. Influence swung again and again from one military man to another.

For around 25 years after the revolt, intrigues and assassinations marked the power shifts at the top of control in Koryo. At first, political power was shared among Chong Chung-bu, Yi Ui-bang, and Yi Ko, the three leaders of the military revolt. Decisions were made jointly within the council. This ended with Yi Ui-bang's murder of Yi Ko. An indication that the prestige of the aristocracy still lingered in the fabric of the military mentality was Yi Ui-bang's move to consolidate his power by marrying his daughter to the crown prince. This attracted the ire of a rival, Chong Chung-bu, whose faction murdered Yi. Chong ruled then but in such a dictatorial manner that many abortive attempts by his own followers were staged to depose him. His conduct eventually attracted the sword thrust of a young commander marked or marred by an aristocratic background, Kyong Tae-sung, in 1179. Kyong's lineage, however, set many military men's teeth on edge as he attempted to lead men who were antagonistic to royal blood in their ranks. Quickly he became targeted for elimination.

Aware of his tenuous position, Kyong gathered around himself a force of approximately one hundred hand-picked men. He named them discreetly his *tobang* or "residential reinforcements." Times were tense for Kyong; records show that before long he "took ill" and died, much to the interest of a rival, Yi Ui-min (also Eui-mun or Yi Eui Mun) who avoided the court during Kyong's reign. Originally a slave, not royal, Yi was not burdened with the onus of noble lineage that doomed Kyong. He did, however, have an uncompromising personality as a ruler that manifested as extreme tyranny. Perhaps his most infamous act occurred when General Chong ordered him to kill a king who returned to Koryo despite banishment. He was taken to the brink of a pond behind a monastery where General Yi, a man with a huge and powerful physique, seized him in his arms and crushed his ribs, killing him instantly. The body was wrapped in blankets, placed in two large kettles which were set mouth-to-mouth, bound, and thrown into the pond. (Later a monk who was a good swimmer raised the body and gave it a traditional burial.) Yi was killed in 1196 by the brothers Ch'oe Ch'ung-hon and Ch'oe Ch'ung-su who made their move when they could stand no more of him. (Hulbert, 1962)

Ch'oe Ch'ung-hon's appearance on the top rung of the political ladder signaled the end of these several decades of military mayhem. He declared goals of national revitalization, elimination of corrupt officials, fair distribution of land, and a high tax on luxuries. Although he could be ruthless, Ch'oe (1149-1219) brought order to Koryo society after years of constant upheaval. His status has been compared to a Japanese *shogun*. He was eclectic in eliminating those who posed a threat as agents of continued chaos. Among those who fell victim to his interest in utter compliance were his nephew, Pak Chin-jae, and his former partner in revolt, his younger brother Ch'oe Ch'ung-su. The latter raised a force of 1,000 soldiers to try to usurp his older brother's position.

Ch'oe was determined to wipe out royal influence and bring the throne to its knees. Within a span of 16 years he deposed two kings, Myongjong and Hui-jong, and installed, in succession, four of his own royal sycophants who ruled through 1259. One of the kings who came to oppose Ch'oe finally considered it prudent to eliminate him first. He enlisted a number of armed monks to go to his quarters in the palace. When Ch'oe heard them attack his servant, he quietly slipped into a chest to hide. His personal guards, becoming aware that these were the king's agents, rushed through the palace, killing every royal loyalist in their path. They would have assassinated the king himself had not the general stepped out of his hiding place and prevented it. Instead, the king was banished and Ch'oe installed upon the throne yet another king of his own choice.

A Century of Rule By Military Overlords

1170-1179	**Chong Chungbu**		
1179-1183	**Kyong Taesung**		
1183-1196	**Yi Ui-min**		
1196-1258	**Ch'oe Clan**		
		1196-1218	**Ch'oe Chung-hon**
		1219-1249	**Ch'oe U**
		1250-1256	**Ch'oe Hang**
		1257-1258	**Ch'oe Ui**
1258-1268	**Kim Chun**		
1268-?	**Im Clan**		
		1268-1270(?)	**Im Yon**
		1270-?	**Im Yumu**

Military Backing for the Ch'oe Regime

Personal guards *(tobang),* household retainers *(mun`gaek),* and house armies *(kabyong)* effectively nullified the authority of the throne under Ch'oe's dictatorship. With the throne disabled, his rule lasted for decades, whereas others had been short-lived.

Ch'oe eventually organized his private soldiery into 36 watches which stood guard in turn at his residence. He selected for his private guard those who were "brave and strong," identifying skilled martial artists versatile with both weaponry and open hand technique. The number of men involved was much greater, in his expanded guard, than the 100 or so soldiers in King Kyong Tae-song's private guard. This caused the regular army to deteriorate markedly with its function gone, since it's most able men joined Ch'oe's armed retinue. He later added a cavalry unit to his private army.

Further military backing for his regime came from the Three Elite Patrols *(Sambyolch'o),* derived from the Night Patrol he had instituted to curb vicious marauding gangs of young toughs that had appeared among the new military. Later as it grew larger, other units formed from this group included the *Sinuigun* or "Army of Transcendent Righteousness," composed of wily soldiers who had escaped after being captured in the wars with the Mongols. Three of these units came to be known as the Three Elite Patrols which functioned as both police and combat forces. They were tantamount to an additional private armed force under Ch'oe's control, and were further evidence that Koryo's original Six Divisions had been preempted by Ch'oe.

The size and strength of the house armies of military rulers is illustrated by Ch'oe's personal force. At the time it was sent to augment the Koryo army against the Khitan, its soldiers were described as "skillful and brave" while the government army was "weak and unable to be used" (Henthorn, 1963). Records state that Ch'oe's "house" army stretched 23 *li*, not to mention the considerable companion force of his son, Ch'oe U. The elder Ch'oe had such a loyal and competent army that, when the armies of Koryo monks that fought against Khitan plotted to overthrow Ch'oe, his house force easily crushed them.

In addition to the "Army of Transcendent Righteousness," Ch'oe's reign founded patrols with equally colorful names, reflecting the evocative designations still important in Korean culture today. These included the "Hawks on the Wing" and "Dragons and Tigers" of the Koryo army.

The Mongol Invasions

Koryo's interaction with the Mongols is an intriguing historical amalgam of military, religious, political, and cultural influences, focused on a 30-year period, starting in 1231. Throughout their armed encounters with the Mongols, the Koryo military distinguished itself with bravery, skill and strategic ingenuity, repelling attack after attack and repeatedly sending the Mongols home to regroup. Only a great martial art tradition that included superior fighting techniques as part of its culture could have withstood such a rampaging force. The peasants of Koryo also displayed courage in the face of extreme hardship and lack of support from the aristocrats who had regrouped in the absence of the preoccupied military. When Koryo finally submitted to the Mongols, it was due to internal events rather than military inadequacy. (Henthorn, 1962) The legendary ferocity of the Mongols played a minor role compared to their sheer numbers and, most significantly, the opportunistic forces at work within the Koryo elite.

Koryo, Mongols Form Military Alliance

The first major military encounter between Koryo and the Mongols involved a joint effort: to destroy a motley army of Khitan who had fled from Manchuria across the Yalu to escape the Mongols. When Chin came under sustained Mongol attack, the Khitan had seized the opportunity to voice their independence. However, following the fall of the Chin capital in 1215, Mongol pressure drove them into Koryo territory where they were unwelcome visitors, penetrating within eighty *li* of the capital. Civilians obtained swords and other weapons and manned the city walls. At this time a sudden civil rebellion occurred in the city, led by priests. Ch'oe killed 1100 of them, creating "mountains of dead and rivers of blood" in the capital, but curbing their action was a costly interference in the task of driving back the Khitan. (Hulbert, 1962) To this end and, hopefully, to eradicate the Khitan problem, the Mongols offered their help.

Masters Harmon demonstrate a form of promise sparring using spear vs. open hand.

A Koryo-Mongol Martial Arts "Performance"

During the time when the Mongols and Koryo were allies against the Khitan (also called Chi-tan), Mongol Marshals Ha-chen and Tzu-yuan welcomed the arrival of Koryo Commander Kim In'gyong with a feast and music at their camp at Tok Mountain, west of the Khitan walled city of Taeju. Afterwards, the leaders had their soldiers provide entertainment in the form of a martial arts performance.

In'gyong moved his men into a military square outside the west gate of the Khitan-held city. The two Mongol marshals climbed a height to watch while the real-life defenders, the Khitan themselves, looked on from the city walls close by. Forty-six Mongols dressed in armor and with swords opposed each other in mock combat. Kim had some of his men perform various techniques with a great clamor in front of the army and then, selecting twenty skilled archers, he had them discharge their arrows into the city in a single volley. The Khitan spectators deserted the walls "hurriedly," according to records. The two marshals, not to be outdone, invited Kim to a second feast and gave him the seat of honor. (Henthorn, 1963)

This type of pre-arranged, mock combat is still practiced today in traditional martial art systems such as Kuk Sool Won. Pre-arranged combat is sometimes mistakenly identified as a creation of modern martial artists, however, as recorded here it dates back to ancient times.

Masters Harmon demonstrate long sword vs. double short sword sparring. The double short sword was a favorite weapon of women body guards in ancient Korea.

Poet-Warriors Reinforce Nationalistic Sentiment

Nationalism by this time was stronger than ever. Citizens of Koryo had consolidated their determination to remain intact on numerous occasions in the face of attacks by various surrounding neighbors. This is reflected in their literature that emphasized the country's pride in possessing a long history and tradition of intertwined military and cultural achievement. Famed Koryo man of letters Yi Kyu-bo (1168-1241) authored an example of his country's awareness of its ancient military culture in a narrative poem called *The Saga of King Tongmyong*, a tale of the legendary founder of Koguryo. He wrote it, he said, "simply to let the world know that our country always has been a land of hero-sages."

Another famous poem was written by the Uiju District Commander Kim Huije. In 1223 he led a raiding party across the Yalu against the Chin Marshal Yu-ke-hsia whose forces were still repeatedly sacking border cities of Koryo. It was likely this daring move led to his quick appointment as Deputy Commissioner of Men and Horses of the Northwest Frontier-District. Later, in 1226, he directed another small raiding party across the Yalu against Yu-ke-hsia after the latter's forces had made attacks on Koryo border cities. Not content with this, Kim evidently decided on his own authority to bring an end to Yu-ke-hsia's insolence by attacking and defeating his main army. With the help of other officials of his district, he raised a force of 10,000 men, and with a twenty day supply of food, crossed the Yalu to attack the Chin stronghold of Shih-cheng. Although Yu-ke-hsia was able to marshall reinforcements to support the garrison, Kim conquered the city. Then, in the tradition of the Koryo military, he wrote a lengthy poem expressing his belief that the generals' halberds had not yet wiped out the shame inflicted by Yu-ke-hsia, reinforcing the earlier association between this weapon and the Korean military. (Henthorn, 1963) The halberd is often thought to be non-existent in Korea, but as we see here, it dates back a thousand years and was already considered a general's weapon in the Korean military.

Kim Huije precipitated his own end through an unfortunately candid remark he made to the wrong person, a Buddhist priest, who promptly reported it to Ch'oe as proof Kim Huije was plotting against him. At a time when Ch'oe was ill, Huije believed that his leader would not recover and was rash enough to mention his forecast to the priest. Due to the intrigues and protocol of the times, this prompted Ch'oe to send officers to arrest him. Kim met them without fear, and then asked for permission to speak.

"I wish only a word, and then I will die," he is recorded as saying, putting into verse his fatal predicament:

I beg to say that the clear river has one hundred streams
of benevolence,
And East, West, North, and South
forget themselves.
What shall I do, now that I have suddenly encountered
heaven's ire?
Thus, a man of the Imperial Path
becomes a man of the blue-green sea. (Henthorn, 1963)

With this poem about the hopelessness of a military man out of favor with his commander, Huije bowed to the Koryo soldier's code of honor and, before a less noble execution were to take place, threw himself into the sea. Bound to the honor of their head of household, his son, Hong Sa, and three other persons also killed themselves.

Mongols Attempt Take-Over of Koryo

Although the Mongols helped discourage the Khitan, afterwards they demanded an annual tribute. Koryo thereby lost interest in its Mongol allies, ignored their demands and subsequently killed one of their envoys in 1225. This was the incident that the Mongols used as a pretext for launching their first invasion of Koryo in 1231. (Lee, 1989)

In August of that year, a large Mongol force commanded by Marshal Sartaq crossed the Yalu and surrounded Hamsin-chin. Convincing the inhabitants to quickly surrender under threat of slaughter, the city's Defense General, Cho Sukch'ang, seized the opportunity to ally himself with the Mongols and opened the town granary for them. He then wrote letters instructing the towns of Sakchu and Sondock-chin to submit to the Mongols. Collusions such as this with the enemy by corrupt individuals could be found throughout the Mongol wars and undermined potentially successful military efforts. Acts of bravery such as those at Chong-ju and Ch'olchu counterbalanced the treachery, more typically reflecting the Koreans' lineage of martial fidelity to country.

At Chong-ju, District Commandant Kim Kyongson led a 12-man "dare-death squad" on a march to meet the Mongol forces that were advancing on Chong-ju. But as fresh Mongol troops continued to pour in, the people abandoned the city and scattered to hide. When Kyongson and his men returned, they found the city completely deserted. Taking his men into the mountains, Kyongson headed on a seven-day "nights-only" march to Kuju, a rendezvous point for forces from Sakchu, Wiju, and T'aeju. This march stands out in world military history as an early example of the tactic of eating without using fire. (Henthorn, 1963) Marching at night, thus eliminating the tell-tale smoke from fire, is a military strategy long considered more recent in origin.

At Ch'olchu, the hero was Mun Tae, a Koryo colonel captured by the Mongols at Soch'ang-nyon and brought with them to use in negotiating. The Mongols escorted Tae to the city walls and instructed him to call out to the people that genuine Mongol forces had arrived, since the less-feared Jurchen forces had previous been known to disguise themselves in Mongolian clothing. Hoping for a quick surrender of the city, the Mongols instead heard Mun Tae shout "They are not really Mongol troops!" The city, as a result, saw surrender as more than premature. Again, the Mongols prodded Mun Tae to identify them correctly or lose his head, but the brave patriot, once again hoping to inspire his compatriots, announced that the troops were not Mongols. He was executed and the Mongols immediately launched an attack on the town.

The defenders offered a spirited resistance and many Mongols met the fate Mun Tae felt they deserved. Unknown to Mun Tae, the amount of provisions in the town was critically short, inadequate to last the amount of time a successful defense might take. When Ch'olchu's food ran out and the city appeared doomed, city administrator Yi Juijok knew what he had to do to rob the aggressors of a rich victory and save his people from a miserable, dishonorable end. He assembled all the women and children, put them in the granary and then set fire to it. He then led the male adults in cutting their own throats. Death appealed to them more than the usual fate of Mongol captives.

When word of the disaster at Ch'olchu reached Ch'oe, the Three Armies were called up and levies made on the provinces for troops as they prepared for intensified conflict. Meanwhile, the Mongol force in the northwest was experiencing a mixture of success and failure. The successes were often aided by a number of ambitious Koryo traitors, such as the infamous Hong Pogwon who, as commander at Inju, turned over 1500 Koryo households to the Mongols and subsequently served as a guide for Mongol attacks. The motive of these turn-coats was likely resentment at not having sufficient opportunity for the acquisition of the power they sought. Perceiving the Mongols as superior in number, they banked on an alliance with them as guaranteeing posts of influence and affluence in short order.

The Mongols, after failing to take the walled city of Kuju, turned on secondary targets, cities they previously by-passed in this march. A second Mongol force failed similarly at Chaju and the Western Capital where they met stiff resistance. Continuing southward they forced the inhabitants of Hwanju and Pongju to flee to coastal island sanctuaries.

The nature of these conflicts and the Mongol defeats refute any attempts to denigrate the Koreans as indifferent warriors, particularly considering the well-known ferocity of the Mongols. Also corroborating Koryo's skilled resistance and adding further credence to the Koreans' capabilities with bow and arrow was the performance of Koryo's Three Armies under the command of General Yi Chasong in 1231. His army marched from its capital for 12 days, but failed to find signs of the enemy. At sunset the general instructed his men to relax and remove their saddles. Shortly thereafter, soldiers who had climbed a height shouted "The Mongols are arriving!"

A force of approximately 8,000 Mongol soldiers suddenly appeared. Generals Chasong and No T'an, among others, fought valiantly to save the situation. Chasong was hit by an arrow and General No was plucked from his horse by a long lance, but both managed to escape with the aid of their men. Slowly the Koryo forces assembled and began to repulse the surprise attack. When the Mongols launched an attack on the right flank, they met stubborn resistance on the part of Koryo and its allied bandit and brigand warriors. Their success was inaugurated by two crack archers. At each pull of the bowstring a Mongol soldier fell. (Henthorn, 1963) The outcome of this Mongol surprise attack: defeat and withdrawal for the Mongols. This is again indicative of the Korean prowess in archery and the serviceability of the unique Korean composite bow, short and strongly re-curved as opposed to the English long bow or the Japanese bow. This bow, rather than being just an anomaly, ornament, or piece of sports equipment, as some historians have suggested, was obviously quite effective in the hands of Korean martial artists. Some authors have said that the bow was introduced to Korea during the Mongol invasions. As we have seen the bow had been well developed in Korea's arsenal for at least a thousand years prior to the Mongol invasions. In another note on Koryo archery expertise from the attack on Cho-im fortress by General Sal Ye-t'ap, it was mentioned that a "notable archer" participating in the defense "shot with unerring skill, and every arrow found its victim." Aided by this warrior, the garrison offered such a stubborn resistance that the Mongols at last fell back in disorder. (Hulbert, 1963)

When, in the northwest, the Mongols tried a second assault with catapults on Kuju, the walled fortress still prevailed despite being smashed in over two hundred locations by projectiles. Well-ordered and quick repairs mended the breaches under the protection of the Kuju soldiers' defense and the Mongols were driven off again.

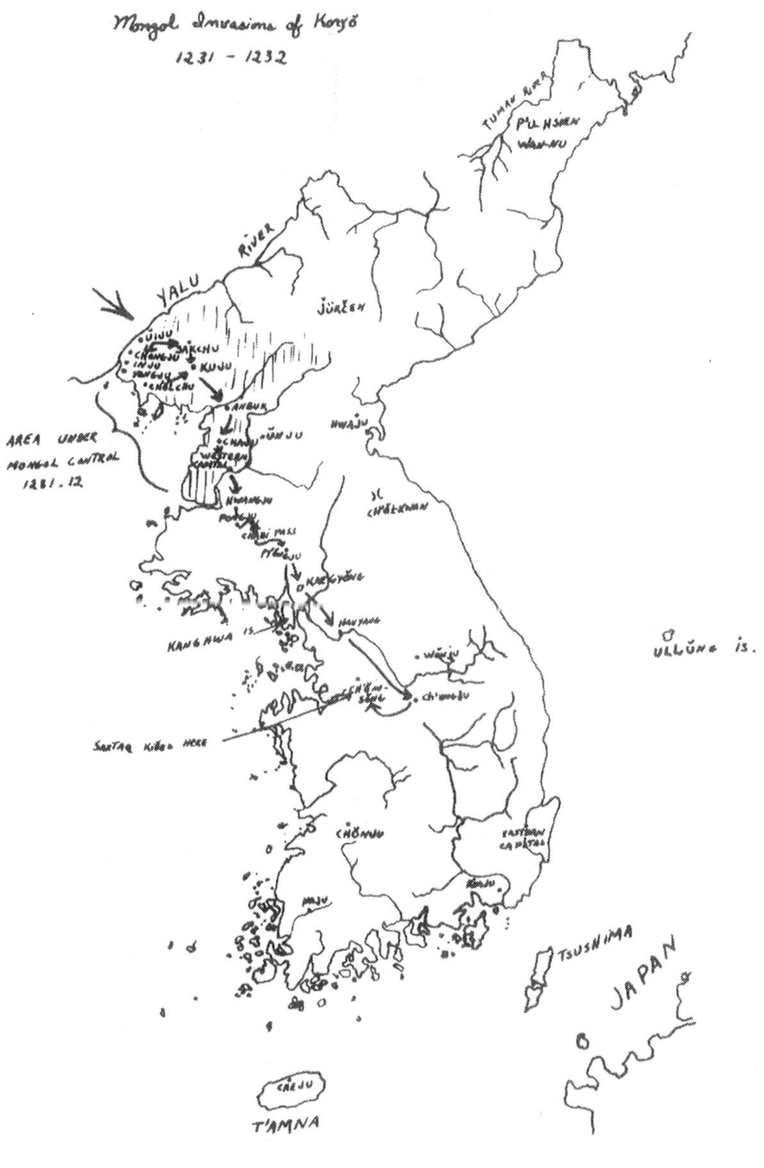

This map shows the Mongol invasion route through Korea in 1231 – 1232.

A Perspective on Koreans as Skilled Fighters, Fortress Builders

There have been some attempts to credit their famous fortresses with the success of the Koryo soldiers in resisting the Mongols as long as they did. That such intelligently constructed and useful redoubts played a key part in their defensive strategy is indubitable, as otherwise the sheer numbers of the enemy would have exhausted them early. However, no enemy as persistent and plentiful as the Mongols could be put off for three decades by fortification alone. Historical records give ample evidence of victorious Korean engagements with the Mongols that show their shrewd tactical talents, courageous initiatives, and legendary abilities with weapons. Additionally, Korean fortresses were not merely piles of stone behind which armies and citizenry hid, but were the products of strategic scheming requiring the skill of master militarists to situate the fortress, design them, and use them well in an active defense. Korean fortresses were only one component although certainly an important and obviously provident one of Korean commanders' tactical planning, and were vital as civilian sanctuaries in those areas where the younger fighting men had been called away to distant military action.

Remnants of old walls and fortresses can be found throughout Korea.

Secondly, however, the many documented military engagements, many on open field of the Koryo against numerically superior forces make it quite clear that the Koreans' offensive martial arts were on par with, or superior to, that of the Mongols.

At Wiju: Koryo Fortress Defense Strategies

According to existing records, one of the finest strategic uses of the Korean style of fortification was carried out by Koryo commander Pak So and his men at Wiju. Kim Kyongson was given the task of defending the southern section by Pak So. When the Mongols arrived with a large force at the south gate of the city, Kyongson, leading his twelve soldiers (a "dare-death squad") as well as all the patrols of the city, gave this order to the soldiers as they were going out of the city gate: "Do not think of your own lives. If fate decrees, die, but do not fall back." The patrols all threw themselves on the ground and would not obey. Kyongson ordered them all to go back into the city and then with only his dare-death squad of twelve soldiers he advanced into battle. Kim himself shot an arrow and knocked down one mounted soldier who rode with a black flag in the vanguard of the Mongol force. Consequently, Kim's twelve soldiers were encouraged and fought strenuously. Hit by an arrow, Kyongson's arm was dripping wet with blood. Still he pressed his men forward without stopping. Battle was joined four or five times and the Mongols finally withdrew. Kyongson then formed his lines and called his small group to return. Pak So met him and saluted, crying. Kyongson also saluted with tears in his eyes. From this episode, Pak So commissioned Kyongson to handle matters pertaining to the defense of the city. The Mongols surrounded the city, attacking the west, south, and north gates of the city repeatedly and heavily. The defending army of the center suddenly went out and attacked them. The Mongol soldiers captured Pak Munch'ang, the Deputy Commissioner of Wiju, and ordered him to go back into the city and instruct them to submit. Pak So beheaded him. Then the Mongols selected three hundred of their finest cavalry and attacked Wiju's north gate. Pak counterattacked and drove them off. The Mongols besieged the city, attacking day and night. They loaded carts with grass and wood, to turn over and burn at the gates as they advanced to the attack. Kyongson used catapults to hurl molten iron to repulse them. Pak So had his men tip pre-positioned barrels of water over the top of the entrance, extinguishing the fire carts.

Next the Mongols constructed towers, as well as a great platform wrapped with cowhide in which to hide soldiers who were working on the excavation of a tunnel under the fort. Pak's response was to bore a hole in the city wall through which he poured molten iron onto the tower base, setting fire to the structure. The ground also collapsed, crushing a few dozen Mongol soldiers in the tunnels. Burning bundles of thatch were directed against the wooden platform which was soon incinerated. The bewildered Mongols scattered.

Reconsidering, the Mongols quickly attacked the south wall, instead, with fifteen large catapults. Pak matched them with platforms erected on the city walls. Mounting catapults on them, he hurled stones and drove the attackers off.

The Mongols' next step was to soak bundles of sticks, reportedly with human fat. Igniting them, they catapulted the bundles over the walls. When Pak tried to put them out with water alone, they burned more fiercely, so he used mud to extinguish them.

Before retreating, the Mongols lit accumulated brush near the wood gates. After they regrouped, they returned to the assault. Kyongson had positioned himself in a chair to direct the fighting, during which a Mongol catapult slung a missile his way. It crossed the wall and landed directly behind him, killing his guards. His men begged him to move to a safer location. He refused, telling them, "If I am moving, then the hearts of all the soldiers will move also." The expression on his face was adamant and without concern and, in the end, he did not move.

For thirty days the Mongols besieged the city and attacked it hundreds of times. On each occasion, Pak would adapt his tactics successfully in order to defend his city. Demoralized, the Mongols withdrew and were forced to call for reinforcements from the cities of the Northern

Frontier District. Thirty catapults were brought in and placed in a line. The wall was breached in fifty places, yet immediately Pak was ready with rapid and effective repair, chaining iron bands across the holes and repairing them with temporary walls. Exhausted, the Mongols gave up the assault and Pak rapidly assessed and took advantage of their situation, coming out to do battle and winning a great victory.

Months after their defeat, the Mongols determined to attack again with large catapults. Pak also employed catapults to repulse them, flinging rocks and killing so many that they withdrew to camp in a wooden palisade in order to defend themselves. Sartaq still tried to intimidate them into surrender, sending a Koryo interpreter and the Recorder of the Academy with a dispatch from Chong, the Duke of Hoean, to instruct them to submit. Pak ignored the demand.

Next the Mongols built scaling ladders to assault the city. Pak countered with "large implements for slashing" (Henthorn, 1963). These inventions destroyed the ladders, along with many soldiers. During the siege, an old Mongol general, 70 years old, was touring beneath the city walls to inspect the ramparts and equipment. He sighed and said: "I have followed the army since I bound my hair [into plaits as a youth] and so I am accustomed to seeing the cities of the earth attacked and fought over. Still I have never seen [a city] undergo an attack like this which did not, in the end, submit."

The Mongols said: "This city has withstood many with few. Heaven protects it, not the strength of men." Thus satisfied that they had saved face by identifying their victors as sustained by supernatural power, they abandoned their siege and left.

For his valiant defense of Kuju, Pak was appointed Senior Councilor of the Royal Chancellery. Ch'oe told him, "Sir, in the nation, [your] fidelity is really incomparable."

The Ch'oe U Surrender: A Tactical Delay

As Sartaq closed in on Ch'oe's capital city, the military man found himself in a situation where placating both the Mongols and his ministers was desirable. Too many Koryo cities had exhausted their resources, whereas the Mongols seemed to have an unlimited supply of reinforcements. The upper echelons of his capital city were restless with anxiety over the possible loss of their wealth and positions as the Mongols pushed closer to a takeover of the seat of government.

Not convinced he had reached the end of his possibilities, Ch'oe needed to sue for peace to buy time as he explored alternatives. He tendered a surrender to the Mongols, but had not anticipated the high level of tribute they would demand. The Mongols regarded everything and everyone in a conquered nation as absolute chattel, a concept that differed considerably from Chinese and Korean policy. They usually took captive all artisans, women, and children upon the fall of a city, while the rest of the population was often slaughtered.

In addition to their demands for vast amounts of goods and animals, the Mongols required from Ch'oe the king's sons, daughters, grandsons, offspring of the provincial lords, 15 hundred other boys and girls, plus a daughter from each high official. The Mongols made captive all of the famed artisans of Koryo they could locate, contributing to the general decline of the classical Koryo celadon ceramics industry.

Koryo presented an enormous amount of this tribute, but had no intention of sending hostages. Diplomatic maneuvers continued while attempts to limit the catastrophic loss were considered. Ch'oe's ministers had been for some time quietly advocating a quick move of the capital to offshore islands where their luxurious mode of living and assets would not be under continual jeopardy from the invaders. Although the Mongol armies would leave resident commissioners in strategic locations in the north, they planned to go back to their homeland soon, expecting the required tribute to be paid. By taking advantage of their absence and their unfamiliarity with the sea on their ultimate return to exact payment, Ch'oe could essentially nullify the surrender.

The wisdom of moving to Kanghwa Island was apparent even beyond the need for a shelter for government. Government storage granaries were located primarily at coastal harbors and maritime transport of grain was already the norm. Kanghwa was separated from what is now modern Inch' on by a strait famous for treacherous rocks, rapids, and a rushing tide. Ch'oe relocated his capital to Kanghwa Island, installing the upper classes and Koryo's bureaucrats in a haven safe from the sea-leery Mongols who had no familiarity with amphibious warfare. The Mongol forces could stand on a hill on the mainland opposite Kanghwa Island and watch their goal just visible across the water. However, their utter lack of seamanship and naval fighting skills would moor them on the shore where they futilely would, one day, try to entice the Kanghwa elite with transparently bogus offers of withdrawal.

Eventually, lodgings for the entertainment of the frequent Mongol envoys began to appear at Sungch'on-pu, the debarkation point on the mainland for Kanghwa. While the Mongols were, some years later, able to get the then-king of Koryo to cross to the mainland for short periods to meet Mongol envoys, Ch'oe U and his immediate successors remained on the island for the rest of their lives. Ch'oe U and the military faction that supported him used the period after the move to recover and rearm. One of the covert measures taken was to send men called "Special Supervisors for the Encouragement of Agriculture" to the southern provinces, actually to prepare further defenses.

At Chaju and Kuju: Integrity, Bravery, Defiance in the Korean Martial Spirit

A heroic postscript to what turned out to be Ch'oe's marginal surrender was written by the cities of Chaju and Kuju. This well illustrated not only the Korean fighting spirit but the nature of armed conflicts in that time.

The communication of victories and defeats was often suspected, resulting in a greater autonomy of commanders at garrisons remote from the capital. Even after Koryo had formally submitted to the Mongols, the garrisons at Kuju and Chaju still held out. Song Kukch'om had been sent to instruct the Chaju Deputy Commissioner, Ch'oe Ch'unmyong, as its commander, to surrender his city. Ch'unmyong's response was to close the city gates in the envoy's face. Kukch'om could only curse him and return to the capital.

In 1232, after the submission of Koryo's Three Armies, the Mongol Commander Sartaq was able to pursue resolution of the situation at Chaju with backing from a Koryo official. He asked the Duke of Hoean, Chong, to insure that Chaju surrendered. Chong sent General Tae Chipsong, with a Mongol official, to Chaju where, arriving at the city gate, he informed Ch'unmyong, "The Court as well as the Three Armies have already submitted. You should speedily come out and submit."

Ch'unmyong refused to dignify the occasion with a personal reply but instead had his men answer. They said "[Since] an edict from the Court has not yet arrived, how can we trust you and submit?"

Chipsong replied, "The Duke of Hoean has already come to request that you submit. Since the Three Armies have also submitted, is this [order] unbelievable?"

Ch'unmyong's men answered, "The people in the city do not [even] know that a Duke of Hoean exists!"

Outraged, the Mongol functionary told Chipsong to enter the city, regardless. Their first move toward the walls brought a hail of arrows from the fort, driving away the delegation.

At about the same time, Sartaq sent the Koryo official Min Hui with some Mongol functionaries to bring about the long-awaited submission of Kuju. A similar message was sent to Pak So, the commander of Kuju, concerning the wishes of the Duke of Hoean to negotiate peace. Despite endless argument, Pak So refused to submit. Min Jui became so exasperated that he wanted to draw his sword and kill Pak himself. Finally, after he was convinced that further resistance would be contrary to the Koryo King's commands, Pak capitulated and submitted his city.

Pak So and Ch'oe Ch'unmyong were scheduled for execution for their stubborn resistance, as both the Court and Ch'oe U feared the Mongols' anger. However the Mongols felt otherwise towards them. In fact, they admired their courage. They were lauded by both the Mongols and also by other Koryo authorities. The Mongol appreciation for their loyalty to country was stated eloquently by a Mongol functionary at the Western Capital where Ch'oe Ch'unmyong was being held for execution:

"Although he went contrary to our orders, he is a loyal subject of yours. We are not going to kill him now that you have already pledged peace with us. Would it be proper [for you] to kill the loyal subjects of all [your] cities? (Henthorn, 1963)

Priorities of the Elite Collide With Military Perspective

An example of the influence of the Koryo ruling class in suppressing overt resistance to the Mongols by their military can be found in an anecdote from a meeting in the spring of 1232. At that time, Ch'oe assembled all the officials of the fourth rank and above at his residence. The subject was transferring the capital to Kanghwa.

During the previous year, Ch'oe U had been advised to relocate the government to Kanghwa Island by Yun In, the Deputy Commissioner of Sungch'on-pu, who had, with a colleague, already secretly sent his family and servants to the island when the Mongol forces threatened the capital. Ch'oe sent men to inspect the island but on the way they were seized by the Mongols. Ch'oe, however, kept the option in mind, and even considered the feasibility of going to distant Ullung Island in the Sea of Japan.

At the spring meeting with his officials to bring the plan out in the open, Ch'oe heard no word in opposition, although, privately, several military leaders favored defending the capital instead, feeling that refuge on Kanghwa was not feasible as a long-range solution. Only Commander Kim Sech'ung of the Night Patrol dared voice his frustration with the suggestion when he heard that the topic was being seriously discussed. Pushing open the door to the council meeting and entering, he told U sharply, "Successive generations have held [our present capital] since T'aejo for all of two hundred years [sic]. The walls of the city are strong and the soldiers' provisions are sufficient. Assuredly we should combine [all] our forces and defend it in order to protect the fatherland [*sajik*, lit. "altars of the earth and grain"]. How can we abandon the capital?"

Ch'oe then asked Kim for his plans to defend the city but Kim was speechless. With strong walls, provisions, and competent militarists in abundance in the Koryo nation, what trap was he being led into, to propose what no one else seemed to think was obvious?

General Tae Chipsong, Ch'oe U's father-in-law, then told Ch'oe that Kim's advice was the prattle of a young girl. He wanted to behead him for such talk, and others at the council meeting supported the idea. Kim was summarily executed. (Henthorn 1963)

Mongol Commander Sartaq Killed by Modest Monk

Koryo's decision to resist the Mongols provoked a second invasion by Sartaq which proved fatal to the Mongol commander. In his attack on the city of Ch'oin-song (Yongin) in 1232, he was struck and killed by an arrow sprung from the bow of the Buddhist monk Kim Yunhu. Records alternatively say that the monk completely denied being armed or that it was a "chance" shot. Kim, clearly observed to have shot Sartaq, declined an appointment as Supreme General as a reward for killing the great Mongol commander, saying, "At the time of the battle I was without bow and arrows. How can I presume to falsely receive an important reward?" Such a high command would not have been offered if there had been the slightest doubt on Ch'oe's part that it was the monk who brought down Sartaq. However, such an attitude on the part of highly adept monks was not unknown.

Kim was then given a temporary appointment as colonel and, subsequently, was appointed Special Supervisor of Defense of Ch'ungju's citadel of refuge where he played a major role in the 70-day siege of the town in 1253. He was promoted to Supreme General for his feats at Ch'ungju and appointed to the post of Commissioner of Men and Horse of the Northeastern Frontier District but, as the district had just fallen to the Mongols at that time, he did not serve. (Ha, 1972)

That a monk so highly skilled in martial arts as to penetrate a massive fighting machine such as the Mongols should deny the feat or claim it happened only with an arrow "accidentally" lethal to such a leader as Sartaq is as fantastic a story as the probable truth. More likely, considering the history of Korean monks' involvement in martial arts and military action, this is a typical Buddhist retelling of an event in which that which seemed obviously intentional is modestly claimed to be misunderstood, possibly only fortuitous, or perhaps a product of divine intervention. It may also have been the reluctance of a good Buddhist to claim the taking of a life.

The Mongols withdrew from Koryo, and left the Koryo traitor Hong Pogwon in charge of conquered areas. (The other prominent Koryo deserter was Cho Sukch'ang who submitted the city of Hamsin-chin.)

Koryo Explains Its "Shortcomings" to Mongols

The reaction of the Mongols when they discovered the unauthorized abandonment of the Western Capital in favor of an island retreat was no less irate than their pique over non-delivery of hostages and tribute. The government of Koryo presented an imaginative "explanation" for its failure to perform according to the terms of the surrender, for the killing and detention of Mongol resident commissioners, and for the unauthorized transfer of the capital.

Among the imaginative reasons they gave for relocating to the island was that a fictitious individual named Song Ipchang had fled from the household of Chi Uisim but returned with the news that the Mongols were raising a large force to attack Koryo cities. Understandably, hearing Song's report, the people became alarmed and fled from the cities. This, in turn, they said, caused Koryo to fear that they could not produce the annual tribute since the cities were being deserted. The imaginary Song had been exiled to a distant island for his false statements, they assured the Mongols. Following the immediate Mongol demand that he be produced, the government claimed that, although they had sent for him, it was feared that he was "lost at sea" on the return journey, since nothing had been heard of his party.

When the Mongols demanded to know what had become of one of the two leading Koryo turncoats, General Cho Sukch'ang, who allegedly had returned to his countrymen, the blatantly inventive Koryo government-in-exile sent word that they couldn't produce him because, unfortunately, he had fallen ill and was still sick, very sick, in bed.

In response to the Mongol demands for a census of the Koryo people and, also, for an army they could use against P'u-hsien Wan-nu, Koryo was similarly unhelpful. Although they had managed to furnish some ships and seamen, no action was taken to send either troops or settlers to help the Mongols pacify the Liaotung area.

The Mongols' renewed demand for hostages fell on deaf ears. Mongol instructions for the king, the high officials, and Ch'oe U to show themselves were ignored, as were the demands for a list of the names and positions of civil and military officials.

Clearly Koryo felt, at least temporarily, that it held the strategic edge. Distance from the Mongol court, the sudden demise of Mongol administrators in Koryo territory, and their island sanctuary made them rather audacious in their stance, colored by their overall contempt for a people they considered culturally and intellectually inferior.

Additionally, Koryo had other projects in mind. Perhaps encouraged by the killing of Sartaq and the taking of many Mongol prisoners at that time, Koryo approached the Eastern Jurchen people and made an alliance with them in 1233.

By the spring of 1233, the Mongols had formulated a response to Koryo's insolence. A Mongol envoy arrived at the Koryo court with an edict listing its "crimes" and requesting its king to appear at the Mongol court. It read, in part:

Your memorial reporting the facts involved was drawn up entirely in false statements and phrases of excuse. How difficult it is to know one from the other! If you were not false, you would come for an audience. From the previous pacification of the Khitan until the slaying of Cha-la, you have not sent a single soul to [our] gates. You have never acted in compliance with the laws and statues of [our] Great Nation. This is your first offense. And when those who were sent to offer the precepts and instructions of Immortal Heaven summoned you, then you dared to kill [them]. This is your second offense. Moreover, with regard to Chul-ku-yu, you plotted to harm him and claimed Wan-nu's people killed him. If you had seized [and turned over to us] the man (Wang Hao-fei) who made the original report, then it would be clear. If Wan-nu had really tried to cause the downfall of your country, [then when] we ordered you to attack Wan-nu, why did you hang back without advancing? This is your third offense. We commanded you to raise an army and, as before, we ordered you to present yourself at Court, but these clear instructions you dared to resist. You did not appear at Court [but] sneaked away to the islands of the sea. This is your fourth offense. Furthermore, [when] we ordered your households to come together and be counted, you claimed that if the people left the cities to be counted, they would fear being killed and flee to [the islands of] the sea and that, when you once cooperated in an expedition with the troops of Heaven, your people were enticed to leave the cities under the pretense of being counted and then were wantonly slain. Now, you dare to submit false statements to this effect. This is your fifth offense. In addition to these offenses, you have been deceitful and evil innumerable times. When we sent you the precepts and instructions of Immortal Heaven, you were not attentive and wished to do battle. But when we, trusting to the powers of Supreme Heaven, attack and smash your cities and villages, there are cases that those who are blind and will not submit are exterminated; yet there are also those who submit and work hard and, whether man or woman, they have never been wantonly slain...

The edict continued to point out that the officials of ten Koryo cities, including the Western Capital, had already taken a census of their households and were remitting taxes, and that all were living peacefully as before. The edict called upon Koryo to field an army against P'u-hsien Wan-nu or suffer the consequences.

The answer from Koryo was a renewed offensive aimed particularly at ousting Hong Pogwon from the Western Capital, still under Mongol control. In June-July of 1233 what the Koryo records term a "revolt" broke out in the Western Capital. The Pacification Commissioner and two Grand Generals were killed. Ch'oe U sent three thousand of his house troops to capture the leader, P'il Hyonbo, and escort him to the capital where he was cut in two at the waist with a massive sword (likely a moon knife), indicating beheading wasn't the only means of execution. Hong Pogwon escaped, but not his family. The remaining people of the capital were then moved to islands and the site sank into desolation.

In the spring of 1234, the rebel Cho Sukch'ang was beheaded. Hong Pogwon had fled northward to Liaotung, with a large number of settlers. He was charged with repopulating this area of old Koguryo, and was given control of the northwestern portion of Koryo. At this time a Mongol edict was circulated, instructing the people of Koryo that anyone who would capture and bring to court the Koryo monarch and instigators of the resistance, including Ch'oe, would be placed on an equal footing with Hong Pogwon and settled in the Tung-ching area. Those who resisted would die.

None of this came to pass. Koryo excuses to the Mongols mounted: the king could not appear at the Mongol court because his queen had just died and a three-year mourning period was needed; the king was ill; he was mourning for his mother. And, finally: he was "too old."

Yet the Mongol demands for hostages could not be ignored forever. Koryo's first ploy in that regard was to dispatch the Duke of Sinan to the Mongol court, where he was passed off as the king's younger brother. For the next several years he scurried back and forth, conveying Mongol demands and Koryo's evasive replies. Eventually, the Mongols demanded a higher-ranking royal person. The Koryo court instead produced a low-level royal relative of the court, proclaiming him to be the crown prince. The substitution was not discovered by the Mongols for 14 years. Meanwhile, the Mongols were so happy to have finally received the "crown prince" that they highly honored the great Mongol General Uyer who escorted him successfully from Koryo to the Mongol court. Uyer was made Supreme Military Commander over seven provincial administrations for this long-awaited act of Koryo "submission."

The Tae Up'o:
The Sword That Became a Knife

The usual translation of this word found often in Koryo historical records is "large knife." According to Henthorn, *tae* indisputably means "large." *U,* however, should be read in its sense "to go" and *p'o*, "a stream," and by closely studying the intricate evolution of the Korean language, he found a more accurate translation than "knife" would be "a large implement for slashing," a large blade or, in other words, a big sword perhaps a type of moon knife. This is significant in adding to the considerable number of references in historical records supporting the ancient and prevalent use of the sword by Koreans of old, even though they are still thought by some to have favored daggers.

Abandoned Peasants Seek Refuge in Citadels

While Koryo's military leaders and government contended with the Mongols for their own strategic and political gain, the peasants of Koryo were left to deal as well as they could with the chaos that followed each power shift. After the exit of the aristocracy with its government administrators to Kanghwa, the peasantry in the rest of the country was given only the advice to seek refuge in the mountain fortresses and on islands off the coast. Records show residents of the northwest cities of Sunju, Ch'angju, Unju, Pakchu, Kaju, Kwakchu, Maengju, T'aeju, and Unju all fled to islands to escape Mongol attacks. These peasants and lowborn classes, at first, supported the resistance to the Mongols. Even the brigand bands on Mt. Kwanak, always opposed to Koryo influence, gave themselves up to Koryo and joined them in the battle against the Mongol enemy.

Martial Skill Advances Ch'ungju Slave, Monk

The army of slaves at Ch'ungju, led by Chi Kwang-su, became famous for their courageous defense of the town, which had been abandoned by its aristocratic officials. The town at this time is also famous as an example of the infighting, intrigue, and lack of organization that weakened much of 13th century Koryo at all levels.

Just before the Mongol attack on Ch'ungju in the winter of 1231, U Chongju, the deputy commissioner and Yu Hongik, the administrator of the town, had a falling out during a discussion of defense strategies. U assumed command of a "Selected Force of the Upper Classes," while Yu took control of the slave army and another special force. The leaders were mutually suspicious of each other but when the Mongol troops arrived, the two men chose the same personal course: to flee. However, Hongik's two forces not only remained but routed the Mongols. The Buddhist priest Ubon also played a significant role in Chongju's winning strategy.

After the victory, the erstwhile "commanders" returned to Ch'ungju and determined that their best course was to immediately accuse the slave army of stealing the government and private silver utensils. The slaves claimed the Mongol troops had made off with them. Meanwhile, a plot was formulated among some of the town officials to kill the head of the slave army, Chi Kwangsu. Learning of this, the slave army accused the officials of deserting the city and then charging the slaves with the Mongols' crime.

Gathering under the pretense of a burial party, the slaves then assembled their followers with blasts on a conch shell and took over the city. They threatened the families of any who dared to flee, setting fire to the homes of the murder plotters, and then hunting down and killing those against whom they held grudges.

In retaliation, the runaways, U and Yu, requested Ch'oe to appoint temporary military governors. These men went to Ch'ungju, investigated the scene, and determined that Chi Kwangsu and the priest Ubon were heroes, taking them back to Ch'oe U who rewarded them. He appointed the slave Kwangsu as a military officer with the rank of captain and made Ubon head of the important temples of Ch'ungju with the high rank of *samjung.*

Ubon, however, was not satisfied and determined to set matters more to his liking in Ch'ungju. He stirred up a revolt that required Koryo's Three Armies to march on Ch'ungju. Counter-insurgents contacted this force as they neared Ch'ungju, offering to kill Ubon and surrender. The government forces accepted the proposal, and the rebels who didn't flee were captured and executed. All of this in fighting was going on at the same time as the Mongol invasions of Koryo further reducing Koryo's defense.

At the previously mentioned siege of Ch'ungju when the town held out through a 70-day siege, the monk Kim Yunhu addressed the issue of class. When provisions ran out, Yunhu, who was in charge as Special Supervisor of Defense, advised his men to forget their class differences. By way of encouragement he burned the government slave registers and divided up livestock which had been captured. He also promised that all who put forth their best efforts would be given official rank. (Henthorn, 1963) This account confirms two aspects of Koryo culture working both for and against national welfare. Class differences were at the core of that lack of unity. This frequently resulted in defeat despite the availability of expert soldiers. Rewarding of martial abilities was a continued incentive to both learning martial arts and to guarding the secrets of these skills that could also advance family status. The titles and land granted to outstanding warriors upgraded not only the immediate family but generations to come and honored the ancestors. Special fighting techniques were kept within the families to help preserve the reputation of its soldiers and earn continued rewards for their battlefield successes. Martial arts secrets at that time were as guarded as national defense secrets today, such was their vital importance. Within Kuk Sool Won today there are still certain martial art techniques and training methods that are closely kept secrets.

No Defense Against Hunger; Peasant Support Declines

The Koryo mountain citadels of refuge known as *sansong* and located near every major settlement, including the walled cities achieved renown for their invulnerability in the Mongol wars. The Mongols were no match for them. However, the fortified Koryo armies still had to eat grain from the fields to survive. The ripening fields, easy to burn, became the new targets of the Mongols. The armies in the mountains weakened, the fortresses were taken, and the people were slaughtered, cut off from economic support by the upper classes.

By the autumn of 1252, the Mongol emperor had reached the end of his patience with the Koryo refusal to produce their king and follow other instructions. Koryo, sensing a climate of change for the worse, quietly began sending Supervisors of Defense to all the mountain citadels. In early 1253, three hundred Eastern Jurchen cavalry surrounded Tung ju in the northwest. Then a raiding party was reported. The worst was confirmed by a report that the Mongol Emperor had ordered a force of 10,000 to enter from the Eastern Frontier District, with A-mu-k'an and Hong Pogwon to proceed to the Northern Frontier District. Despite these moves, when the Mongol Prince Yeku sent a delegation to the Koryo court in 1253, there was no change in the Korean position. Mongol troops therefore crossed the Yalu and later the Taedong River. An attack on Kanghwa was evidently anticipated. Ch'oe Hang still refused to send more envoys as he noted they were treated as hostages and 300 persons previously sent had not yet returned. Except for raiding patrols, the king ordered his countrymen to remain in a defensive position. On the mainland, Mongol forces rode largely unchecked with garrisons left to their own resources.

One of the worst of the campaigns against the mountain redoubts was led by the Mongol commander Jalairtai in 1254. Records claim the number of Koryo captives reached more than 200,000. The corpses of the dead were too many to be counted, and the entire region through which the Mongol force passed was reduced to ashes. The population declined severely and whole villages fell into ruin, along with many cultural treasures. With no sign of Koryo's willingness to submit, Jalairtai's forces swept southward to renew the attack on Ch'ungju. A violent storm drove them back. As the Mongol forces rode south, dispatches from the Eastern Frontier District reported many Eastern Jurchen troops crossing the border.

During this period a Mongol force attacked the mountain citadel at Sangju where their fourth-ranking official was shot by a Buddhist monk from Hwangnyong Temple. The siege was finally lifted after the Mongols had lost an estimated fifty percent of their force. (Henthorn 1963)

Mongols Attempt Broader Naval Operations

The Mongols decided an increase in amphibious warfare would have to be undertaken, despite their lack of expertise in this area. They built ships and attacked Cho Island unsuccessfully. When Koryo heard that, in the beginning of 1256, the Mongols were planning to attack the southern islands, a fleet of 300 men was sent south under Generals Yi Kwang and Song Kunbi. Song devised a ruse to defeat the Mongols and captured four of their officials.

Although the Mongols captured Sinwi Island and invaded Ch'angnin Island, Koryo, with its long maritime tradition, completely outclassed them. (Henthorn, 1963) The Koryo fleet also provided transport for forces sent against the Mongols. One instance occurred in the summer of 1256, when Koryo sent General Yi, Chun (One-Thousand) with a fleet of over 200 men to ward off the Mongols in the southern provinces. He fought the Mongol forces at Onsu-hyon in modern S. Ch'ungch'ong Province, "took several tens of heads and seized over 100 men and women who had been taken captive. [Upon their return] Ch'oe Hang rewarded the soldiers with six *kun* of silver." (Henthorn, 1963)

Mongol Commander Acknowledges Koryo Military Skill

To one of the numerous envoys riding back and forth between the Koryo and Mongol camps, Commander Jalairtai again expressed the familiar Mongol proposal that if the Koryo king came out to welcome his envoys, and if the Crown Prince went to the Mongol court, then the Emperor would cause the army to be withdrawn. However, by mid-1256, Koryo patrols were again active on the mainland, attacking small Mongol detachments. The effectiveness of the Koryo sallies was noted when Jalairtai angrily told a Korean envoy, "If you desire peace and friendship, then why do you kill our soldiers in great numbers"? But as long as Mongol forces were on the peninsula, action against them could be expected.

Kanghwa Island Life Draws Resentment From Peasants

While the life of the peasants deteriorated seriously, the officials at Kanghwa continued to spend their days in luxury among its palaces, mansions, temples, and entertainments imported from Kaesong to the sanctuary of the island. A gigantic polo field was built west of Ch'oe's residence with an enormous observation tower said to seat 1,000 people. Both Ch'oe U and his successor Ch'oe Hang were fond of polo, chiefly a military sport in Koryo and often played by the Koryo cavalry units. Matches often featured javelin throwing and mounted archery.

In addition to the irritating rumors of high living on Kanghwa, the island-based administrators continued to exploit the peasantry, crushing them with taxes, making their lives more precarious, and considerably dampening their desire to fight against the Mongols. To the bureaucrats of Kanghwa, the resulting hostility and alienation posed a serious threat with import they refused to acknowledge. Isolated and comfortable, they pursued their pleasures, undermining the efforts of the military. Once again, capitulation to an outside force was becoming inevitable, in spite of Koryo's martial superiority.

Horseback archery is still practiced today in the martial art of Kuk Sool Won.

Healing for Schism Sought Through Monumental Tripitaka Carving

As the exploitation continued, peasant support of Ch'oe's resistance against the Mongols declined even further and the nation's crisis deepened. Koryo's survival now depended not on military capabilities but, again, on healing the schism within its own people. (Lee, 1984) The Koryo administrators' answer was to commission a *Tripitaka*, a monumental carving of the Buddhist canon, including all the sacred teachings of the Buddha in 81,137 woodblocks. Such a pious project had been completed in 1087, also as a form of prayer, during Hyon-jong's reign to bring a halt to the Khitan invasions, but the Mongols destroyed it while attacking the Puin-sa monastery in Taegu where it was housed. The new *Koryo Tripitaka*, completed after sixteen years in 1251, became famed for its exquisite artistry and survives to this day at Haein-sa Temple near Taegu. Despite its creation under wartime conditions, it is regarded as the finest among some twenty versions of the *Tripitaka* from East Asia, in terms of its accuracy, the beauty of the calligraphic style, and the exquisite carving of the woodblocks. (Lee,1984) This art was another area in which Korea innovated and proved itself second to none.

Special prayers to the deities of heaven and earth were offered at the same time the carving of the *Tripitaka* was under way. A ceremony designed to cleanse or purify the nation, the *chaehoe*, was also undertaken, and involved the feasting of "30,000 monks" (a symbolic number meant to indicate all the monks in the nation). This, like the carving, was a religious act designed to exorcise or scourge invaders from the land, conducted mainly by the court, rather than the military.

The result seemed to be an astonishing turn of events. A sentiment for peace with the Mongols took over Koryo in the nature of a fever for appeasement which swept Kanghwa. Leading in enthusiasm were the scores of civil office holders who for some time had been completely ignored by the military. However, since Ch'oe had been leaning increasingly on these men of letters, they had become bolder. There had always numbered among them those who opposed the move from Kaesong, and now they took every opportunity to urge peace.

Ch'oe U's Death Inspires Interest in Monarchy

The death of Ch'oe U in the winter of 1249 should have resulted in his son's ascendancy to military power, the old commander having given him 500 men of his own the previous year. However the *Tobang*, the Guard Corps, had other ideas, immediately assembling at Ch'oe Hang's residence. Subsequently, when the new commander attempted to consolidate his position, he found several obstacles. The first attempt to overthrow him was abortive and led to a purge by Ch'oe Hang that included his stepmother, her family, and slaves. Ch'oe Hang thereby laid claim to his superiority as military leader, reinforced by considerable land holdings.

Koryo Moves Toward Prosperity, Peace With Mongols

Behind the apparent interest in ending the conflict with the Mongols was an even greater interest in securing and expanding their influential posts. By attempting to curb the power of the military men through reaching an accommodation with the Mongols, they could survive and extend their authority as bureaucrats. In order to achieve this, the cessation of the wars was a prerequisite. The conflict-ravaged mainland had to be returned to revenue-producing land and trading had to be normalized. The road to peace lay through arranging the downfall of those who advocated continued resistance to the military. (Lee, 1984)

End of the Ch'oe Military Clan Rule

In 1258, the last of the Ch'oe dictators, Ch'oe Ui, was beheaded by a civil official, Yu Kyong, and a military official, Kim Chun (Kim Injun), who assumed Ui's leadership role. Ch'oe Ui not only failed to maintain good personal relationships with those who had formerly served the Ch'oe clan but failed to issue doles during drought and the famine brought about by the pillaging of the Mongols. He even instituted private tax collectors on Kanghwa Island. His executioners charged him with watching his people starve to death without aiding them, and praised his assassination as an act of righteousness. Lavish rewards and promotions followed the overthrow of the Ch'oe clan.

THE PYOLCH'O: KORYO'S CIVIL DEFENSE UNITS

The Koryo *pyolch'o* were often spontaneously and hastily organized groups. They had the potential of developing into highly professional military units, sometimes becoming a permanent part of the military system. They were frequently capable of fighting extremely effective, localized actions against numerous invaders throughout the Korean peninsula. Usually they were temporary drafts of men who disbanded when an emergency passed. There are many references to the pyolch'o in records of the Mongol invasions.

In late 1253, the pyolch'o on an island off Hwanghae Province hid soldiers outside the walled city of P'yongju and entered the Mongol camp at night, killing many of them. Captain Chang Chabang grasped a short sword in his hand and killed, including the chief of the encampment, over twenty men. The unique history of this weapon has been preserved by practicing the double short sword form taught in Kuk Sool Won. In the eighth month of 1254, Mongol soldiers and cavalry camping at Koeju were routed and crushed by a pyolch'o.

These forces were actually the one means to maintain order available to the regional authorities after the government shifted to Kanghwa Island. (Henthorn,1963)

Koryo Submission to Mongols Not Backed by Military

Two groups were involved in the struggle to bring down Ch'oe U. The Confucian-Royalist faction, led by Yu Kyong and supported by the aged *literatus* Ch'oe Cha, wanted to send the crown prince as a hostage to the Mongols in order to bring an end to the fighting. The militarists headed by Yu Kong sided with this faction only because of its interest in eliminating the Ch'oe clan. They had no desire to drastically alter Koryo's policy of continue resistance to the Mongol forces, although they advocated a temporary cessation of the fighting. As a withdrawal of the Mongol forces could only be gained by concessions to them, they supported these gestures. But, as later events testify, complete submission to the Mongols was the goal of the Confucian-Royalists, not the military establishment.

Power Remains in Hands of Military

Overthrow of the Ch'oe clan did not mean that the monarch would regain complete control of the government. The real power still remained in the hands of the military, with its individual leaders struggling for supremacy.

Meanwhile, the Koryo authorities continued to be concerned with the concoction of excuses that would pacify the Mongols and reduce their skirmishes on the mainland. In the spring of 1258, when the Koryo king heard that Jalairtai had sent an envoy to spy on Koryo's avowed intentions to return the capital to the mainland, he became concerned since nothing had actually been done in that regard. He quickly dispatched all the civil and military officials across the straits to Sungch'on-pu where repairs were made to the palaces and to the homes of the officials. The Mongols, however, were beginning to suspect all Koryo feigns in this regard and soon conveyed a threat from their emperor that Kanghwa would be sacked unless the Koryo authorities came to the mainland and submitted.

The Koryo king's response was predictable. He was much too old and ill, he replied. Yesuder, a high-ranking Mongol negotiator, again demanded of the Koryo envoy that at least the crown prince be handed over. The envoy agreed, as usual, and, in keeping with the well-established pattern, after a few days the Mongols were informed that the crown prince was ill and unable to come. The Mongols let loose their forces to pillage over the countryside, increasing their raids even to remote mountain villages when a subsequent request that the crown prince show his ill face was again denied. "How can he come out?" responded the Koryo king.

The Mongols by this time decided to occupy Koryo themselves and were aided substantially by an assortment of Koryo deserters. Koryo had lost her northeast area and Mongol forces occupied both Uiju and the Western Capital on a permanent basis.

Koryo resistance during this period, while stubborn, was weakening. There was a great increase in the number of revolts, especially those led by the local officials themselves, and in many cases the people would simply kill the local Supervisor of Defense to end the conflicts and gain peace. Some measures were taken by Koryo in an attempt to inspire loyalty and resistance. Rewards included the presentation on one occasion of white silver and two bolts of black silk gauze to each district magistrate. It was too little, too late. In 1258, the grain of all the provinces was exhausted due to Mongol pillaging. Koryo yielded to Mongol demands to send Crown Prince Chon to the Mongol court to convey Koryo's desire for rapprochement. On this morose trip north in the summer of 1259, Chon encountered the Mongol Prince Kublai, the future Khan, returning from an expedition against Sung and submitted to him. At this meeting in the field, Prince Kublai is said to have exclaimed, "Koryo, a nation 10,000 *li* [distant] T'ang T'ai-tsung himself led an expedition [against them] and was unable to obtain their submission. Now their Heir Apparent himself comes to me. This is the will of Heaven."

At this same audience, Chao Lang-pi, then Pacification Commissioner of the Chiang-huai provinces, is said to have told Kublai, "Although Koryo is called a small nation due to its perilous mountains and seas, our nation has used troops [against them] for over twenty years and they are still not our vassals." (Henthorn, 1963) Not mentioned were the Mongols' repeated defeats at even less-perilously-located garrisons and the wily maneuvering of Koryo strategists.

Unfortunately for the Mongols, the will of Heaven soon reverted to something resembling the status quo when, after finally obtaining a Koryo king's heir after so many years of virtually begging, Chon's father, Kojong, died and the Mongols were compelled to escort the soon-to-be-crowned prince all the way back to Koryo the following spring.

NOT REALLY SURRENDERED

Twenty years after Koryo's theoretical surrender, in the spring of 1260, a Mongol envoy arrived at the Koryo capital with yet another entreaty for the nation to behave properly conquered: "Of all beneath Heaven who have not surrendered," said the envoy's missal, "there is only your nation and Sung [the modern Szuchu'an Province]." (Henthorn, 1963)

As a demonstration of sincerity, Kanghwa's walled fortifications had been torn down, and reconstruction of palaces in Kaegyong begun, but it was still to be many years before Koryo's promise to move back to Kaegyong was kept. Crown Prince Chon was escorted back to Kanghwa Island by the Mongols themselves.

With a peace agreement concluded in the third month of 1259, Koryo hastened to turn its attention to agriculture, "to lead the people who had fled from the disorders back to the mainland to plow and plant [the land]." (Henthorn, 1963)

Opposition to Peace Making

Kim Chun, along with the rest of the military, never had his heart in the peace movement, although he took no active role in thwarting it. Another military man, Im Yon, resented his fence-straddling and murdered him to seize power. He then deposed the last Koryo king to be granted a temple name King Wonjong, who had put the pro-Mongol (and, thereby, pro-royal) policy into effect. The opposition to peace-making was out in the open but it was too late. Rapprochement had already reached the point where Mongol interference had become entrenched in the wheels of government.

Additionally, national solidarity and the will to resist the Mongols had disintegrated to the point where there was no hope of rallying adequate numbers to the military's cause. Pressure from the Mongols soon restored Wonjong to his throne, where upon he welcomed Mongol troops into his capital, pledged his son's hand in marriage to a Mongol princess, and quickly assassinated Im Yu-mu, the son of Im Yon (who had recently died) and heir to his military authority. These events occurred in 1270, the same year Kanghwa Island was ultimately abandoned and the capital returned to Kaesong. On June 15, 1270, the transfer of all ranks and organizations back to the old capital was ordered by the ministers on Kanghwa in accordance with King Wonjong's instructions. This transfer marked, both symbolically and in fact, the transfer of power from the military government back to the monarch and Koryo's final submission to the Mongols. For official Koryo, the Mongol wars were over. Governance was effectively removed from the province of the military and returned to civilian authority. The only thorn in the side of both the Koryo administrators and the Mongol overlords was the indomitable Three Patrols, who remained on Kanghwa Island and refused to obey the transfer order.

PROFILE OF KORYO'S LAST MILITARY STRONGMAN

Im Yon presented an impressive appearance in line with his reputation of being able to knock a man flat or, alternatively, toss him to the rafters with ease. His military career began as an aid to a general. He later returned to his native village, only to flee when the Mongol forces arrived. Joining the army, he became a lieutenant, and in this rank created a scandal when he seduced another man's wife in retaliation for a similar offense to his own by this individual. His trespass, however, resulted in a charge by the authorities which was suspended when the great Kim Chun became apprised of his physical strength. Kim Chun had the charges dropped and appointed him as a colonel, winning his devotion. Thereafter, Im Yon habitually called Kim Chun "father," that is until he became a powerful enough leader in the Three Patrols to overthrow his Mongol-appeasing benefactor. Although he represented the last of the major military figures with the fighting spirit to oppose total surrender to the Mongols, he arrived on the scene at a time when Koryo had exhausted its physical resources for successful resistance.

With little description of ancient martial art techniques remaining we can only guess at what type of technique Im Yon could have used to "knock a man flat or toss him to the rafters". However, the fact that such technique is mentioned indicates that it was a powerful force within the society. It also gives us another historical reference that points to the fact that Korea indeed had a powerful empty hand martial art deeply ingrained within its culture.

Rebellion of The Resentful Sambyolch'o

The Three Elite Patrols *(Sambyolch'o)*, as the central unit of the military governing body, were in the forefront of the resistance to Mongol invasion. When the Kanghwa-based king capitulated, this cadre of skilled veterans, famous for their bold forays and well-plotted attacks, were outraged and bitterly resentful. They responded with an immediate revolt under the leadership of Pae Chung-son. First, they blocked all traffic between Kanghwa and the mainland. A royal kinsman, Wang On, was chosen by them as king, and a government was established. This opposition government selected as its base the island of Chindo, off the southwest tip of the peninsula. Kanghwa was no longer practical to defend as in years past. The fortifications had been dismantled as one of the conditions of the peace negotiations of 1259. The Mongols had acquired more competence on the water (aided considerably by Koryo sympathizers for peace), and there was no shortage of manpower or vessels at the command of the allied Mongol-Koryo administrators.

Reaching the mainland and moving south, the Three Patrols looted and plundered Mongol-captured regions. As their successes against the Mongol-Koryo forces continued, their fame spread. This, in turn, inspired others to rebel and join them, increasing their size and range of activity. The weather was also working against the Mongol-Koryo forces; the blazing summer heat was causing steam to rise from the sea and the power of their bows was retarded as a result.

On Chindo the rebels built a palace complex on a large scale, outlined a capital city, and brought the nearby islands and adjacent coastal region under their control. This hastily formed maritime kingdom had only a year of life when, in mid-1271, a combined Koryo-Mongol assault destroyed their initiative. The survivors, led by Kim T'ong-jong, fled to Cheju Island. There they were left alone for two years. Then, in 1273, they were attacked again and finally defeated. Those remaining were sent to the mainland and executed.

On the 24th day of the fifth month of the year 1273, the king in Kaegyong received the report that the Three Patrols had been subdued, and the next month word was sent to the Yuan court. The disillusioned struggle of the Three Elite Patrols was ended. However, their spirited resistance indicates the fiery loyalty and finely honed traditional fighting proficiency of these elite Korean soldiers. That it was even partially successful against the vast armies of the Mongols says much about their martial art, their skill and their zeal for combat. Despite their smaller numbers, they could be defeated by neither the Mongols nor the new Koryo government but only by a teamed effort of these two forces. "They manifested the spirit traditional of the Koryo military men," said Korean historian Yi Pyongdo.

The rebellion of the Three Patrols impacted the last hours of the Koryo-Mongol conflict with several consequences. It drove King Wonjong further into the Mongol camp to seek a stronger alliance against military control. It brought to light the still-considerable support for Koryo autonomy existing in the south. It worried the Mongols into tightening control over Koryo and establishing more Mongol offices in Koryo. It disastrously doomed by delay the Japan invasion expedition until the following year. By cementing the Mongol-Koryo alliance, it made Koryo a full-fledged partner in the Mongol adventure of conquest.

In 1274, the marriage of Crown Prince Sim to a Mongol princess finally was formalized, the first of seven such marriages of Mongol princesses to the Koryo royal family in the coming century. The offspring of three of these marriages held the throne. One of them, King Ch'ungyol, pursued a policy which aimed to restore Koryo sovereignty over its former territory and was successful to a surprising degree. (Henthorn, 1963). His initiatives were reversed, however, by his immediate descendants.

The story of the last days of the Three Elite Patrols is part of the legacy of skilled resistance to foreign influence inculcated into Koreans for thousands of years. When the victories of Korean fighters were thwarted, it almost invariably was political intrigue or cultural upheavals that undermined their military successes. (Henthorn, 1963) Ultimately, it was the civilian authorities who wanted to gain in authority by initiating peace that brought an end to Koryo's resistance to the Mongols.

5

Confucianism, Foreign Intervention Impact "Land of Morning Calm"

At the same time the Mongols were completing their pacification of Koryo, they were proceeding with their takeover of China, achieved by 1271. Kublai Khan, the grandson of Genghis Khan, who by now had stretched his influence to the Mediterranean, was ready to style himself "Son of Heaven." The Mongols, his nomadic people, were proud of their military conquests but were frank in admiring the established culture of the lands they overwhelmed militarily. So appreciative were they of the splendor of China, they even assumed the Chinese dynastic title of Yuan. The capital Kublai Khan established at Peking was also in the Chinese style.

The Korean peasantry bore the brunt of Mongol ambition under their rule, having to pay for the lavish court and its members' frequent trips to Peking to visit their intermarried relatives. Furthermore, there was a huge annual tribute to be delivered in gold, silver, ginseng, and hawks (since the latter were so popular for falconry among the Mongols), in addition to artisans and slaves. Added to this were the mammoth expenses of the abortive Mongol invasion of Japan that the Mongols attempted to extract from Korea. Records show that perhaps the only Korean who found this situation acceptable was Ki Cha-o, a farmer from Haengju, whose daughter was taken hostage to the Peking emperor, rose to become his second wife, and gave birth to his heir. As the unexpected grandfather of an emperor he reveled in wealth and idleness for the rest of his life.

Mongols Ruin Koryo Economy

Koryo warned against the likelihood of failure of an expedition to Japan by sea but the Mongols were determined to proceed. Some 35,000 Korean workmen were forced to build nearly 900 ships which debarked with 20,000 Mongol and Chinese troops and 5,000 Korean seamen. Japanese resistance, plus a major storm, doomed the effort. Undaunted, Kublai Khan sent another 900 ships and half the original number of crew again in 1281 with the same results from the weather and the Japanese. By this time, the Korean economy was in ruin.

The Mongols, by a variety of means, kept Koryo politicians from again forming a patriotic core, making sure they were constantly in turmoil through rumors, intrigue, and destabilizing efforts. One Koryo monarch was even made ruler of a non-Koryo territory in southern Manchuria and the Liaotung peninsula, creating rival factions in the Koryo court. Another, a crown prince doing his turn in Peking, came back to Koryo when his Mongol queen mother died, became suspicious that the court was to blame, and executed dozens of its members.

Cracks began to appear soon in the Mongol power structure, also infected with internal struggles. Emperor turnover became frequent. Famine and flood contributed to destabilization, and the Chinese took advantage of their conquerors' crises. From the 1340s on, rebellions simmered and broke out continuously. One of the self-styled Sung states to establish itself in northwest China based its power on one of several secret societies, the Red Turbans. These especially aggressive fighters eventually occupied the Liaotung peninsula. About 40,000 of them fled, after an engagement with the Mongol troops, into the Koryo kingdom where a Koryo army finally drove them out. However, they returned, more than twice as strong, forcing the Koryo court to flee to the south, relocating the capital. The court drew upon its military forces there and drove the Red Turbans back, slaughtering them in such numbers that they were permanently eliminated as a threat to Koryo. (Han,1970) This was achieved in spite of the Koreans' meager financial resources. Only through martial art prowess would such a feat be possible especially considering the condition of the Korean economy and government.

Ming Dynasty Supplants Mongols; Koryo Kingdom Reforms

A young Chinese commoner named Chu Yuan-chang had joined a rebel band in 1352, and his abilities promoted him to its leadership. In 1356 his men seized Nanking, and the next 10 years saw Chu Yuan-chang extending his power base. When he assumed control of most of China south of the Yangtze, he was ready to attack the Mongols. In 1368 he declared himself the first emperor of the Ming dynasty, which was to rule China for the next three hundred years.

Free from Mongol domination at last, the Koryo kingdom began to restyle its government and arrest the decline of the country. King Kongmin, in 1351, began removing pro-Mongol aristocrats placed by the Yuan rulers in influential Koryo positions. The northwest territories which the Mongols had been ruling directly from Peking reverted to Koryo control. The army was reorganized under direct control of the court and the old royal names and titles that had been replaced by the Mongols were restored.

Still, stability was a goal not at hand. Several problems plagued the Koryo ruler. The Manchurian Mongols plotted an abortive takeover of Kaesong with the pro-Mongol faction. Then the Manchurian ruler coaxed the Koryo deserter Ch'oe Yu to lead 10,000 troops across the Yalu in an attempt to restore Mongol dominance by force. Routed by Koryo defenders, the Mongols acquiesced, opened peace negotiations, and sent Ch'oe Yu in chains to Kaesong, where he was executed.

General Choi and the World's First Paratroopers

Japanese pirate ships invading the west coast, as well as the red-hooded bandits from China, were challenges met by a Korean hero, General Choi Young (1316-1389). Known for the rare trait of standing by his principles, he became a national hero by putting down Cho Il-shin's rebellion in 1352 and subsequently fighting 17 battles which spread his fame across the continent. He defeated hundreds of Japanese pirates. While serving as mayor of Pyongyang at the end of these wars in 1360, his efforts to eliminate famine and promote new crops attracted national attention. He suppressed the Kim Yong rebellion and annihilated about 10,000 Mongols. In 1374, his typical ingenuity was displayed when the Koryo court sent a fleet under his command to the island of Cheju-do, the last Mongolian bastion in Korea. After repeated failures to scale the high cliffs along the coastline where the defenders were positioned, he is said to have penetrated to the rear and recovered the long-lost island by use of paratroopers riding big kites—believed to be a "first" in warfare. (Yun, 1989)

Although he was highly decorated and at the pinnacle of his profession, he lived his life as a poor man, condemned extravagant officials, and discharged his duties with so low a profile that he was recognized by few of his own men. He focused his later years on defeating an influx of better organized Japanese pirates, assisted for the first time in world history by naval guns and by other capable warriors such as Yi Sung-kye, Chung Ji and Choi Mu-son. He became the hero of seaside villagers, whose descendants elevated him to demigod. Even today one can find General Choi Young's shrines dotting the south coast. (Yun, 1989)

Another difficulty was the proliferation of fraudulent documents, foreclosures, and the forces of private guards. In addition there were extensive private land holdings, which withheld taxes from the government. The government could not exist without the support of the great landowners but many of these were the same officials charged with reforming this practice. The uncooperative military was pitted against civil officials in Koryo's traditional power struggles. To end this stalemate, the king selected an obscure monk, Sin Ton, to re-establish royal authority and a more enlightened bureaucratic government. He was quickly targeted for assassination by the landholders. Crushed with defeat, King Kongmin was forced to compromise with the landlords but was still assassinated after retreating from his positions on reform.

Confucian Values Enter Political Arena

What these men couldn't achieve within Koryo government, was brought about by a philosophical movement that began not at the top but at the lower end of the bureaucracy. These offices were increasingly occupied by Confucian scholar-officials. Their credo of life and work was based on the thinking of a 12th-century Confucian scholar named Chu Hsi, whose view of governance swept China before arriving in Koryo. While Confucianism could previously be found in the Koryo government, control over the royal court and the culture of society had generally been directed by Buddhist monks. Although Buddhist priests were often interested in politics as well as religion, their loyalty was always to their sense of what was best at the time for their country. Confucians looked at their nation solely through the Chinese concept of the "world-state" system which could revolve only around the Chinese emperor as the supreme earthly figure. This philosophy, which initially was an asset to reassembling the Korean nation, would prove to be, in a few hundred years, the downfall of its culture as the neo-Confucian scholar-officials became authoritarian, rigid, factious, then corrupt. Two originally non-Korean concepts they introduced to the detriment of Koryo society were implacably rigid class distinctions and the subjugation of women.

Another feature of neo-Confucian doctrine was the dividing of existence into two inseparable components: *i* and *ki*. The first is form or structure and the second is its animating principal, the energy which figures so prominently in the classic instruction of Asian martial arts.

Yi Song-gye Wins Approval of Neo-Confucianist Reformers

Chu Hsi's "practical" reformed Confucianism required its adherents to look askance at Buddhism. Particularly targeted were the cost of its public festivals sponsored by the government, the power of monasteries, and the practice of so many men serving these monasteries rather than serving the government directly. It took the appearance of an outstanding reformer in the person of Yi Song-gye, later King T'aejo, before Koryo bureaucrats, who had become enthusiastic Confucians, could hope for change. Yi was a renowned military leader, having suppressed two local rebellions, participated in driving out the Red Turbans, and shut down the rebellion of Ch'oe Yu.

Portrait of Yi Sŏng-gye(1335-1408), founder of the Chosŏn dynasty. Artist unknown. Kyŏnggi-jŏn, Chŏnju, N. Chŏlla province.

Portrait of Yi, Song-gye (1335-1408), founder of the Choson Dynasty. Artist Unknown.

General Yi Song-gye Moves Against Japanese Pirates

The military challenge that would first bring Yi into focus as a national savior was his success with the piracy problem. Until Japanese piracy was under control, Koryo could not function with any order. The rulers of Japan at this time, the Ashikaga Shoguns, were only in nominal control and not of all Japan. A social revolution had passed through the country, depriving many Japanese *samurai* of their occupations. At the same time, an extreme economic depression visited the country and the hungry people formed wild pirate bands called *waiku* ("little barbaric thieves") by the Koreans. Many of the people of northern Kyushu and the islands off its coast had taken to regularly plundering the coasts of China and Korea. No longer attacking coastal towns only, they would march overland or navigate the rivers, raiding larger cities. Their policy on capturing a town was to sack it and kill everyone.

An Appreciation for Archery

One of the many stories concerning the prowess of General Yi indicates the Korean enthusiasm for skilled bowmanship. During an attack on Japanese pirates hiding in the Koryo hills, Yi had two horses shot out from under him and an arrow pierced his leg. Drawing it out and continuing the fight, he sighted a huge man among the enemy who was dancing about with spear in hand, urging on his men. Encased in armor, he wore a copper helmet protecting his entire head. Still, Yi was determined to fell his target and said to his lieutenant, Yi Tu-ran, "Make ready an arrow and when I strike off his helmet, you aim at his face." Yi drew his bow and sent his arrow powerfully and directly to the helmet, knocking it off. His lieutenants' swift arrow flew directly after Yi's, bringing the man down. This demoralized the enemy and they were soon routed. Yi took 1600 horses along with a large amount of spoil. (Hulbert, 1962)

Campaigns against the pirates by military commanders like Ch'oe Yong and Ch'oe Muson succeeded in reducing the strength of the attackers. They were aided by a variety of gun powder weapons produced at the government's cannon foundry. The manufacture of firearms by Koreans began in the reign of King U (r. 1375-1388), earlier than some give credit, according to the texts *Hart Guk-sa Sajon* and *Nihon Chiri Taikei*. (Henthorn, 1963) General Yi Song-gye repelled pirate attacks in his own northeastern area and then fought a series of engagements over the next several years that reduced their power and kept them under control.

Yi Song'gye's acquisition of even more status grew through his solution of the two main factional differences behind the assassination of King Kongmin: the group promoting an alliance with the Mongols, and the more realistic group who wanted to establish ties with the new Ming dynasty in China. Kongmin's successor, King U, favored the Mongols who had asked him to send troops to attack a Ming fortress and capture it for a renewed Mongol foothold in China. Even Mongol supporters in Koryo were unwilling to urge their king in such an aggressive move against the Chinese.

When Ming forces occupied a former Mongol fortress on the northern Koryo border, military strongman Ch'oe Yong took personal control of the government to block any hasty pro-Mongol conflict with the Chinese. This did not placate the Ming emperor who escalated tensions. Finally Ch'oe Yong charged Yi Song-gye to move against the Ming forces, despite Yi's misgivings. Yi was aware of the diminished state of the Koryo army, especially against such a large force. He was reluctant to withdraw troops from piracy patrol, and lose the gains made on coastal security. Furthermore, the rainy season had unwisely been chosen for the campaign.

Regardless, Yi followed orders, but by the time his army was crossing the Yalu, heavy rains, disease, and desertion crippled his force. Convinced that the expedition was headed toward disaster, he sent a courier to Kaesong to convey his conclusions. However, neither Ch'oe Yong nor King U would abandon the campaign, and ordered him to proceed against the Ming fortress.

Certain defeat, disgrace, and probably death faced Yi. The alternative was to bring down the king and Ch'oe Yong, thus changing the course of Koryo history. His army sided with him in rebellion; they marched back to Kaesong, deposed the king, and took charge of the government. Ch'oe Yong was banished to Ki-yang and as Yi sent him off, he is said to have wept at his former comrade and said, "Go in peace." Ch'oe may well have recalled at that time a prophecy made many years ago to General Ch'oe by Yi In-im that one day Yi Song-gye would become king. At that time General Ch'oe is said to have laughed. A popular song composed at this time stated that:

Outside the wall of P'yung-yang there is a red light,
Outside the wall of An-ju, a snake.
Between them comes and goes a soldier, Yi.
May he help us.

With Ch'oe removed, Yi turned to the king, summarizing his actions: "It was impossible to carry out the plan of conquest. The only thing left was to come back, banish the man who gave such bad advice and make a new start. We must now be firm in our allegiance to the Ming emperor, and we must change back to the Ming costume." The later remark refers to putting away Mongol dress affected by those supporters. Yi's call for respect of the Ming neighbors was based on his interest in stabilizing Koryo in a peaceful environment in which to renew his country.

The emperor, however, was still not appreciative of any plans other than his own. He called 80 of his most trusted eunuchs, armed them with swords, and sent them to kill Yi. It was another plan ill-conceived; the general was well guarded.

King U was not of Koryo royal stock, so a plan was devised to depose him and replace him with a blood relative of the Wang family. Yi was not interested in proclaiming himself king, as yet. King U's son was elevated to the throne while Yi Song-gye began a deep-seated reform of government. He broke the power of the landlords by enlisting the support of the Confucian scholar-officials. These under-compensated bureaucrats saw that Yi was a true reformer rather than the usual military dictator.

A scholar, Cho Chun, drew up the articles of reform and all land was nationalized and redistributed for the support of government officials. The king and his successor were discredited and deposed. The great estates were broken up and the bulk of land returned to the government tax rolls for revenue. The old land registers, which were the legal basis of the landlords' power, were burned.

In 1391 Yi Song-gye completely reorganized the military as commander-in-chief. All civil and military officials were assigned tracts of land for their support, while coastal lands, islands, and newly reclaimed land were reserved for the support of the army. Slaves, artisans, tradesmen, and, significantly, Buddhist monks were specifically struck from the list of the land-grant eligibles. Rent control was instituted, tenant eviction required sure cause, and tenants were forbidden to sell their rights of tenancy without permission. Exploitation of farmers was thus prevented, farmers felt secure on the land, and revenues were guaranteed.

To obtain office, examinations were given and, in theory at least, individuals became nobles by qualifying for high position. Aspirations for economic power thereby began with academic or professional attainment for entry into either military service, the so-called literary classes, or royal service. The generals and admirals came to share the economic favors of the king with the civil officials, reducing the likelihood of civil-military conflict.

Military examinations tested martial art skills such as archery, lance marksmanship, and low-saddle maneuvering (for examples, see the *Mooyedobo T'ong:, Manual of Ancient Korean*

Martial Arts), as well as knowledge of classical and military texts. This form of testing to qualify entry into the military made possible the regular recruitment of military officials and became an avenue through which even the lowborn might advance. (Lee, 1984)

In 1392, the Supreme Council of Koryo formally declared that the Koryo dynasty had come to an end and that Yi Song-gye was the rightful king. Like the founder of the Koryo dynasty, he was given the posthumous title *T'aejo* (Grand Progenitor) by which he is known historically. A new dynasty was about to be founded.

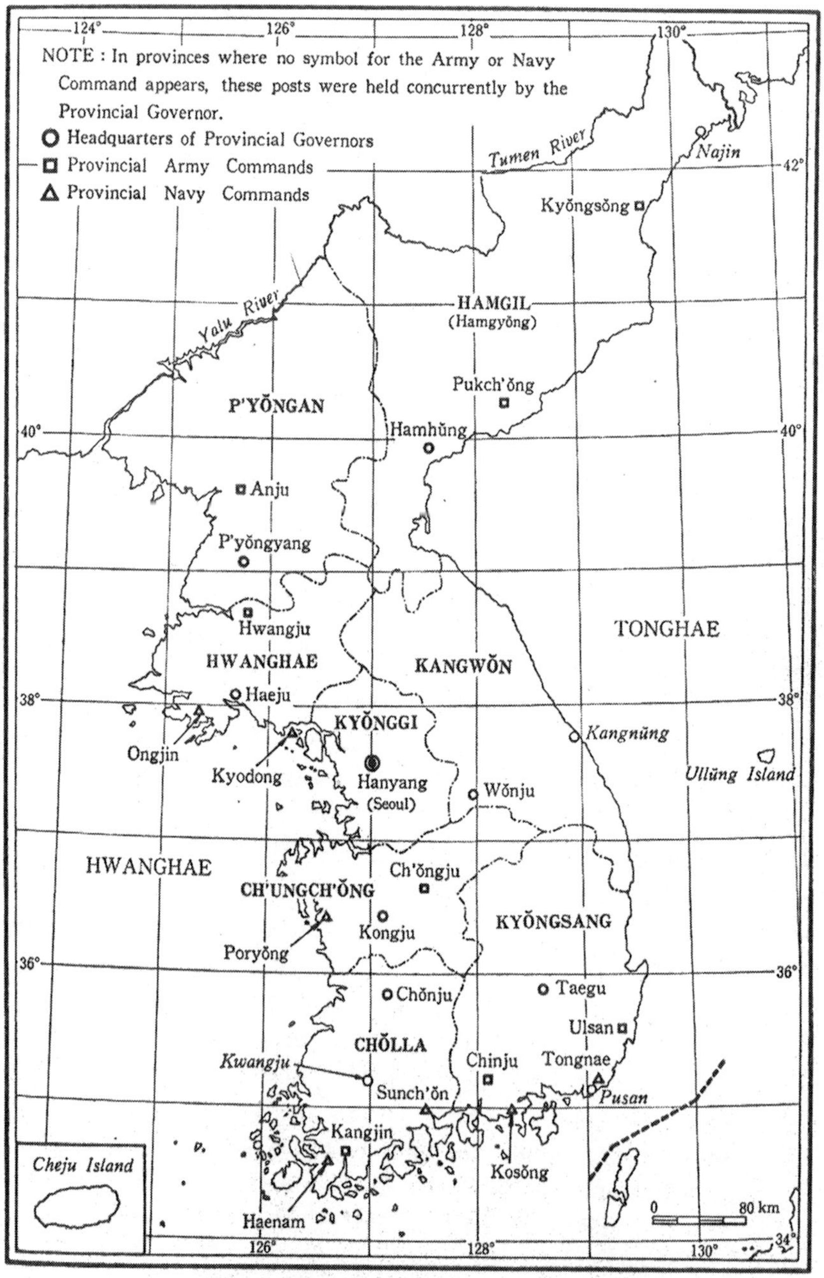

CHOSŎN'S EIGHT PROVINCES AND REGIONAL MILITARY COMMANDS (15th CENTURY)

This is a map of 15th century Choson showing its eight provinces and regional military commands.

Yi T'aejo Reorders Koryo Military System

Bringing order out of the chaos of the military system during the late Koryo period was a high priority of Yi T'aejo's. He established the Three Armies Headquarters to assume control of the nation's defense. The personal armed retinues of members of the royal household, "merit subjects" and others stood in the way of centralization and were abolished. In 1400, he called up their soldiers and brought them under the Three Armies Headquarters. This command was reorganized by Sejo in 1464 as the Five Military Commands Headquarters. "Five" refers to the divisions of Center, East, West, South, and North, each of which had military jurisdiction over the corresponding region of the country. Each division consisted of five brigades which contained four regiments, followed by battalions, companies, and platoons. The troops that formed the core of the Five Commands were professional military men selected through tests of their martial skills. Commoner peasant-soldiers, formerly the core of national defense, became simply conscripts called from the fields as needed, matched by the Paired Provisioner System to two or three able-bodied men who supported their daily needs.

This five-phase (element) theory is integral to Oriental philosophy and found in various disciplines, including Oriental Medicine (Acupuncture and Herbs) and Korean martial arts. One cannot help but conclude that the "five-phase theory" so prevalent in Korean philosophy may have influenced the organization of the military divisions.

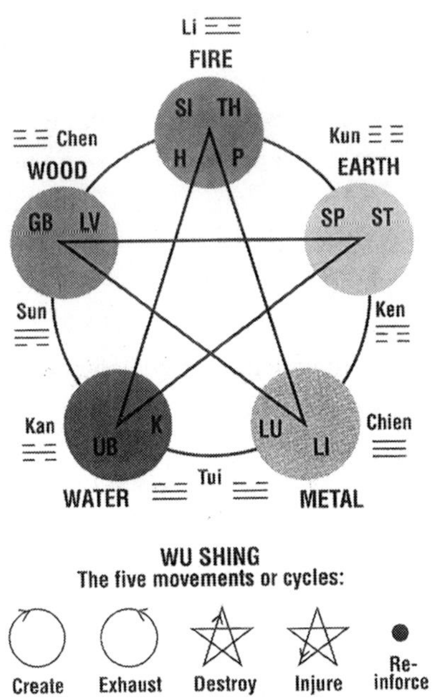

This is a commonly used Asian chart of the five phase (element) theory. It is used in acupuncture and oriental medicine and is also used in higher levels of martial art theory and philosophy.

Koryo's Hostile Neighbors Pacified Through Trade

The area near the Tumen River, the northern tributary of the Yalu, was inhabited by a Jurchen people known as the Yain or "barbarians" by Koryo. They originally survived by farming and hunting but had to obtain additional food, clothing, and tools by trade from Koryo. There were no convenient markets for this trade; they often raided a town for what they wanted. One Yain chief became of considerable concern in this regard as his power grew. The solution to this strife was the opening of markets in the area and the presentation of titular rank, food, clothing, and houses to those who ritually submitted to Koryo or immigrated.

Similarly, a relatively final solution to the problem of Japanese marauders was to eliminate the cause for their raids which were prompted by their meager mountainous existence and Koryo's trade embargo. The Yi government took a conciliatory position, granting the Japanese limited trading privileges, opening three ports, and working out a treaty in 1443 that would set certain restrictions on the sale of goods to the Japanese. In 1510 the Japanese at these ports rose in arms against the Korean garrison commander and trade was once again abolished. In 1512 another agreement was negotiated, at half the terms of the 1443 treaty. This trade resulted in an infusion of cultural items into Japan, including handicrafts like mother-of-pearl inlay, porcelain ware, carvings, Confucian writings, and histories. The Japanese offered minerals, medicines and herbs not found in Korea.

Neo-Confucian Revitalization Promotes Koryo Inventions

Between 1401 and 1544, the improved moral climate, level of ethics, and discipline brought about by the neo-Confucian influence resulted in an atmosphere of stability and productivity conducive to creativity and invention. Among military advances were bows which were shot by putting the feet against the bow and drawing the string with both hands. They were especially designed for women to use in defending walls. Another new bow devised was small, powerful, and shot metal "needle arrows." These bows propelled the arrows four times farther than the ordinary bow; one of the needle arrows could penetrate three men. A bomb was also invented, probably projected from a catapult. Another innovation was a spring trap that released an arrow weighing 125 pounds. (Hulbert, 1962)

Prominent among the achievements that advanced Korean culture into its "golden age" at that time was a world "first," the production of the first movable metal type, probably of copper. It was first cast and used in Koryo between 1232 and 1241, and produced in mass quantities in 1403. (Kim,1990) (Ha,1977) (Hulbert, 1962) This made possible the distribution of such works as, in 1433, *The Compilation of Native Korean Prescriptions*, establishing an independent Korean medical science. Ten years later a medical encyclopedia was published. The flexible Han'gul alphabet phonetic system was developed by King Sejong's scholars in 1443, as "the sounds of our language differ from those of China and are not easily conveyed in Chinese writing." This important step towards national literacy was followed by the compilation of the monumental Han'gul-Chinese dictionary in 1536. These achievements stimulated the development of an unprecedented volume of literature to appear in both forms of writing. (Hulbert, 1962)

Military texts whose contents were to be kept secret from outsiders were also written for the first time in Han'gul. (Han, 1974) References exist in extant records to various national chronicles and histories of successive reigns, the keeping of which was promoted by Confucianism, but only one has survived: *Che-wang Un'gi*, a book of poems eulogizing various Chinese emperors and Korean kings. A portion of a book on great Korean monks also has withstood the ravages of time. This level of destruction in respect to Korea's military history has contributed to the difficulty in documenting the details of achievements indicated in such records as are available.

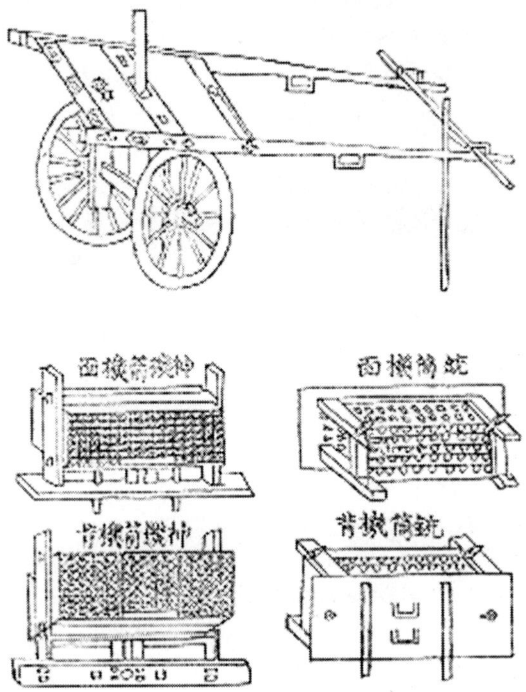

Rocket artillery piece devised by King Munjong, Chosŏn dynasty, to fire arrow-like projectiles by means of wick-ignited gunpowder charges. 1451.
plate page 6? ANHK

Drawing of an artillery piece that shot arrow like projectiles using gunpowder. Devised by King Munjong during the Choson dynasty in 1451.

In the area of military technology, improvement was made in the manufacture of cannons, helping to shift their use to offensive weapons. Techniques for their manufacture were now possible to describe in detail with diagrams and accompanied by Han'gul text. A projectile-launching vehicle was invented soon after, with an artillery piece that used gunpowder and was ignited by fuse wicks. It fired a hundred arrow-like missiles and other rocket projectiles mounted on an undercarriage. For use in naval warfare, a close-quarters attack galley was constructed by adding a protective covering to the standard Koryo warship used to ram and sink enemy vessels.

The general thought among Westerners following the centuries-later Japanese interpretation of Korean military history was that these weapons never existed in Koryo because Koreans' reliance on them was not as significant as elsewhere. However, the records exist to show that they were well developed on the Korean peninsula and not of Chinese origin as generally thought.

Further T'aejo Reforms

In foreign policy King T'aejo considered it most prudent to defer ceremoniously to the Ming court, even sending an envoy with the request that the emperor choose a new name for the kingdom. He suggested "Choson," the name of the earliest of the Korean states, and "Hwa ryong," the name of the new king's birthplace. T'aejo chose Choson, saying it was both beautiful and hallowed by history. However, the emperor was not fully satisfied with T'aejo's behavior, feeling he had not produced a sufficient amount of tribute and because he had refused to repatriate the numerous Chinese residing in Korea. He did not at first grant him the golden seal customarily given to tributary kings for use in dealing with the emperor's court, and thus he was unable to use the title of king before the Ming court.

In 1395 King T'aejo was ready to transfer the capital from Kaesong to Hanyang, modern Seoul. This made a symbolic break in the minds of the people between Kaesong, identified with the old aristocracy, and the new era of central government.

The implementation of neo-Confucian ideals was accelerated in government and in the home where each family member's deportment was outlined. However, the closing years of King T'aejo's reign were characterized by in-fighting among his numerous sons for the succession. Prince Pang-sok had been appointed crown prince, whereas his half-brother, Pang-won, was an able, intelligent man who had been of great service to his father in establishing the dynasty. Pang-won's supporters finally assassinated Prince Pang-sok and another brother. But when King T'aejo abdicated in 1398, Pang-won, rather than admitting his guilt by ascending the throne himself, maneuvered another brother into power. Pang-gwa was crowned and is known under the posthumous title of Chongjong.

Chongjong, encouraged by court fortune-tellers (geomancers) who predicted more doom for Hanyang, tried to transfer the capital back to Kaesong and leave the new capital, full of his still-quarreling brothers, to its intrigues. Nevertheless, Pang-won ultimately obtained the power to banish his brother, more or less tactfully having himself made crown prince instead of king. These power struggles largely were made possible by the fact that corps of personal bodyguards still remained from the early days of the dynasty when central power was not yet secure.

In 1400, when all serious rivals had been eliminated, private bodyguards were decreed illegal, and mercenaries were brought under the control of the government. That year Pang-won also felt secure enough to persuade his brother to abdicate, finally achieving his goal. For the next 18 years of his reign he dedicated himself to completing the reforms started by his father. The main thrust was the elimination of all structures through which the Koryo dictators and bureaucrats had governed, and the expansion of royal authority. In October of 1404 the capital was returned to Seoul, where it remained throughout the Yi dynasty.

Korean Culture Blossoms Under Yi Dynasty

The Yi dynasty experienced its greatest monarch, and was most creative culturally, during the reign of King T'aejong's son and successor, Sejong (1418-1450). He enthusiastically promoted the ideal that cultivation of the literary arts is the path to individual virtue and virtuous government, as well. He established the Chip-hyonjon, a royal research institute that conducted political studies, compiled commentaries and histories, issued monographs, sponsored lectures, and furnished royal tutors. The range of publications he sponsored encompassed military, political, social, scientific, and artistic topics.

Eight years after Sejong stepped down as ruler due to illness, King Sejo assumed control after bloody in-fighting among his relatives. The welfare of his armies was paramount to this leader. He distributed large quantities of medicine among the soldiers on the northern border, and made generous gifts of land to the troops. This guaranteed a certain degree of loyalty and fostered a military spirit among the people. He also published a book on military topics. Throughout his reign, his soldiers were trained by staging sham fights, both in the palace enclosure and outside the city walls. These exercises, called "promise sparring," are still in use today in martial systems such as Kuk Sool Won to preserve ancient tradition, train techniques, and sharpen skills. Sejo innovated the use of the split bamboo as a sign that a military messenger from him was properly accredited. The courier would carry half of a split bamboo to a general previously given the other half.

Sejo recruited all soldiers who could wield a bow of 120 pounds in order to subdue the troublesome wild tribes of the north. This is a clear indication that archery was a leading martial skill among the fighters of Choson. He also instituted a census of the people for the purpose of making army recruitment estimates.

Korean Society Falters With Decline of Confucian Idealism

In Sejo's time the seeds of the corruption and strife that was to curb the creative spirit of the Yi dynasty were sown. The promise shown by land reform was compromised by its administrators, the class of civil and military officials or *yangban* who owned the land for which they were also supposed to collect the required tax. The interests of these clan-centered, land-rich administrators whose duty was supposed to be first to the king and country deviated increasingly from the Confucian ideal.

Resolution of disputes over the awarding of posts or disbursement of authority weren't easily mediated in the Confucian system. It had no provision for opposing points of view or compromise because it assumed that there was always a single policy that was right and that all other policies were wrong.

Another element of divisiveness was the spread of the *swoon*, private Confucian academies established by the *yangban* on their estates. In times when central authority was weakening, the *swoon* not only competed for students with government-run schools but were focal points for a commitment to clan solidarity that extended into the later lives of students who became government officials.

As historian Ki-baik Lee noted, the dominant characteristic of factional conflict in Choson was the struggle among political cliques, membership in which was essentially "foreordained and forever." The descendants of members of a particular faction inherited their factional affiliation generation after generation. Their land holdings and clan affiliations sustained partisan feuds. Even with the rise and fall of factions, descendants of the victims merely awaited the time when they might again rise to exonerate their ancestors. This system involved conflicts among both officials in the central government and the neo-Confucian literati.

In 1455, Sejo was usurped, and in the following years, during the reign of his son and grandson, dissatisfaction with the government structure increased. A steep turn for the worse occurred in 1494 when the grandson, King Songjong, died suddenly and Yonsan'gun ascended to the throne. He was a willful, arbitrary and dissolute ruler so despised he was never given a posthumous title or called king by historians. He was intolerant of divergent opinions and purged his court, executing many. In 1504, when he discovered the court secret that his mother had been deposed and executed during his childhood, he instituted another, more violent, purge. During the remaining two years of his reign, his megalomania was fully unleashed. He ignored Confucian decorum, stabled his horses in Buddhist temples, banned the use of Han'gul, and ordered the destruction of all documents written in Han'gul (due to the fact he had received a critical letter in that script). These were only a few of his many destructive excesses. In 1506 he was deposed.

Under King Chungjong (1506-1544), some semblance of order returned but court favoritism regarding land allotments increased dissent. The former idealism of the neo-Confucianists deteriorated into factional fights and blatant power struggles. Chungjong's successors saw the situation worsen. Factionalism rose during the reign of King Myongjong, and junior and senior officials raged against each other. Because attention was devoted to personal vendettas, the military fell into confusion.

Japan Consolidates Power, Initiates International Aggression

Embroiled in internal conflict, Korea had no awareness of the political climate in neighboring Japan. Korean diplomatic missions to encourage Japan to control its pirates were unproductive. After a devastating attack by pirates on the coast of Cholla Province in 1555, Korea suspended relations with Japan.

In 1543, Portuguese ships began trading with the western Japanese islands and eventually introduced firearms to the local warlords. Quickly, upon seeing the advantages of this new use of gunpowder, they were eager to compete with their rivals in the granting of accessions to the Portuguese. One of the most influential of these was permission to introduce Catholicism into Japan, even to the point of turning over whole villages to the Jesuits. Catholicism soon became fairly widespread in western Japan.

In 1588, Japan decided to approach Korea again, this time with a delegation headed by Yoshitoshi, a young man described by the Koreans as coarse, violent, and of such a fierce nature that the other members of his delegation entered his presence only on their knees and did not dare look him in the face. Month after month he waited for the Korean king to agree to send an envoy to Japan. At last the king relented on the condition that the Japanese government would capture and send back for execution some Korean renegades who were conspiring with Japanese pirates on coastal raids. This done, the Korean king agreed to meet Yoshitoshi and presented him with a handsome steed. Yoshitoshi gave the king a peacock and a gun or guns. It has been written that this marked the introduction of guns to Korea, but as we've seen in King U's reign, firearms already were being used one hundred years previously in Korea.

In 1590 the Japanese leader Nobunaga was succeeded by one of his followers, Toyotomi Hideyoshi. Hideyoshi would be the first leader to succeed in imposing his rule over the entire country of Japan.

As the Japanese found they could manufacture their own muskets, they elevated the importance of firearms to a strategic level in their military training. Eventually, Hideyoshi banned Catholicism, primarily to eliminate the exchange of guns and goods for conversion and to position himself for a personal takeover of the Portuguese trade. (Han, 1974) It is likely that he was also interested in diminishing foreign influence. He sent many of the Japanese Catholic converts to Korea, including General Konishi (who had received the baptismal name of Augustine Arimandano).

When Hideyoshi felt his control over Japan was well established, he looked toward his western neighbors with expansionist plans. He sent envoys to Korea, suggesting that they reopen relations, beginning with Korea's permission to allow Japanese soldiers pass freely through Korea to invade China. Amazed that Japan was actually capable of such a campaign, Korea flatly refused but sent envoys to Japan as a precautionary measure to determine whether the Japanese plan was bombast or truly underway. Each messenger returned with opposing views.

Picture of Hideoshi (artist unknown)

The Korean government chose to believe that a Korean invasion was unlikely, laughing off Hideyoshi's approaches by saying, "The Japanese attempt to attack the Celestial Empire is like that of a snail which strikes a rock." Considering the deteriorated condition of its neglected military, it was the preferred deduction. Farmers had been buying exemption from service with a tax paid in textiles. The standing army was usually employed on public works projects and had little training. Some active units did exist to guard the northern border and to repel Japanese pirates, but there was no full-scale field force anymore. Professional training and mobilization would have taken years. Korea had not been aware of the Japanese investment in firearms manufacturing and had no similar industry. Swords, bows, arrows, and spears were the mainstays of their arsenals; they had few firearms.

(1) Hideyoshi's First Invasion (1592-93)

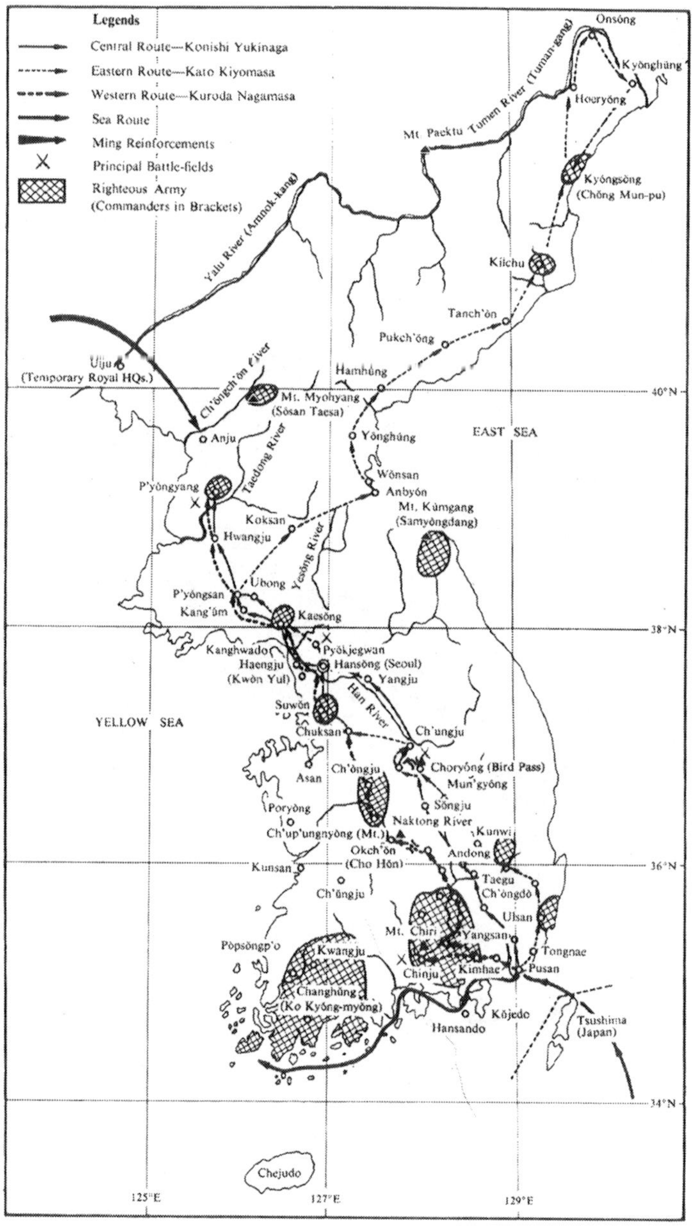

This is a map of the first invasion route traveled by the Japanese invasion force.

The Origins of Korea's Martial Unreadiness

For centuries before the Japanese caught them unawares, Korea had been largely at peace, with its army scaled back merely to units dealing only with the occasional border disturbance. The martial arts had receded in practice to the province of the families of traditional martial art adepts and those few still training the scaled-down military. The people in general had been preoccupied with the arts and occupations of peace.

For example, in 1591, a program of building walls around towns in the northern part of Kyongsang province was implemented. The Korean court felt some minimal defense measures such as these might pacify those who saw Japan's Hideyoshi as a threat. Emphasis was on enlarging areas to accommodate more people rather than to fortify vulnerable areas by taking advantage of features of the terrain. (Kim, 1978) The court also ordered the governors of three provinces to conscript men to manufacture weapons such as spears and swords. These workmen, not perceiving any threats to Korea's peace, complained loudly.

When, in Kyongsang province, a military training center was established in 1589, local peasants were forced by order of the governor to undergo a six-month training period each year. Those selected were the least needed in the work force: old men and teenagers, some volunteering only for the pay. These circumstances were not likely to yield any combat-worthy soldiers. (Kim, 1978)

Poor administration of military affairs was a chronic characteristic of the Yi dynasty and contributed seriously to the weakening of Korea's military readiness. Preference was given to civil officials over military experts in army administration, and slights to officers were frequent. The Chungch'ubu, the highest military organization in the central government, was considered virtually a retirement home for aging officers, and had no real function. (Kim, 1978) For nearly two centuries, until the reign of King Sonjo, Korea's antiquated defense system had no substantive functions. Until Sonjo's renovation, which was done only as a temporary measure against the Japanese invasion, military affairs were part of the duties of the provincial governor. Unfortunately, the reorganization added another negative element friction between the governor who now had to split his military duties with a new official sharing administrative duties with him. Moreover, at the time of King Sonjo, all able-bodied males 15 through 60 years of age were subject to military service, but the sons of the *yangban* (privileged rank) were exempt. That left the commoners and the *ch'onmin* or low caste, who did not read or have access either to the martial ideals and preparedness of their ancestors, or to those monks and recluses who still harbored these ideals. According to the deteriorated ethics of the civil servants administering the military, anyone with the cloth required to obtain exemption or the money to hire a proxy to take their place were not required to serve. Sometimes a proxy would represent more than one man. Military officer posts were sold and the purchaser then sold military duty exemption. Military rosters were no longer kept current either, and as a result, military units were below prescribed strength. It was impossible to ascertain military strength or readiness with any accuracy. (Kim, 1978)

Morale among the Korean military forces was particularly low. The *Sonjo Sillok* records for the year 1585 show that when the people were starving following a crop failure, certain *yangban* blithely went on with their banqueting and merry-making despite the growing resentment of the populace. Banditry increased, and the idea of looking out for oneself predominated in many quarters. (Kim, 1978)

Koreans, without use for a large standing army, had for a long time not been oriented in large numbers to military life as they had formerly, and the ideals that motivate great warriors had faded away. The sudden appearance of close to 250,000 Japanese soldiers on the Korean coast caused panic not only due to the enemy's obviously superior preparedness but because they were well supplied with a formidable new weapon lacking in the Korean arsenal: firearms.

A third factor contributing to a defeatist attitude lay in the psyche of the country: the tendency to become jealous of any outstanding leader, prompting envious peers to plot his ruin. As a result, according to historian Hulbert who considered this the main cause of Korea's weakness at the invasion's onset, the morbid resentfulness existing between opposing parties in government made certain that no popular military figure was available in the early hours of need. The Japanese, on the other hand, newly united with idealistic energy freshly minted from centuries of feudalism, were well practiced in warfare from their continual forays into one another's territory and their coastal raids. Their courage was also reinforced with an abundance of the latest technology, guns, and experienced sharpshooters.

Participation of the Monk-Soldiers

One of King Sonjo's critical moves to bulwark the inadequately prepared armed forces was to return the exiled Master Hyujong from his retreat on Myonhyang Mountain. Hyujong had commanded wide respect among the Buddhist monks for his role as arbiter between the two sects of Buddhism during the restoration of that faith under King Myongjong (predecessor of King Sonjo). Sonjo felt that he would be able to organize the monks with little difficulty. Hyujong had gone into retreat after being unjustly implicated in the Chong Yorip rebellion of 1589 during which the real ringleader had taken his name to win support. King Sonjo discovered the truth and had Hyujong released. It was certain that Hyujong would help him now, and he did his duty as national commander of all monk-soldiers. He dispatched an impassioned plea to monks throughout the country for them to participate in the defense of Korea. It read:

Alas, the way of heaven is no more. The destiny of the land is on the decline. In defiance of heaven and reason, the cruel foe had the temerity to cross the sea aboard a thousand ships. The miasma is filling the air. The innocents are falling dead at their sword by the thousands. With the three capitals taken, a thousand years of our forebears' achievements are

(3) Hideyoshi's Second Invasion (1597)

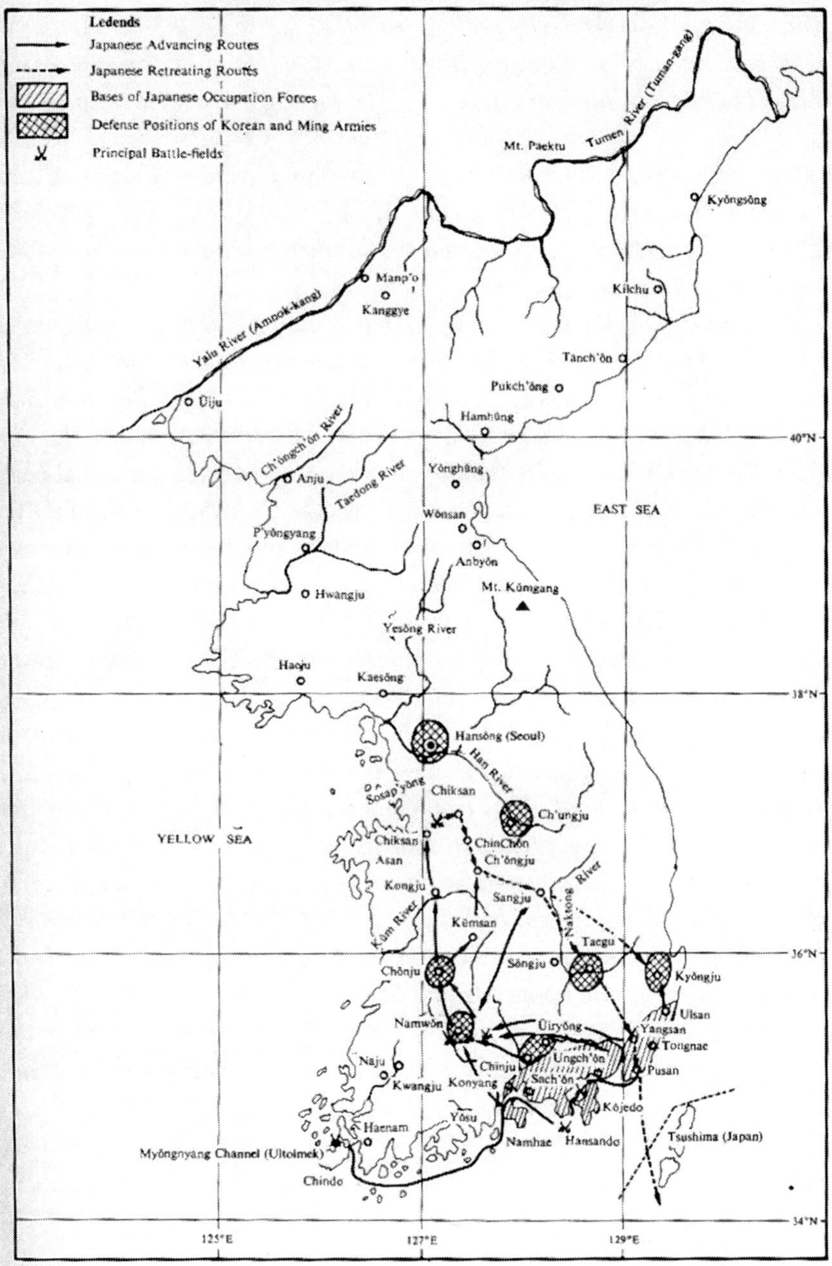

This map shows the route of Hideyoshi's 2nd invasion of Korea.

brought to naught in one fell swoop. The ruthless enemy, as the devil and sea monster, laid the land to waste, slaughtering the people. The ancestral land is taken. Can this be the way humans behave? These poisonous devils are as virulent as snakes or fierce animals.

Hold your banners high, and arise, all you monk-soldiers of the right provinces! Who among you have not been given birth in this land? Who among you are not related by blood to the forefathers? Who among you are not subjects of the king? Confucius taught us to lay down our lives to achieve benevolence. Sacrificing oneself for a just cause and suffering in the place of the myriad souls is the spirit of Bodhisattvas. Master Won'gwang [hero-scholar of Silla] *enjoined us not to retreat from battle. To defend the country and save the people is the tradition of the ancestors and Buddha's teachings.*

You monk soldiers of all the monasteries! Abandoning a just cause and swerving from the right path in order merely to survive in hiding how can this be the proper way? The cunning enemy, the monster, will never take pity on you. Once the land perishes, how then do you propose to stay alive? Put on the armor of the mercy of Bodhisattvas, hold in hand the treasured sword to fell the devil, wield the lightning bolt of the Eight Deities [spiritual beings commissioned to guard the law of Buddha], *and come forward. Only then can you do your duty. Only then can you find the way to life. Let the aged and the weak pray in the monastery. Let the able-bodied come out with their weapons to destroy the enemy and save the land.*

Whether or not the people will survive, whether or not the land will remain, depends on this battle. It behooves everyone with the sacred blood of Tan'gun flowing in their veins to defend the country with their lives. When even the trees and grass rise as warriors, how much more should red-blooded people? The people are indignant. Lose no time but arise, beat back the sworn enemy. Buddhist law is just this to save the world. People fall victim to the foe's weapon, their blood staining the land. How can you just sit back in the mountains and watch? When the land is no more and the people are in distress, your survival would be betrayal of the people. I regret to hear that famed ministers are locked in partisan feud and that commanders flee before the battle. They seek survival by asking for aid from abroad. Deplorable, indeed.

Only our monk-soldiers are able to save the country and deliver the people. You have been training day and night to rise about life and death. You are not burdened with families. Bodhisattvas will give you protection. Arise, onward to the battlefield to destroy the enemy. There can be no victory without fighting. No life without death. Why be afraid of the enemy's weapons? Monk-soldiers, arise! Assemble at Pophung monastery in Sunan. I expect you to be there. Unite, and onward to the battlefield!

June 15, 1592
Hyujong,
Commander of the Monk-Soldiers
of the Eight Provinces
(Kim, 1978)

This document illustrates that ideals and military capability were not entirely moribund in Korea but were latent and emerging in the warrior-monk class. Korea's particular brand of

Buddhism is evident in the citing of Won'gwang, believed to be the originator of the ideal of the Korean Buddhist patriot's vow of no retreat when in battle. Although the attitude of stopping at nothing for the sake of the state may be said to be foreign to Buddhism in general, it was characteristic of the tradition of Korean Buddhists ever since the Silla dynasty. (Kim, 1978) Elsewhere, the central Buddhist precept against taking life was observed by Buddhist monks.

The reference to Tan'gun in Hyuyong's document widened its appeal to Confucianists and the result was more favorable than expected. More than 8,000 monk-soldiers from across the country enlisted for war duty during June-December of 1592. This may seem small when compared to the 50,000 soldiers of the regular army, but the monks' performance in guerrilla warfare and their influence on the rest of the soldiers was very influential. Sometimes as few as 22 monk-soldiers (the number of the group at P'yongyang) directly affected the outcome of a campaign. Their individual performance was extraordinary, and more than made up for what they lacked in numbers. Frequently it was the monk-soldiers who spearheaded an attack, a role the regulars and righteous army shied away from. Although their casualty rate was high, their daring charges often turned the tide of major battles.

An added incentive to the monks to aid the army, even on an unpaid basis, was the possibility that their reduced social status would be negotiated for such participation. Unfortunately, unlike volunteers who received food rations, sometimes the monk-soldiers, who received no such government support, had to disband simply for lack of food. The whole recruitment campaign suffered from extreme adversity. Half of the area from which monk-soldiers came was under Japanese control and a number of their monasteries had been reduced to ruin. Nevertheless, the monks also volunteered for transporting military provisions, cultivating crops, and performing some fortification work after the initial negotiations for a truce failed.

Another interesting factor in the stepping forward of the monks was the fact that they responded in greatest numbers from P'yongan and Cholla provinces, two areas spared the initial direct impact of the Japanese invasion. The reasons for the enthusiasm of monks from these two places included the history of neglect to which they had been subjected by the central government. Excluded from government service for so long, the war provided them with an opportunity for social advancement through military service, as well as service to their high ideals. Since P'yongan province was the former territory of Koguryo, known for its warlike tradition and military valor, it is likely, too, that its inhabitants "still retained the readiness to confront danger for a cause." (Kim, 1978)

"Although monks had taken up arms against foreign invaders before," said historian Samuel Dukhae Kim, "their performance during the Imjin wars was without precedent in scale and was even more remarkable against the background of the government policy of repressing Buddhism. The fact that some aged monks and novices of tender age also joined the ranks tends to show how pervasive was the enthusiasm among the Buddhists."

In Korea, Buddhist patriotism was nourished by the belief that it would avert foreign invasion. In contrast Buddhist patriotism in the other countries, like China and Japan, was believed to ward off natural disasters and civil disturbances. The Buddhist monks' participation in the wars against foreign invasions is a unique characteristic of Buddhist patriotism in Korea, and there are numerous examples of monks engaged in this model throughout its history. The Buddhist belief "to never kill anything" was circumvented by the idea that it was necessary in order to relieve the distressed masses. Korean Buddhist demonstrated their belief in relieving the distressed masses by going to battle many times; quite different from Chinese and Japanese Buddhist actions as a group.

The **Sonbi** *Spirit*

At this turning point in the history of Korea, it is appropriate to say a few words about the Korean spirit which dominated the nature of the people for the 500 years prior to Japanese Annexation and directed the course of the Choson period.

Like the spirit of chivalry in medieval European history and the *Samurai* spirit of the Japanese, the Koreans of Choson were identified for centuries with the ideals of the classical Confucian scholars called the *sonbi.* Their value orientation as a concept, at least, has survived even down to contemporary industrialized Korea, largely in terms of popular political slogans.

Everyone in the Choson period was influenced by the *sonbi.* The title could only be obtained by academic achievement and not by inheritance. Lower class men were approved when they met the requirements and practiced good conduct. The *sonbi* spirit was a highly idealistic model based on a metaphysical belief system which explained life as centered on ancestors, family shrines, rites, duties, loyalty, and filial piety. The sonbi played two roles as scholars and administrators. They were extremely concerned with how later historians would view their behavior. For example, they would ignore claiming a tremendous fortune if it were not "righteously" obtained.

A Sonbi from the later Choson dynasty dressed in yang-ban (gentlemans) cloths practicing archery.

Sonbi lauded bravery but their literary pursuits did not prepare them for action on the battlefield. Therefore, they were mistakenly thought to be effeminate and timid. However, they sometimes sent memoranda to the kings or even demonstrated in front of the palace, objecting to some policy at the risk of their lives. Even though they could be banished to a distant region or be given poison as a death penalty, they dared to speak out without reserve for the sake of moral duty to the king. When the Sonbi found that the royal policy was not oriented to righteousness and that they could not promote their king's aspirations, they voluntarily resigned from their official posts and retreated to their native towns where they could devote themselves to more intensive study and guide younger disciples. Even when repeatedly entreated by the kings, they would turn down offers to return. One Sonbi, Yulgok (Yi I), was recorded to have been called back to service 107 times by a king. Sometimes their integrity actually caused a ruler to change his mind.

Although not strong or capable of defending their country physically such as professional soldiers were, they rallied soldiers throughout the nation in the crises caused by foreign invasions, during which they showed unexpected bravery.

Unfortunately, some of the Sonbi attitudes had extremely negative consequences for Choson, particularly when the foreign invasions began after years of peace. Scholar Dr. Yoon Ki Lee, a former professor of politics at Hanyang University in Seoul, tallied their weaknesses in terms of their position of influence. (Lee, 1989) They admired poetry and literary affairs excessively to the neglect of defense matters. They wasted more time in the elegant arts and conversation while practical preparations and special reformation were ignored. The Sonbi led the descent into self-absorption and closed-minded attitudes in complete ignorance of foreign affairs. They retarded the adoption of enlightened policies because of their insensitivity to new thought.

Sonbi lacked the will to compromise. Their "black or white" logic and sense of "either an enemy or a friend" aggravated factional strife and brought about many merciless purges of Confucian scholars. They did not understand the concept of "loyal opposition." As the doctrine of popular sovereignty replaced that of the monarchical, their political views did not fundamentally change from subordination to participation politics.

Understanding the pervasive influence of the Sonbi gives a heightened appreciation of the heroics of the later-Choson-period military men. A strong impression that the failure of Korea to defend its borders at the end was certainly not for either lack of martial art or martial skill but the availability of skilled martial artist at that time.

1592: Japan's First Invasion of Korea

Hideyoshi, confident of his army's superiority, dispatched 190,000 soldiers to invade Korea in the spring of 1592, with a reserve of 60,000 to follow. The army was provided with 5,000 battle axes, 100,000 long swords, 100,000 spears, 100,000 short swords, 500,000 daggers, 300,000 firearms, large and small, and 50,000 horses. The flotilla which crossed the 120-

mile strait to bring this huge army to the shores of Korea consisted of 3,000 to 4,000 boats, 40-50 feet in length (12-15 meters) and 10 feet wide (3 meters). (Hulbert, 1962)

A dense fog concealed the expedition from the unguarded beach near the Korean port garrison of Pusan. The commander of the Pusan force happened to be hunting that day on Deer Island at the entrance to the harbor and was first to become aware of the fateful invasion. His town fell quickly under a rain of bullets. Surprised, outnumbered, and panicked by heavy gunfire, a relatively small number of rusty spears, bows, and arrows pitted against a very large number of muskets, swords, and long spears were no match.

Acts of heroism contrasted with acts of cowardice as the stunned Koreans attempted to cope with the invasion of their country and imminent death. As the invaders marched around the bay to the ancient city of Tong-na, the general of the province, approaching from the north, panicked on hearing of the fate of Pusan. He pulled back six miles from the targeted town of Tong-na, reportedly stating, "As commander of all the provincial forces, I must not risk my life in actual battle but must stand outside where I can direct affairs."

However, Song Sang-hyun, the prefect of Tong-na, hurriedly gathered all the citizens and soldiers he could find to defend his city. The Japanese took the town, and the next day they prepared to storm the city's fortress where the brave prefect assumed his position in the upper story of the great gate. There, according to Korean custom, he beat upon a great drum and urged on his soldiers in the fight. For eight hours the gallant defenders fought until they were no more. Seeing that all was lost, the prefect called for his official robes and seated himself in state in the upper gateway. He bit his finger till the blood came and with it wrote a note on his fan to be taken quickly by his friend Sin Yu-go to his father: "The duty of a subject to his king comes before that of a son to his father, so here I die without seeing you again."

Sin Yu-go was told by the prefect, "There is no need of your staying here to die. Make good your escape while you can."

Sin replied, "I have enjoyed pleasures with you and now I prefer to suffer with you." The intruders entered, and when Song Sang-hyun was disrespectfully pulled by his garments in an attempt to force him to bow to the enemy, the offender was given such a kick in the stomach by Sin Yu-go that he rolled over on the floor. The prefect was instantly struck down by a sword and his friend put to death. But the Japanese general in command was so impressed with the bravery of Song Sang-hyun that he had his body decently buried and erected over his grave a wooden monument on which he wrote, "A Loyal Subject."

The blow to the stomach by Sin Yu-go, could well be an indication that kicking techniques were not only taught to Koreans but they were so well trained that they could deliver them with power enough to send a warrior, presumably in battle armor, instantly to the floor. Even today the Koreans are well known for their powerful kicking techniques.

There is a legend that for two years after this event a red light could be seen glimmering at night above the gate where this man who honored his heritage met his end.

When General Yi Kak and another commander with him, General Pak Hong, heard of the fall of Tong-na, they fled. This kind of cowardice, as Hulbert pointed out, revealed itself almost exclusively among certain kinds of officers, such as U Pok-yong, prefect of Yong-gung. He was elevated to the rank of district general as a result of his false claim that he had destroyed a band of two hundred robbers. They actually were two hundred Korean soldiers from the town of Ha-yang who had failed to recognize his rank as they passed him on the road and so had not dismounted. He summarily executed them all.

Cowardice was rarely encountered among the rank-and-file soldiers who defended their country to the end. Illustrative of this is the response of men under the timid General Yi Kak. His troops became disgusted at his flight from place to place in the opposite direction from the invaders. They made crude guns that would shoot pebbles, hoping for a chance at the enemy.

Four days after the Japanese landed, the alarming news reached Seoul and the ministers rushed to the palace to draw up a plan for defense. Three generals were assigned by the king to head south by way of the three approaches to the city. Chief commander General Yi Il proceeded by the middle road to a garrison at Cho-ryung, the most important strategic point in the Japanese line of March.

In the haste of the moment, few were aware that these generals were practically without forces. When the military rolls were consulted, it was found that the army was mostly on paper. A majority of the men were either "sick" or "in mourning." General Yi Il could muster barely 300 men but not even in time for his departure. He went alone, trusting that this pitiful handful of soldiers would follow him, and hoping to recruit at least the semblance of an army as he rode south.

At this time another situation occurred which indicated the military incompetence of the king. Prime Minister Yu Sungl-nyong was made Minister of War and charged with the duty of organizing an army. Sil Yip was appointed Vice-Minister of War, given an elaborate sword, and sent south with the injunction to kill anyone who should prove unfaithful to the throne, even though it might be General Yi Il himself. This elaborate sword could very well have been a sword decorated with bats or butterflies. The author has a sword decorated with bats and it is said that this type of sword was given by the king to special investigators. The oral tradition says that anyone with this sword had the power cut off the head of any nobleman deemed to be disloyal.

In effect, Sil yip was given an independent command over the head of his commander-in-chief, a confusion of authority often disastrous. As Sil Yip exited his audience with the king, he slipped on the stone steps and lost his court hat. The attendants noted this omen of bad luck with dismay.

Three columns of Japanese fanned out from Pusan, marching north unchallenged up through the central part of the peninsula. General Yi Il fled in panic over what he saw to be the hopeless conditions at Cho-ryung and left it undefended. His followers objected to remaining under the command of such a coward and he was finally stranded in the town of Sang-ju without a soldier at his back. Enraged that the local prefect had not been able to find additional soldiers among the farming population, he threatened to decapitate him unless he produced some troops immediately. The prefect managed to coerce 900 raw recruits to form a band. They had never before borne arms or fought anyone.

Meanwhile, General Sil Yip had contrived to acquire a force of approximately 8,000 men, intending to push straight for the key city of Cho-ryung. He abandoned that idea and fell back to Ch'ung-ju when he heard of General Yi Il's disaster there. After the latter joined him with his

This sword was made by master Korean sword maker Kang, Sung Sik who recently passed away. It represents the type of sword the Kings secret inspectors would carry. Inspectors who carried this sword had the Kings authority to cut off the head of anyone under inspection, even a general.

new troops he made a doomed decision. He tried to draw the Japanese into a valley with only two narrow passages, a river passing through both. His idea was that his men could use their battle-flails on the Japanese very effectively as they tried to squeeze through these passages. Conversely, the Japanese employed their muskets and swords on the Koreans even more effectively. They maneuvered to drive those who survived to escape into the deep river waters where they drowned.

Seoul stood defenseless as the next target of the Japanese. The king called a council of his advisors. Many of the opinions reflected the lack of preparedness of the Koreans for such a national emergency. The minister of war was in favor of the court moving to P'yung yang. Yi Hang-bok, an official who would later figure prominently in the war, suggested that this would not be enough and that Chinese aid should be sought immediately. A number of other officials, on the other hand, agreed with the king that they should stay in Seoul.

The king said, "The ancestral temple with all the tablets of my illustrious ancestors is here. How can I go and leave them? Let the ministers of war immediately detail troops to man the walls."

A quick head count of men available and the number of battlements showed this was not practical. With 30,000 battlements on the city walls, each having three embrasures, and only 7,000 troops in the city, there was not a tenth of the force needed to man the walls. Long centuries of peace never called for attention to this level of readiness for war, and, instead, the

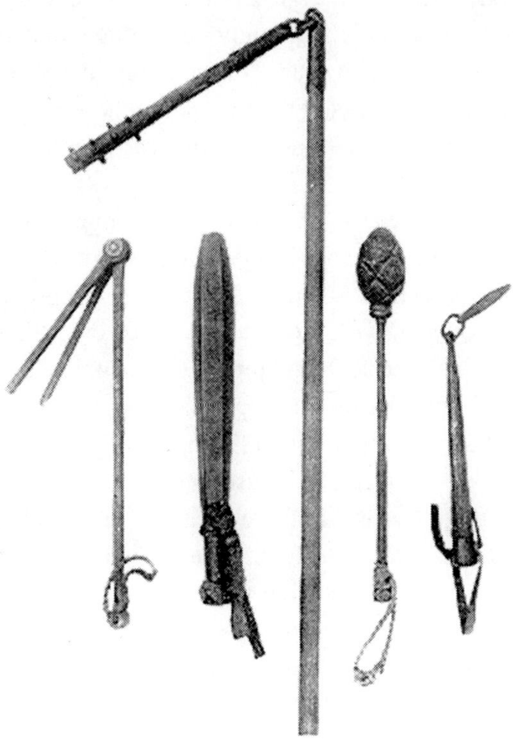

Battle flails are a unique Korean weapon used from ancient times through the last dynasty.

practice had been instituted of requiring male citizens to submit a remittance in lieu of military service. Only the poorest of the poor became soldiers. While the custom was discriminatory, the resultant low level of proficiency among government troops does not indicate either an incapacity for competence in the martial arts or the absence of courage and loyalty among Koreans of the day. Quite the reverse became apparent.

The alarmed Chosen court finally realized it had only one option: to depart for Uiju—with Seoul's outraged citizenry attempting to block their path, hurling insults at them. The king had charged two princes with raising fresh troops in defense of the kingdom in Hamgyong and Kangwon provinces, but they could not find anyone willing to cast themselves, inadequately equipped, into the path of the Japanese. Finally, they were seized by a turncoat district constable and handed over to the Japanese. They were later rescued by a loyal Korean general who himself was captured. He in turn was rescued by yet another band of Korean loyalists. Chaos was the order of the day.

Koreans Secure Victories Without Firearms, Cannon

In those desperate times during the flight from Seoul, another story of remarkable courage stands out that carried a Korean city to victory in the face of superior numbers and weaponry.

As the king fled north, a high official named Yi Chong-um raced to the walled town of Yun-an in Whang-ha Province, where its prefect had already fled. When a Japanese force of 3,000 men approached, the people begged Yi to take charge of the town's defense.

He consented, advising the residents of their peril, the likelihood that they would die, and inviting any who wished to run away to do so. To this it is said they replied with one voice, "How can we let our leader die alone?"

The following day the Japanese arrived. When they attempted to storm the walls, buckets of boiling water were thrown on their heads. They withdrew, but when they renewed the attack at night, piles of burning straw met their advance. At a third try, approaching with broad planks over their heads, they were pounded with huge stones rolled over the walls. By these improvised means persistently applied, the Koreans repelled their attackers for three days, finally forcing the Japanese into withdrawal after burning their dead.

Another encounter at the town of Chin-ju in Kyung Song province illustrates the Koreans' capacity for perseverance, even when facing a vastly larger and better equipped force. In this battle, the Japanese advanced on the town in three divisions numbering 10,000 soldiers. Their musketeers numbered 1,000, and made a deafening roar. The Korean general, Kim Si-min, had already decided to begin the battle by causing the enemy confusion and doubt. The city's response to the fusillade was silence. Its walls were deserted, not a man to be seen.

The Japanese thought this over and then next day remounted the assault, discarding the muskets and using fire arrows. Soon all the deserted houses outside the wall were in ashes. General Kim's response was a feign; he climbed to the south gate and in view of the enemy, sat in a leisurely manner, listening to one of his flute players. Hopefully, the Japanese would conclude that he was so confident in the superior strength of his own force that he had no concern for the activities of the enemy.

The effect was to make the Japanese very careful. They chose to prepare elaborately for the assault. Bamboo and pine trees were cut down to make ladders about eight feet wide and as high as the wall. They also made straw mats for head protection against missiles.

The Koreans used the extra time gained by the enemy's extended preparations to put together counter measures. They formed bundles of straw with little packages of powder fastened inside to cast down on the attacking party. Piles of stones and kettles of hot water were also made ready, and to welcome the Japanese in the event of a night attack, planks bristling with nails were thrown over the walls.

The latter tactics were especially provident as the attack did take place that night, raging fiercely for a time. However, so many of the Japanese were made lame by the spikes in the planks that at last they had to withdraw, leaving half their comrades behind. Most of these wounded were killed by the defenders. It is commonly thought that only the Japanese *ninja* used spikes such as these but as we have seen, they had been used in Korea for hundreds of years previously.

The General of the Red Robe

General Kwak Cha-u led a group of three former military men in the south who felt it was their moral imperative to show leadership in the face of the unexpected Japanese invasion.

Kwak, who cashed out his family's wealth to equip an army of 5,000 men, became famous for his rapid changes of bases. He appeared now at one point and again at another with such bewildering speed as to be regarded as possessing magic. He is said to have worn a fiery red cloak, and was dubbed Hong-eui Dae Jang or "General of the Red Robe." A glimpse of the flaring red robe he wore in battle was enough to send the Japanese scurrying off. He was a master at setting traps in passes and of cutting off small contingents of troops that the harassed and demoralized Japanese withdrew entirely from the three districts of Eui-ryung, Sam-ga, and Hyup-chun where the "General of the Red Robe" was active.

Ironically, his career was cut short ignominiously as had been General Yi Kak's. The villain was the cowardly Kim Su, governor of Kyung-sang Province, who had fled from the Japanese. Furious when he heard of this, Kwak sent Kim Su a message naming seven valid reasons why he deserved execution. Kim Su replied with the ridiculous charge that Kwak was a robber and obtained the ear of the king in this regard, accusing General Kwak of disloyalty.

Kwak hotly denied the charges to the king and retired in disgust rather than be forced to engage in debate on the subject. He dismissed all his supporters and retired to a hermitage at Pi-p'a Mountain in Kyung-sang Province, "living upon pine leaves for food," according to records. Though later offered the governorship of Ham-gyung and Chulla by the king, he refused to exit his retreat, changing his name to Mang U-dang or "House of Lost Passions" and thus acquiring a reputation for great sanctity.

As Lee says, "Here is another instance in which the king lost an able leader through mere wanton caprice." Lee also charges the general with "forgetting country, king, kindred, honor," all due to wounded pride, but in those times the life of a Renunciate was considered a highly honorable alternative and a sacrifice that would benefit the country as a whole.

Korean Victory Ends in Bare-Handed Battle

The final conflicts that ended Japanese advancement in the province of Cholla were engineered by General Cho Hon in company with the monk warrior Yung Kyu. His band of soldiers had successfully stormed the important town of Ch'ung-ju with only stones and arrows, forcing the Japanese into retreat at night out the north gate. General Cho hoped to move forward to the place where the king had found refuge, so he relocated his troops north to On-yang. Upon learning that a large contingent of Japanese had advanced to Yo-san in Cholla, General Cho was eager to turn back and stop them. This, he determined, would be more feasible with help from the troops of Kwun Yul, the provincial general of Cholla. He wrote the general and received confirmation that the two armies could make a simultaneous attack upon the Japanese position from different sides. However, when General Cho arrived before the Japanese camp with a force of only 700 men, General Kwun and his men were nowhere in sight. The Japanese were said to laugh at the size of the army proposing to attack them but, nevertheless, after engaged in battle found they were no match for the Koreans' ferocity and skill.

Despite their ability to drive the Japanese back time after time, the Koreans were running out of arrows. Finally, as the day wore on, they became fatigued and half famished. Even then, General Cho entertained no thought of retreat and kept urging on his men, although victory already was theirs. The Japanese had lost many more men than the Koreans and General Cho's aides advised him to withdraw. Stubborn, he emphatically refused, pressing his men on until every last weapon was gone and they had to fight bare-handed. At last the battle was over. While the Koreans were crippled by victory and required four days to burn all their dead, the Japanese never regained the ground lost in this battle.

Korea Produces Leaders, Attracts Allies

Because the Korean government failed to concern itself with the protection and welfare of the people, farming villages fell into ruin. Nearly the whole country, now defenseless, was trampled by the invaders who were experienced in land warfare and well equipped with firearms. There was no reason to expect that Korea's meager, untrained battalions would prevail against them.

As the Japanese contingents set off to complete the subjugation of the country, the king finally agreed that his best course of action was to appeal to China for help. China responded by sending troops stationed in Manchuria to P'yongyang.

The Korean government's original plan to use monk soldiers and regular troops to retake P'yongyang was abandoned in favor of a joint operation with Chinese expeditionary forces. It was determined that Korean and Chinese troops would attack the walled city while the monk soldiers dislodged the Japanese forward contingent from a nearby hill, a prime vantage point not only for the city but also a broad stretch of the Taedong River and the island of Nungna. Hyujong moved 4,100 men from Pophung monastery 20 miles north to Inwang-ni, located north of the hill, Mount Moranbong. On the following day the monks charged in a surprise assault up the steeper northern slope. Though the Japanese opened fire with small arms, the monk soldiers persevered in the face of certain death. Relief came in the afternoon when a contingent of Chinese troops, led by Wu Wei-ch'ung, began scaling the western slope. At the end of the fierce battle, which lasted two days and two nights, the Japanese retreated toward the northern wall of the city. Both sides suffered heavy losses. The surviving monk soldiers and the Wu contingent pursued the enemy and entered the city from the north in coordination with Chinese troops led by Li Ju-sung, who attacked from the west. Korean regulars advanced from the south. The battle lasted three days, after which the Japanese fled to the south over the river.

In order to retake P'yongyang from the enemy, seizure of Mount Moranbong was considered vital. In anticipation, the Japanese stationed its best contingent to hold the height to the very end. Li Ju-sung of China, then commander of all allied forces, assigned monk soldiers to the Moranbong area in preference to the regular troops in whose performance he had little faith. The staunch patriotism of the monks and their experience in mountain warfare weighed strongly in his decision. After P'yongyang was retaken, Li dedicated a poem in their honor:

Patriotism runs through the hearts of these monk soldiers.
They are not after a name or profit.
The commander Hyujong is indeed a righteous priest of the East...

Again, in every major campaign, it was the monk soldiers who spearheaded charges, with higher casualty rates as a consequence.

The Japanese, weakened by cold weather and losses from an epidemic, were also experiencing a host of other unexpected complications due to the Korean hatred of foreign invaders. Resistance leaders appeared all over the land. They included Korean general Kwon Yul, who was battering Japanese attacks from the mountain fortress of Haengju; a legion of guerrilla forces emerging throughout the country under the leadership of Buddhist monks and Confucian scholars; and the soon-to-be-legendary Admiral Yi Sun-sin. A host of little bands of 50 or 100 men each, headed by what Admiral Yi called "tiger-spirited" generals in the Volunteer Army, were springing up all over the country. They fought separately, a situation which, perhaps at this point, added longevity to their efforts. The small size of the units prevented the kind of envy of power that had brought down leaders of bigger armies.

Chinju and Haengju: Two Monumental Choson Land Victories

Korea's success at turning back the Japanese on land was confined mostly to smaller skirmishes, due to its previously mentioned unpreparedness nation wide. Two major land battles, however, stand out. What is considered one of the three great victories of the war (the others being Chinju and Hansando) took place at the Haengju mountain fortress in 1593. With only 2,000 men, Kwon Yul all but annihilated 30,000 Japanese in a terrifying counter-attack, inflicting mortal wounds on three enemy generals and capturing 727 items of enemy equipment. The victory enabled the king to return to his palace in Seoul eight months later, following the entry of the royal army and the Ming general Li Ju-sung into the capital city.

The alarmed Japanese gradually pulled back towards the south. During the two-year lull in the shooting war as a Ming intermediary, envoy Shen Wei-ching, attempted peace negotiations they built new long-term garrisons along the coastal areas of the Pusan perimeter. It was during this time that Korean patriots rose across the country and defeated the Japanese in many guerrilla battles. (Ha, 1977)

At Chinju in the fall of 1592, the ratio of Koreans to Japanese was even lower than at Haengju 3,000 to 50,000 enemy attackers. Yet the commander, Hwang Chin, and his men withstood the onslaught. Humiliated, the Japanese laid siege to the walled city again in the summer of 1593, pummeling the fortress with gunfire and fire arrows. The Koreans, with all four entrances fast closed, successfully defended the bastions on the city wall. Boiling water was poured down over the Japanese attempting to scale the walls. However, they returned again and again with gunfire and human "suicide bombs."

Eventually, inside the city, all food was gone. Indicative of how poorly supplied they were, was the need for women to cut off their long plaited hair to replace the worn-out bow strings of the men. Finally, the last arrows went over the walls. There was nothing left except patriotism, and with that, Hwang Chin charged into the attacking Japanese. He was quickly struck down by an enemy bullet and the great fortress fell.

A victory banquet was held by the Japanese on a pavilion high over the Nam River flowing through the city. From this event, a story is told of a Korean patriot, a dancer named Non'-gae, who despite the fact she had survived, unlike most of her fellow Koreans in that place, still put country first. She was appropriated by a Japanese general, and asked to join in the celebratory feasting of the Japanese. When she began crying, the general went to where she was standing at the edge of the wall overlooking the ruined city and demanded to know what she as a survivor had to grieve over. She moaned:

"You have come here and driven away our people and our king. I do not know whether my sovereign is living, and yet I sit here and feast. I can hardly claim to be better than the beasts, to sit here and make merry!"

Throwing her arms around the general, she then cried, "I must put an end to my life!" With the spirit of resistance that distinguished her countrymen, she toppled the surprised Japanese back over the wall, so that as she fell with honor to her death, he at the same time died with dishonor at the hands of this unarmed woman. Her avenging act resulted in the veneration of her spirit at the site where she made her sacrifice. (Hulbert, 1962)

Japanese Atrocities Fuel Korean Revenge

While the Koreans of previous centuries were appalled by the Mongols' butchery, 16th century Koreans weren't prepared for the barbarism of the Japanese who created a notorious memorial in Kyoto to their war victims. It was called Mimi-tsuka, the Mound of Ears, said to contain over 100,000 ears and noses from their Korean engagements. General Yoshihiro obtained some 38,700 ears after the battle against the combined Korean-Ming forces at Sach'on. The troops at Chinju sought to beat that record.

Even though Admiral Yi ordered his men to concentrate on shooting the living rather than mutilating the dead, his sailors got revenge by cutting off and taking away the heads of as many Japanese as they could.

Jealousies Result in Attrition of Civil Military Leaders

For centuries, petty envies and mistrust among government and military men in Korea resulted in the abuse of power to execute these rivals, much to the detriment of the country's need for military talent. A striking example of this waste is the fate of General Kim Tuk-nyung, celebrated throughout the Korean army for his strength and prowess. It was said that, single-handedly, he could attack a tiger and pin it to the ground with a spear.

Reportedly, he could ride into battle with a 100-pound iron mace in each hand. He downed so many Japanese in this manner that they gave him the name, "General From Under the Rock."

Some ministers in Seoul were suspicious of his high profile and conspired to discredit him, charging the general with having been in league with the unprincipled ruffian Yi Mong-hak. They convinced the king, and Kim was arrested, subjected to a corrupt trial, and executed. The Japanese, stunned that such a hero would not be revered by his own people, had a portrait made of him. When his death was announced, they held a great feast in honor of his demise, on the eve of their final departure back to Japan. (Ha, 1977)

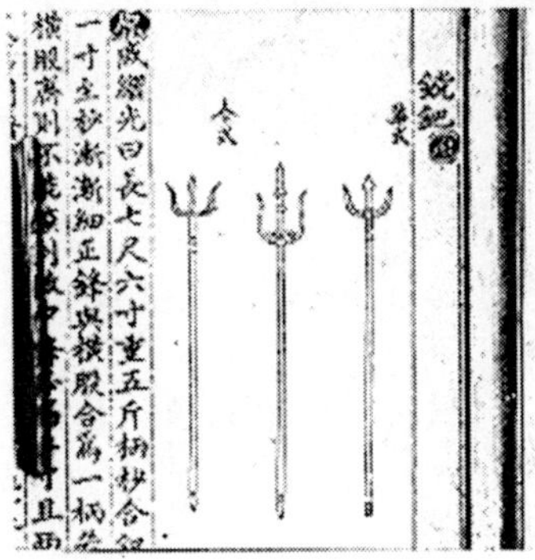

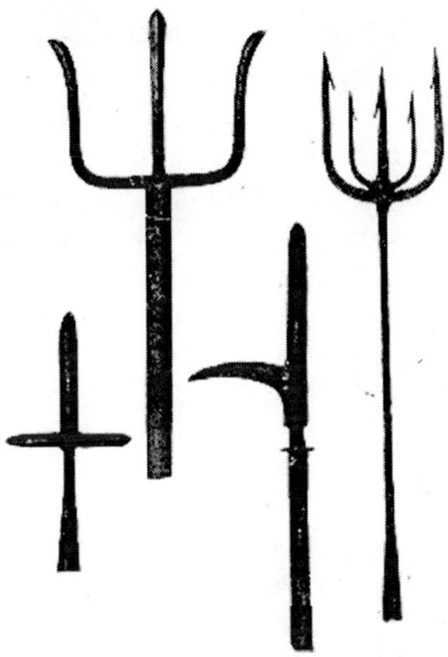

Three point spears, also called tridents, are one of the oldest weapons in the Korean inventory and is said to have been used for tiger hunting from centuries past.

Pictured are but a few types of iron maces that were commonly used in Korea.

6

Admiral Yi Sun-Sin: The “Admiral Nelson of Asia”

Admiral Yi Sun-sin (posthumously titled Ch’ungmu-kong or Duke of Loyal Valor by King Sonjo) epitomizes the Korean martial spirit and ranks at the top of his country’s list of heroes. He diligently compiled a diary, a detailed record of his life and times. It became a rich legacy of inspiration for generations of his countrymen. Frequently referred to as the “Admiral Nelson of Asia,” he was the inventor of the world’s first iron-clad man-of-war ship (one of many of his innovations). He built up his own navy, manufactured his own weapons, and supplied his troops with crops cultivated on their own farms at a time when they were cut off from the rest of the country. His critical and spectacular strategies defeated an invading force which had the advantages of strength, numbers, and surprise against a nation totally unprepared for a military challenge to its survival. He is one of history’s greatest masters of defense.

Admiral Yi, Sun-Sin dressed in full battle armor with his famous long sword.

Admiral Yi's deep sense of Confucian ethics was mirrored in his recorded life. King Sunjo, whom he served, often noted the eloquence of his reports and the extraordinary beauty of his calligraphy.

At the time of his birth on April 18,1545, an astrologer predicted that he would be a top-ranking officer by the age of 50. From childhood he loved to stage mimic battles in which the other children instinctively followed him as their general. Having a superior talent for literature, he could have attained fame as a scholar but always preferred the sword to the pen. He began studying the military arts in earnest by the age of 21, and his strength in fencing, horse riding, and archery was unmatched by his friends.

While awaiting his turn at the wheel of Korea's fortunes, Yi epitomized passion for his country's welfare and the patience of a loyal and dutiful soldier. He entered the navy, rose rapidly, and at the time of the Japanese invasion, was posted in the north. He was appointed Commander of Cholla Left Naval Station in Chwasuyong (Yosu) in 1569 during the reign of King Injong.

Initially stymied from action by the lack of preparedness of his country, regional divisiveness, and dependence on the Chinese, he found himself at one point with a fleet of less than thirty boats. While waiting for reinforcements and chafing for action on the part of his government, he was barely able to control his zeal for revenge on the Japanese:

"My anger and pain penetrate my heart and bones; I am resolved to thrust into the heart of the enemy lair, offering myself courageously to the State. With this loyal mind, I pledge to annihilate the enemy forces by united efforts . . ."

Speaking to a gathering of military leaders, he called for an end to both inaction and reliance on the provincial forces to halt the tidal wave of Japanese invaders. He declared, "At this time when our national safety is at stake before the fierce enemy attacking at all points, how can you stay behind local boundary lines on the plea of being the sailors of another province? I only sounded your opinion to test your loyalty and patriotism. Today we have only one duty, to fight and die. If anyone says no, I shall cut off his head." The only dissenter was a frightened sailor from Yodo who attempted to desert and was caught. Yi ordered his head cut off and passed around the camp as a vivid warning.

When he heard that the royal household was in peril and that he had to stand by while land troops marched away on a rescue mission, he wrote, "Hot tears rolled down my cheeks. I stroked my sword with a deep sigh, wishing to lead my valiant captains of war to destroy the Japanese robbers who have penetrated our heartland, but as a subject defending the frontier, I am not allowed to take such rash actions. So pressing down the indignation in my heart, I patiently await further orders from the Court." The nature of his reference to his sword also indicates how deeply this weapon permeated the mentality of Koreans; it was not only a weapon for fighting but like a companion in a sacred task of responsibility.

As a general, and prior to taking to the sea, Yi attained a reputation for uncompromising faith in the superiority of his cause, his men, and his strategies. He did not tolerate doubt, which had become endemic in the debilitated Korean army. An example of his resolve occurred with his first encounter of the Japanese at Hyang-gyo. He was supposed to have been reinforced by his brother but the latter instead sent an envoy with the message that the engagement was a hopeless case. He should retreat, his brother advised. Yi replied by decapitating the messenger and leading the attack on the enemy, with a warning to his men that the first one to retreat would lose his head

The Japanese commander rode a powerful white horse and carried a staff with a yellow flag which he kept beating with a sword, creating a considerable noise. Yi ignored him at first, choosing not to shoot at any of the Japanese soldiers but to send fire arrows into their camp and baggage, setting the entire base ablaze. Then he ordered his men to charge, singling out the conspicuous leader for his own target. He dropped him with one of the famous Korean "needle arrows." The enemy was soon in full retreat. Their exodus was cut short by a high ledge of rocks. There, it is said, 1800 Japanese perished at the hands of the Koreans. The few who escaped made their way across the straits to the island of Quelpart, where they demanded arms since they dropped theirs in flight. Instead, the prefect of the island attacked them with an enormous battle club, completing Yi's victory. For this sensational rout, the brilliant young Yi was made governor of the province, and the king granted a tax rebate to all prefectures where the Japanese had created the disturbance.

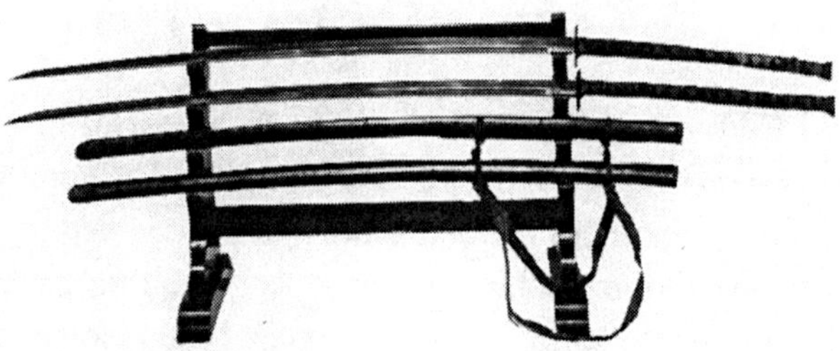

Service-swords of the Admiral.
Inscribed on them is a poem of Martial Theme of his own handwriting.

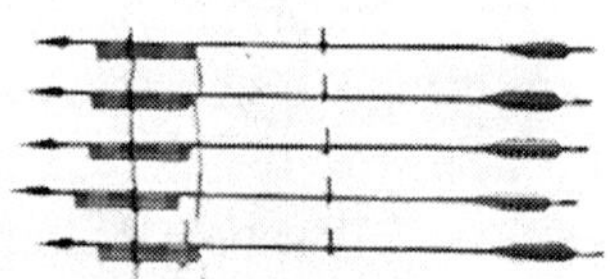

Fire arrows (Hwa-jŏn)
Shot against the enemy with flame at the arrow-head.

Four-clawed long hook (Sa-jo-ku) in boomerang shape, thrown to the enemy vessels to grapple with them.

"Victory" gun (Sŭng-cha ch'ong-t'ong), one of the early models in Korea fired by fuse. Made in 1581 and used in combat with the Japanese "Hinawaju" (Korean name: Cho-ch'ong).

Cho-ch'ong (Hinawa-ju), one of the powerful Japanese weapons used in the Hideyoshi Invasion (1592–98).

These are but some of the weapons use by Admiral Yi and his troops during his time.

"Wiwon" cannon (So-wiwon-p'o), one of the three types of cannons used by the Korean navy: Long, medium, and short range.

Tiger cannon (Hojun-p'o) in the shape of a crouching tiger.

Flying Bomb (Pi-gyŏk-chin-ch'ŏn-noe), Cannon ball with pre-set timer for detonation.

"Heaven" mark cannon (Ch'ŏn-cha-p'o), fired by fuse, shooting lead-balls and arrows (Tae-changgun-jŏn).

"Earth" mark cannon (Chi-cha-p'o), fired by fuse, shooting arrows (Tae-changgun-jŏn).

These are but some of the weapons use by Admiral Yi and his troops during his time.

Initially, Chinese assistance came with a caveat very distasteful to the Koreans: the Ming general's field order forbade slaughter of the Japanese. "All Korean commanders ground their teeth with indignation," said Yi, until the Chinese high command itself finally ordered him to pursue the Japanese. "This message stirred up the martial spirit of our officers and men who are now resolved to revenge themselves upon the enemy at the risk of their own lives."

Yi was firmly convinced that the enemy never should have been allowed to set foot on Korean shores but instead should have been kept at bay at sea. By this time in Korean history, the inhabitants of the fortified towns had drifted too far from martial readiness to perform an effective job of national defense as they had done in previous eras. Yi was that individual chosen by fate to address this deterioration and recall Koreans to the effectiveness of their martial heritage.

The admiral was uncompromising in his views of what ideas and which people constituted a threat to the welfare of his country. He once decried a secret memo written by the Royal Secret Emissary, Yu Mong-in, to the throne in which he denounced the substitute enlistment of sailors from the same family or the sea service of two adults out of four in all families. "Forgetting the national emergency," he said, "Yu Mong-in seeks only the short-run objectives as he listens to the petty officials' crooked words and cunning, which will lead the nation to evil."

For such "disloyal, tricky behavior," he says, "my heart bleeds for the future of my homeland."

Similarly, Admiral Yi characterized as an "unpardonable, evil act" a move by Yu Mong-in to discredit several magistrates in order to "punish valiant subjects and reward crooked cowards. If matters come to this point, the state affairs can never be tranquil; it is as if we are expecting something from a vacant house."

As a naval commander, Yi felt he could do at sea what was less possible on land. His objective was to cut off Japan's reinforcements and supplies from home, keep its ground troops from retreating by water, and annihilate the Japanese navy. While serving as Naval Commander of Left Cholla Province at the beginning of the war, he strengthened the country's naval forces, applying his creative and organizational abilities to the project. Developing both a reserve of provisions and physical strength among his men were among his first priorities. When he was in camp at Hansando Island off the coast of Kyung-sang Province he engaged all his troops in the work of making salt by evaporating sea water, putting together a vast reserve. This also enabled him to offer a bag of salt for a day's work to the carpenters and workmen needed to put together barracks for the soldiers. His energy and patriotism were so inspiring that many worked for nothing, and the barracks were quickly assembled.

After the Hansando and Pusan sea battles, in recognition of his successive victories over overwhelmingly larger Japanese forces, he was promoted to Commander-in-Chief of the Combined Naval Forces in the Three Provinces (Ch'ungch'ong, Cholla, and Kyongsang).

Koreans Improve Firearms Manufacturing

Although Koreans had been using firearms since the late 14th century, they were not motivated to improve on them or to manufacture them in quantity until their encounters with

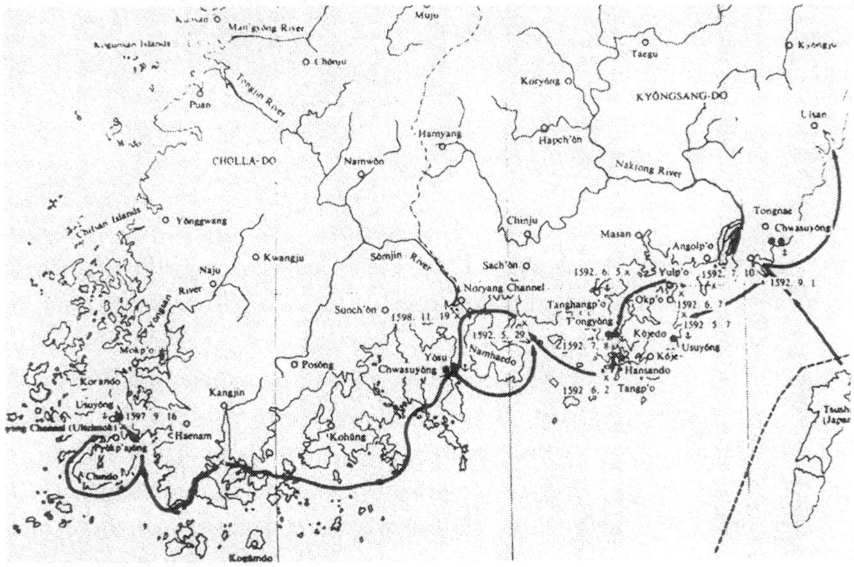

Admiral Yi's sea battles.

This map shows many of Admiral Yi's sea battles along the southern and southeastern coast of Korea.

the Portuguese-styled guns of the Japanese. Admiral Yi had seized many of these hand guns in his battles and was eager to test their capabilities. He compared them with the Korean weapons and immediately took steps to improve them. To turn them out in sufficient numbers, he established manufacturing operations in each town and port under his naval jurisdiction. He also sent a model to be copied in all other parts of Korea.

'Flying Thunderbolt' Invented

Other innovations for defense and offense were appearing throughout Korea. What might have been the world's first mortar and powder was invented by the Korean Yi Yangson. (Hulbert, 1962) Its use was recorded in the attack by General Pak Sin of Kyung-sang Province on the walled town of Kyong-ju after it had been captured by the Japanese.

"The Flying Thunderbolt" was projected from a kind of mortar made of bell metal with a bore of around 12-14 (30.5-36 cm) inches. The mortar was about eight feet long. Records say that it could hurl itself through the air for a distance of 40 paces, undoubtedly meaning that it was cast this distance. It was noted that when the "Flying Thunderbolt" landed over the city wall, the Japanese flocked around it in curiosity. It then exploded with a terrific sound, instantly killing twenty or more men. The Japanese were struck dumb with terror, and fearing the supernatural was at work, in accordance with their superstitious nature, they evacuated the city. The secret of the construction of the "Flying Thunderbolt" died with its inventor but the historian Hulbert said that, at the time he wrote his *History of Korea*, one of these mortars still could be found in a storehouse in the fortress of Nam-han.

First Suspension Bridge Attributed to Koreans

The invasion by the Japanese also inspired the Koreans' to invent what is believe to be one of the first suspension bridges. It was built to take their Chinese army allies safely across the Im-jin River when it was partially frozen but impassable for boats. There was no possibility of driving piles or of erecting any supports from the bed of the river itself. Engineering this daunting situation "and the brilliant success they achieved," according to historian Hulbert, "showed how thoroughly the Koreans were determined to see chastisement inflicted upon the Japanese."

On either side of the river, heavy timbers were planted firmly in the ground about 20 feet apart. Behind these, heavy logs were laid horizontally. Fifteen heavy strands of the tough fibrous vine called "chik" (*Pueraria thunbergiana*) were stretched between these supports on either bank. Because these sagged to the water in mid-stream, stout levers were inserted between the strands and twisted until the cables swung clear of the water by several feet.

With this as a foundation, willow branches were spread thickly upon the cables. Finally, a heavy layer of earth was added and packed down tightly by many feet. (Hulbert, 1962)

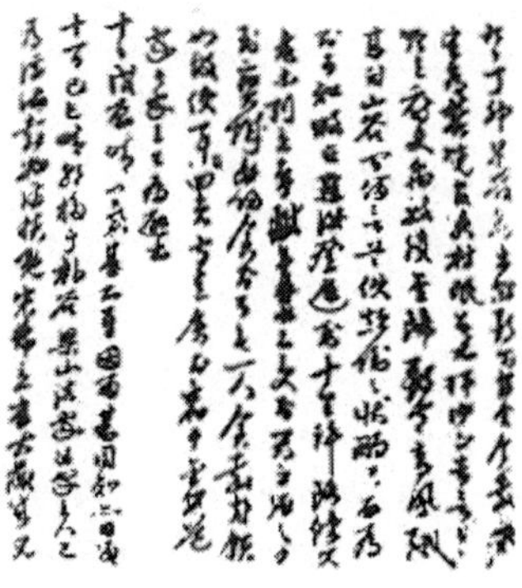

War Diary of Admiral Yi Sun-sin in his own handwriting.

The Turtle Ships: First Ironclads

Novel war machines and devices were a specialty of the versatile Admiral Yi. He is famed, especially, for turning a type of vessel already in use in the mid 15th century into his *kobukson* or "turtle ship," the first iron-clad vessel of record which could travel freely with unparalleled protection in the midst of the enemy flotilla. He built a fleet of these wooden vessels with board-roofed cabins (*p'an-ok-son*). Na Tae-yong, his chief shipbuilding engineer, was ordered to construct the first turtle ship according to Yi's drawn model. Made in the shape of a turtle, it had a flat bottom with no keel, constructed with heavy boards 4" (10.2 cm) thick. It was 64'8" (19.8 m) long, 12' (3.7 m) wide at the bow, 13'5" (4.1 m) wide amidships, and 10' 6" (3.2 m) wide at the stem. The sides were 7' 5" (2.3 m) high, each side made of seven heavy boards, 4" (10.2 cm) thick. In length, these side boards were 68' (20.7 m) at the keel, increasing to 113' (34.4 m) at the dock. Due to the curvature of these boards, Dr. Horace H. Underwood in his book *Korean Boats and Ships* estimates the overall length at 110' (33.5 m).

On its shell-like back it had long iron spikes like sharp reversed sabers which could pierce the feet of any enemy attempting to board the ship. When engaging the enemy vessels in battle, the upper deck was covered with straw mats to camouflage the spikes.

Overlapping double iron plates all over the hull and iron railings made possible its near-invincibility. The only visible opening in the ship was a narrow passage in the shape of a cross on the deck so its crew could go in and out. The head of the turtle ship, called the "dragon's head," was a battering ram on the bow, 4'3" long by 3' wide (1.3 by 91.4 cm). It was mounted with four guns inside which threw "flying thunder" bombs of gunpowder and iron splinters while spreading a smoke screen around the ship. Ten oars on each side of the ship powered it in calm air when the enemy vessels could not find enough wind to fill their sails.

Yi also positioned a turret on the stern which gave the turtle ship its "tail." There were six gun ports at both port and starboard on the lower decks, and 22 gun ports at port and starboard on the upper decks.

A flag bearing the Asian (Chinese) character for turtle flew at the mast. There were evidently some smaller turtle boats of different dimensions, employed as auxiliaries to the principal ship.

Since it was essentially a closed ship, like a turtle, its sailors could see from inside but its interior was not visible to the enemy from outside. There were 24 compartments in the ship. Two for provisions, three for weapons such as fire-lock cannons, bows, arrows spears and swords, 19 for sailors' quarters, and two cabins for the commanding officer and the ship's captain.

With cannons around the entire circumference of the ship so that attack could be made at will from any side, the turtle ship quickly gained a fearsome reputation. Victorious in his first encounter at Okp'o, Admiral Yi continued to enjoy winning victories aboard the turtle ships at Tangp'o, Tanghangp'o, Hansando Island, and Pusan.

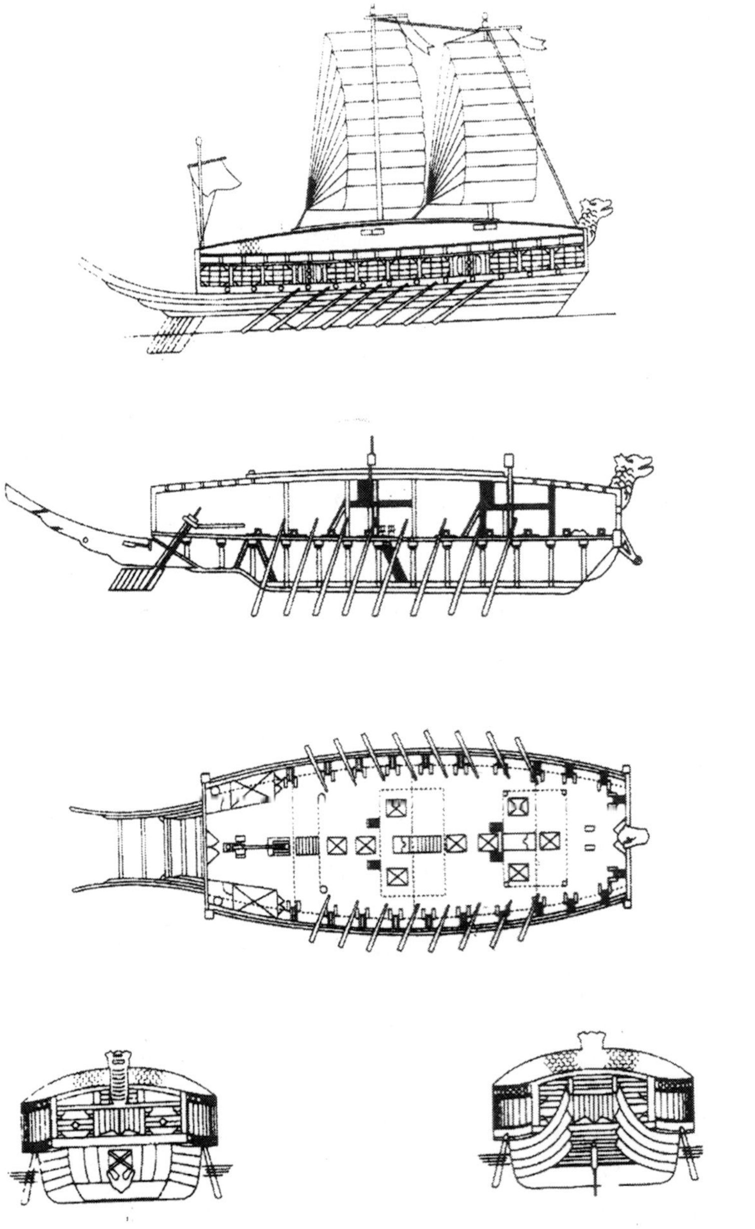

These drawings show's the interior layout of the turtle ship.

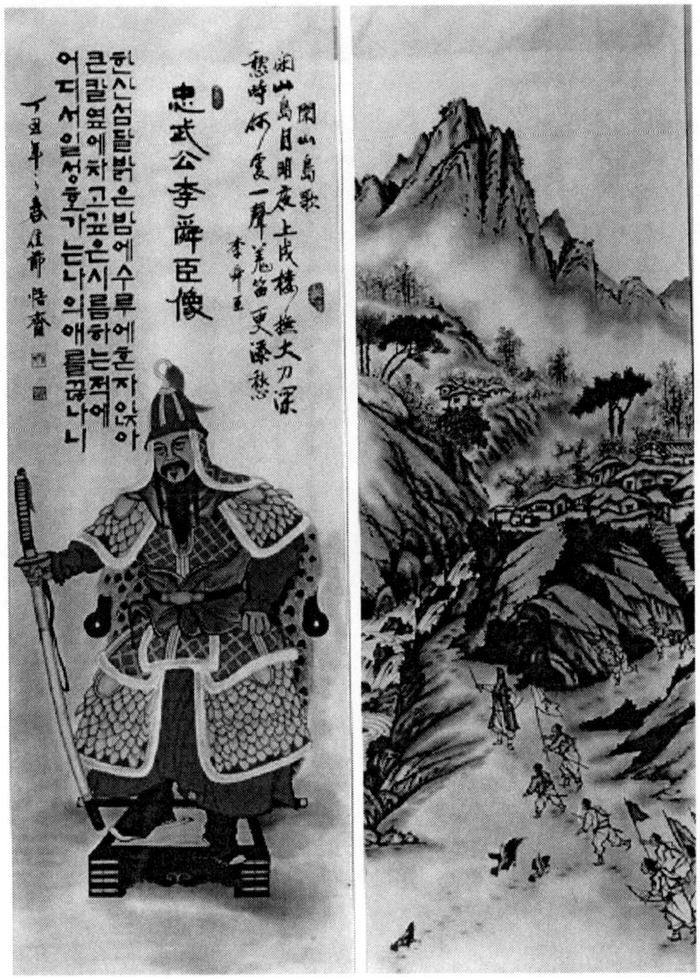

Painting of Admiral Yi on Silkscreen

War Journal of a Soldier-Sage

From January 1, 1592, to November 17, 1598, Admiral Yi, who never lost a battle, also kept a log of Korea's war with the Japanese. The seven volumes of the diary, with other personal objects, are now on display at the Hyonch'ung-sa (Shrine for Honoring Patriotism) for Admiral Yi Sun-sin at Asan, 20 minutes' drive from Onyang Hot Springs. The shrine is built on the site of the Admiral's original home where he practiced archery and military drill in his adolescence. Relics of the admiral were kept by his descendants until Chong-ok, a member of the 13th generation in his line of descent, donated them for display at the shrine.

In addition to his diary there remains a volume of his "memorials" or memorandums to the throne, submitted during his war engagements.

The last entry of his 205 folio pages is dated only two days before he was killed by a bullet, in the final great sea engagement of the war. In the tradition of the warrior-sage, he filled his diary with quotes from traditional proverbs and Zen (Chan) sayings from the 12th century

Chinese texts *Treasured Lessons of Zen Schools* and *Chanmen Baoxum*. Additionally, he made frequent reference to the Taoist classic *Huai-non Philosopher*, a tome of essays compiled by Liu An (180-122 B.C.). In this daily recording he included notes on his men, their hardships, and the many archery competitions he staged, and in which many of these he himself participated. He commented on his ambitions, philosophy, fears, the life he had chosen, and always, the weather, crucial to a naval strategist. There are frequent notations confirming the status of such weapons as swords, spears, bows and arrows, and guns as gifts from the admiral to the king, crown prince, court members, and his military colleagues. The frequency with which he mentions swords being sent back and forth as presents indicates their status and importance to the Koreans.

The successful use of acupuncture on the admiral to relieve discomfort is also documented here, and this remains a skill practiced among some Kuk Sool Won martial arts masters today.

Admiral Yi on Dying and Preparedness (From His Diary):

May 1, 1592 ... I am greatly impressed by [the men's] unswerving commitment to give their lives for their country, they are worthy of the word "heroes."

September 15, 1597... You will live if you are willing to die and you will die if you seek to preserve your own life in battle. We must follow this philosophy. One soldier who uses sound strategy can defend against a thousand. Remember this. I repeat: Never seek to preserve your life in battle.

[Undated] Warriors who embody culture and martial training are invincible. Those skilled in empty-handed combat and the use of arms must first develop their own abilities before requiring it of others. They must be intelligent and mature before they can teach. They must first become invincible before they can achieve total victory.

Kuk Sool Won training today emphasizes culture as much as martial training. Ones own skill is also required before requiring it of others. Scholarship and maturity are also desired from any Kuk Sool teacher. Not so different than five hundred years ago, Kuk Sool continues to connect us to the past while going forward into the future.

Masters Harmon are geared up for horseback archery.

Revitalization of Korean Army

When Chinese General Yi Yu-song gave Korea's king a book on the art of war written by Ch'uk Kye-gwang, the ruler was handed a blueprint he quickly adopted with procedures for military reorganization. A large number of poor and destitute soldiers were gathered to test for their fitness to help reconstitute the royal guard and escort. The examination required lifting a rice bag full of earth and of leaping over a wall as high as their heads. In ten days 2,000 men were found who met the standards. They subsequently were drilled in three areas: firing with guns, shooting with bow and arrow, and using the halberd. (Hulbert, 1962) The number of those similarly tested and drilled gradually increased to 10,000, with 2,000 being attached to each of the government departments. The entire force was divided into two parts. While one was drilling in the city, the other was set to work farming in the suburbs. In this way, the necessary food was raised to sustain the entire force. This plan was extended to the country, and teachers were sent to train the country soldiers. This militia became the foundation of the revitalized Korean army, improving its quality and discipline substantially.

One example of these men, noted by Admiral Yi, was one Cho Chong, a horse-farm supervisor from Sunch'on, "who fitted out a boat with his own funds and participated in the battle with his slaves and cowherds as volunteers, killing many Japanese and seizing many spoils of war."

Korean Martial Monks Show Patriotism

The recruitment of monk guerrillas was accelerated as the war gained momentum. Many had been practicing in secret, despite their public posture. Yi once sent out notices to towns bordering Chulla Province, seeking idle monks and laymen hiding themselves in the Buddhist temples as they were needed for sentinel duty. "Hearing this news, about four hundred monks gladly responded to the call and gathered like clouds within one month." Before he could canvass for even more, three outstanding monk leaders "rose up with patriotic indignation and formed guerrilla bands by recruiting their fellow countrymen;" Pang Ch'o-in, a Confucian scholar of Kurye; Kang Hui-yol, a wandering bowman of Kwangyang, and Son Ung-chi a hermit of Sunch'on.

Another example of the military capabilities of the monks occurred when Yi ordered a dozen warships manned by the Buddhists as captains and sharp-shooters to feign landings at strategic points between Angolp'o on the east and Chep'o (Chedokni, Ungch'on-myon) on the west. Thrown into confusion, the enemy was sandwiched between the forces and the sea. Although they responded desperately, "our valiant monk soldiers jumped up with brandishing swords and thrusting spears and charged into the enemy positions, shooting guns and arrows from morning till night until the enemy fell back... Though they chopped off few heads, they emerged victorious, unscathed," recapturing five Korean prisoners. (It should be noted that monks tended to avoid bladed weapons except in national emergencies, preferring disarming or disabling with canes and staffs.)

A Roster of Some 16th Century Monk Military Heroes

The first official government monk army of Korea was created in 1104 under King Sukjong's reign when they were enlisted to form a "Demon-Conquering Corps" (Hangma-gun). During the Hideyoshi invasion, their devotion to country prompted them to join in many engagements with the Righteous Army of the Confucian patriotic volunteers commanded by Cho Hon, Ko Kyongmyong, Ch'oyong, and others. Here are a few of these leaders, with their principal exploits.

Kwak Chae-u: Defeated enemy troops in Kyongsang Province and captured Chinju fortress.

Cho Ko Kyong-myong: Led revolts in Chulla Province and died fighting at Kumsan fortress.

Hon (pen name: Chungbong): Allied with the Buddhist leader Yonggyu, recruited 700 soldiers who drove the enemy out of Ch'ongju; died at Kumsan.

Kim Ch'on-il: Raised a force in Chulla, captured Suwon 30 miles south of Seoul; died in battle at Chinju.

Chong Munl-bu: Defended Hamgyong Province; instrumental in Japanese retreat there.

Hyujong: Aged Buddhist monk; rallied all monks of P'yongan Province into a fighting force valuable to Chinese troops in taking P'yongyang; previously led 5,000 monks to Sunan.

Praise, Practice and Discipline Under YI's Command

In his diary, a notation made by Admiral Yi indicated that good marksmanship was to be promoted and rewarded. Archery contests motivated sharpening of this skill, with the further incentive that the most adept would receive recommendations for support of their children. One archery contest for the sailors of the Chulla Left Naval Station offered the spoils of war distributed to good shots as rewards. This continued the old traditions of valuing and compensating those skilled in the martial arts. Additionally, the Admiral promoted continual competitions among the officers, examples being hurdle races with high and broad jumps, wrestling matches and fencing contests. Bushels of rice were among those prizes offered to victors.

Photo: Survey of Korean Folk Culture. 1-80.

Plate 7. Kim Hongdo, Ssirum *(Yi dynasty; eighteenth century); album leaf, ink and light colors on paper; 22.7 x 25.7 cm. Collection of the National Museum of Korea, Seoul. The sport of* ssirum *can be traced continuously from its early practice in Korea, at least 1600 years ago. In this painting Kim portrays the universal scenario of the match: struggling bodies, cheering and subdued spectators, and even a boy peddling sticks of sweets called* yot.

Ssirum is a type of traditional Korean wrestling using throwing and grappling techniques that dates back more than 1500 years.

Frequently the Admiral would not only practice archery by himself but would invite visiting officers, his sons, and other relatives to join him. There was one notation citing the use of bows weighing "six yang" at these practice sessions, indicating these larger bows were a weapon used in the war.

The Chinese allied forces were quite impressed with Yi who subtly and diplomatically manipulated them to retain his own power and vision of the development of the war. According to Admiral Yi, when Korea first called for help, the Ming Chinese soldiery took great liberties with the people of the Korean countryside, stealing their valuables, trampling their crops in their marches, and generally causing them "worse evils than those in the war-devastated areas." Yi quietly requested that the discipline, only, of the Chinese force be put in his hands, and from that day on, "the smallest irregularity was severely punished and the most perfect order prevailed." This awed the Chinese admiral Chil Lin. He wrote to the king that Yi was a remarkable man and that the world did not contain another soldier like him. (Hulbert, 1962)

Quick to praise, Yi was as quick to punish as an example to his men of what would be tolerated and what wouldn't in the new Korean army. When a hundred monks once volunteered to gather stones to help construct a city wall, he was pleased. When the head monk neglected to oversee the stone gathering of his subordinates, he had him flogged. Similarly flogged were the artisans, arrow-makers, and weapon inspector at an armory where the bows, armor, helmets, quivers, and swords were allowed to become rusted and out-of-repair.

Deserters quickly lost their heads when brought before the admiral. When the Okkwa naval affairs chief neglected his duties of sailor enlistment, resulting in the escape of over several hundred seamen, the false reports he submitted were well remembered by the Admiral. He was brought before him, his head cut off and then hoisted on a pole as a public warning.

Admiral Yi made certain that punishment was severe and widely broadcast when he felt it fit the crime. This included not only runaways but surrendered or captured Japanese which he would gather together and have decapitated. One of these, a captured Japanese named Magoshiro who was caught in an ambush in a grassland, deeply impressed the Admiral for his expressionless face and bold march up to the executioner. "What a cold-blooded fellow he was!" said Yi.

Flogging was another punishment he dealt to those with weak ethics. His diary shows he had Kim Tu-hon of Kwang-yang flogged 70 times for taking double salary from two magistrates while he was serving on blockade. When he was transferred to the navy as punishment, "he refused to wear a sword or a bow and arrow, and behaved in a haughty manner."

Far from being heartless, however, Admiral Yi concludes many of his entries with the state of his emotions as he attempts to chart his efforts towards the survival of his beloved country. The same night he recorded the beheading of the Okkwa naval affairs chief, he concluded his notations with, "The unceasing mad whistling, high and low [of the wind], shakes my throbbing heart." One lonely, rainy day, as he sat alone in an empty pavilion with the weight of his responsibilities pressing upon him, he wrote, "Hundreds of thoughts ran to my mind. Reminiscences perplexed my heart. It was beyond my expressing. Muddled with speculative thoughts, I felt myself stupid and even crazy." And again, with a day drawing to its close: "Autumn meditations fill my heart and force my body to stroll in the pavilion" and "From early evening the moonlight flooded into my room. My homesick heart was filled with a thousand emotions."

His solicitousness about the proper rewarding of faithful soldiers fills his diary, with numerous mentions of lifting the status of "menials" for their courageous actions. Added to a note he made regarding the prompt submission of a list of undecorated and unrewarded veteran sailors with more than a year of sea duty, he said "I was always alert in memorializing the meritorious sailors and officers who had not been decorated."

Yi's Prowess, Ethics Impress Allies, Foes

One day as they sat in the summer house overlooking the sea, a fleet of Japanese boats appeared, much to the excitement and consternation of Admiral Chil Lin. Yi, however, laughed and said, "Sit here and watch me give those fellows a whipping." He called out his fleet and in an hour had 40 of the enemy boats on fire with the rest fleeing. Admiral Chil Lin could not praise him enough after this and declared again that the universe did not contain another man who could perform the feats that Yi apparently found easy.

Later in the war, there is an incident recorded in Admiral Yi's diary which shows the regard another Ming officer had for the admiral:

"At 2 p.m., Yang Pu, a Ming officer, arrived at the entrance of our camp, so I sent Yi Sol, my Right [Navy Command] staff officer, to meet him. When escorted on board my flagship, he beamed with delight and requested permission to come on board. I expressed my thanks repeatedly for the grace of the Emperor and beckoned him to sit down, but he stood erect and talked for an hour, appreciating the grand appearance of our fleet."

The Japanese were equally impressed with Admiral Yi's strategies and the courage of his men. In his diary, Yi describes an encounter with 21 Japanese vessels anchored alongside the wharf at Tangp'o while 300 Japanese were plundering and firing on the nearby town and its vicinity.

On seeing the approaching Korean navy with its formidably impregnable turtle ship, the Japanese commander, ensconced under a parasol in a towering pavilion aboard one of the larger vessels, "showed no expression of fear, like a man resigned to death," said Yi. The turtle ship dashed close to the commander's boat, firing its cannon balls—designated "Black," "Heaven" and "Earth"—and immobilized it. Its commander was downed with an arrow, the Koreans boarded the boat, and a Korean swordsman slashed off his head "quickly, with a lightning sword-stroke." With its "fire bullets" and arrows, the turtle boat struck many other Japanese vessels behind it. Six enemy heads were cut and recovered and all the vessels burned.

"All the enemy hordes shrieked with fear and ran away as fast as they could, leaving scattered on the field their fallen comrades, hit by our bullets and arrows," wrote Yi.

Yi noted, at the conclusion of another engagement, that "Japanese soldiers feared the Korean arrows, and whenever the Koreans shot, they ran away, no matter how much their commanders shouted to them to charge."

Even soldiers on the boats most poorly equipped could exhibit a fearsome fighting spirit. Once Admiral Yi ordered An Wi, the Magistrate of Koje, not to shrink to the rear but advance on the enemy or risk death or court martial. An Wi's men grabbed sharp-edged clubs, sea-washed stones, and some long spears, the only weapons they had, and jabbed at the enemy boarding their boat until they were exhausted.

Decapitating the enemy was the preferred means of ending him as a threat and those most proficient in this activity were admired, as were their swords. Said Yi one day in his diary, "At noon, I had Yi Hui-nam sharpen my sword. It cuts so well that I can whip off the heads of the enemy commanders."

Yi's personal moral convictions and sense of correct behavior are reflected in his diary and give further substance to his qualities as a leader. Frequent references indicate his disapproval of officers who appeared drunk before their men or chose unwisely the occasions for such indulgence, particularly when confrontations with the enemy were due. Repeatedly he takes Korean Admiral Won Kyun (a man with an "evil heart full of knavish tricks") to task for malfeasance in this regard and for setting a poor example for his soldiers:

At nightfall, Cha Pung came and reported that a boat from Namhae with Ki Hyo-kun aboard, hiding a young woman in his cabin, had pulled alongside my boat. Ridiculous! At this critical moment facing the nation, he takes pretty girls in his boat, betraying his loose morals. How can it be justified? But, never mind, his chief Admiral Won Kyun is such a man and he cannot help it.

Admiral Yi's point was well made after the disastrous defeat of the Korean navy during a time when it suffered under Admiral Won Kyun's command.

Yi was quick to identify the foolish acts of both his enemies and his countrymen, another example of which was Wang Chl'ueh-te of Liaotung, who decided to claim the Korean throne as a descendent of the Wang family of Koryo and was proceeding to raise an army to attack Korea. "What nonsense!" the admiral scowled in his diary.

Despite the breadth of his experience with human nature, Yi was frequently taken aback by acts of disloyalty to the country to which he gave his life. A situation that especially caught him by surprise was the perfidy of one of his fellow Korean commanders, Kim Ung-so, whose character harbored the seed, as Yi sensed, of Korea's downfall.

Text of the Royal Degree Charging Kyongsang Right Army Commander Kim Ung-So With Disloyalty (From Admiral Yi's Diary)

The national distress has reached its zenith of misery and the enemy remains in our country; the gods are ashamed and the people are resentful. Thus, the earth is smeared and Heaven is polluted. Since we cannot sweep away the wicked enemy from our fair land and cure the pains, we are forced to live with the enemy under the same Heaven. Who is there that, in the hot blood of burning patriotism, will not roll up his sleeves and stand forth to cut the enemy down? Nevertheless, you as a general encamped face-to-face with the enemy have been meeting the foe to talk disloyal words without the Royal orders, and you bend your head before him with flattering words through correspondence begging for peace. Your humiliating attitude is known even to the Ming Chinese emperor. You show no sense of shame and do not hesitate to start new controversies. Although your guilt is worthy of death by court martial, with magnanimous pardon I only reprimanded you with a strict warning. But far from heeding my gracious instructions, you have become more stubborn as you fall deeper into the pit of crime, to my annoyance and perplexity. Now I send Kim Yong, an officer from the Border Defense Council, to convey my personal message verbally. You are expected to repent of your ways lest you have cause for greater regret.

"When I finished reading this royal message," said Yi, "I was overwhelmed with awe, myself. What kind of a man is Kim Ung-so? As yet, I have not heard that he has repented and changed his mind. Had he a bit of conscience he would disembowel himself to apologize for his guilt. "

Timid military leaders were not the rule in his experience but when he encountered signs of their inactivity, he was quick to condemn them and to right the damage they caused. In his diary he mentions a trip to Kuch'i where he reprimanded those who fled their home town rather than stand up to the enemy. The people, however, protested that it was their army commander, Yi Pok-nam, who ordered their retreat, and who burned the grain warehouse and his own commander's office. "When we saw the sight, we felt nothing but grief," he said. At Kuch'i, Yi Pok-nam had fled a second time, leaving behind, unguarded, the weapons in his charge. "What an astonishing act!" Yi said. When he reached Sangdong, in the path of the now infamous Yi Pok-nam, he found the town "dead and still," except for one stalwart Buddhist monk, Hyehui, who was rewarded with a written appointment as an army captain.

Yi's Solicitousness Shown Towards Troops, His Mother

His solicitousness about the proper rewarding of faithful soldiers is exemplified by a diary entry concerning a volunteer monk. The monk had performed well and was being recompensed through an official memorandum that abolished his menial status and restored him as a free monk.

The admiral was an especially devoted son, constantly sending messengers to inquire about his mother's health and well-being. He also sent his sons on such errands, visiting her whenever he could, particularly on her birthday, and noted in his diary his despair or delight every time her health took a turn for worse or better. He held his wife in respect as shown by his disinterest in the ribald entertainments of some of his colleagues, and in his worry about his sons' being absent from home when she was critically ill.

Dreams Interpreted by Admiral Yi

Like virtually all of his contemporaries, Admiral Yi was watchful for signs and portents to guide his expectations in a very uncertain world. One incident, one of several recorded in his diary, read: "In my dream at dawn, I begot a son an omen of a man being released from his captivity."

On another occasion he was impressed with a dream that came to him at dawn:

I saw a man shoot arrows too far into the air and another man kick horse-hair hats, breaking them to pieces. I interpreted the dream by myself as follows: The man who shot too far indicates the enemy fleeing to a far place, and kicking and breaking the hats can be understood to mean that the heads of the enemy troops are torn to pieces. So this dream foretells the total destruction of the enemy.

It is interesting to note that one of Admiral Yi's dreams is about kicking horse hair hats. Koreans are famous for their kicking techniques. Kicking hats was one sign of an expert kicker of that time. In previous times, expert kickers were known to have kicked as high as the top knot on a man's head. These same types of kicking skills have been continually passed down to present-day Korean martial artists. For Admiral Yi to have dreamed about kicking only reinforces the belief that kicking must have been deeply ingrained in the Korean psyche.

Yi Cautions Troops Against Killing Korean Captives

Yi gave special instructions to his men regarding their conduct after boarding foreign vessels since the Japanese were known to bring Korean captives on board and cut their hair Japanese-style. The Korean soldiers were told to examine carefully those on board and not to kill recklessly. "To find our people who had been carried away to the enemy and to recapture them alive is a merit equal to beheading the enemy robbers." (Ha,1979)

Admiral Yi Arrested, Demoted for Insubordination

By the year 1597, the celebrated Yi had to answer for the fame he had accumulated in the context of factional strife, the jealousies in the King's court, and the interest of the Japanese in seeing him removed from his post. A charge against him was instigated by General Won Kyun who resented not only Yi's accomplishments but his superior character. Won, in turn, had been given the ammunition for the charge as the result of an elaborate yet ridiculous plot by the Japanese. The Japanese spy Yojiro had given General Kwon Yul, Field Marshal and Supreme Commander of Army and Navy, false information that prompted him to order Yi far out into the open sea to repel the enemy's large re-invading fleet. Yi had several reasons to be suspicious of the order, doubt well founded as, in fact, Kato Kiyomasa's fleet was already in a Korean port, Chang-munp'o, about a week before General Kwon's order was delivered to Yi. The admiral refused to act on the order, convinced certain disaster awaited the Korean fleet. By his diary, which he interrupted on the 11th day of the 10th moon, it can be seen when this situation came to a head. He was placed under arrest by royal order on the 27th day of the first moon, 1597, and imprisoned at the capital, accused of disloyalty and insubordination to royal instructions and the field order of General Kwon.

When the Korean Minister Chong T'ak interceded with the king, the admiral was granted a special pardon but ordered to participate in the war only as a common soldier in General Kwon Yul's camp. On the first day of the fourth moon, 1597, he resumed his diary.

After Won Kyun's crushing defeat in the Battle of Ch'ilch'onnyang in the Hansando area, Yi was reinstated to his former command. He rallied the Korean forces, thwarting once again the Japanese who planned to sail north through the Strait of Usuyong (Myongnyang Channel). On his deathbed the shattered Hideyoshi was forced to concede final defeat, and ordered all the Japanese convoys to evacuate Korea. As they fled, Admiral Yi sank them all, with the assistance of the 5,000 Ming sailors of his admirer Chinese Commodore Chil Li (var. Chen Lien).

Admiral Yi's Campaigns at Sea

Among the other victories won by the Admiral's fleet, the following are the most famous, dated by the lunar calendar:

First Campaign (Okp'o Battle, 5th moon, 4th to 8th, 1592): Prior to the employment of the turtle ships, this campaign consisted of two battles involving 91 Korean ships and a total of 63 enemy ships. The Japanese lost 42 vessels and Admiral Yi lost none, with the only injury to his men being a slight wound to one sailor.

Second Campaign (Sach'on Battle the first to use turtle ships): From the 29th day of the 5th moon to the 5th day of the 6th moon, Admiral Yi and his combined fleet caused the enemy to lose 72 vessels and 88 sailors whose heads were cut off. On the Korean side, 11 were killed and 26 wounded. Admiral Yi was shot in the left shoulder, the bullet exiting through his back, "but the wound was not serious," according to his diary. By this time the revitalization of his naval forces was established.

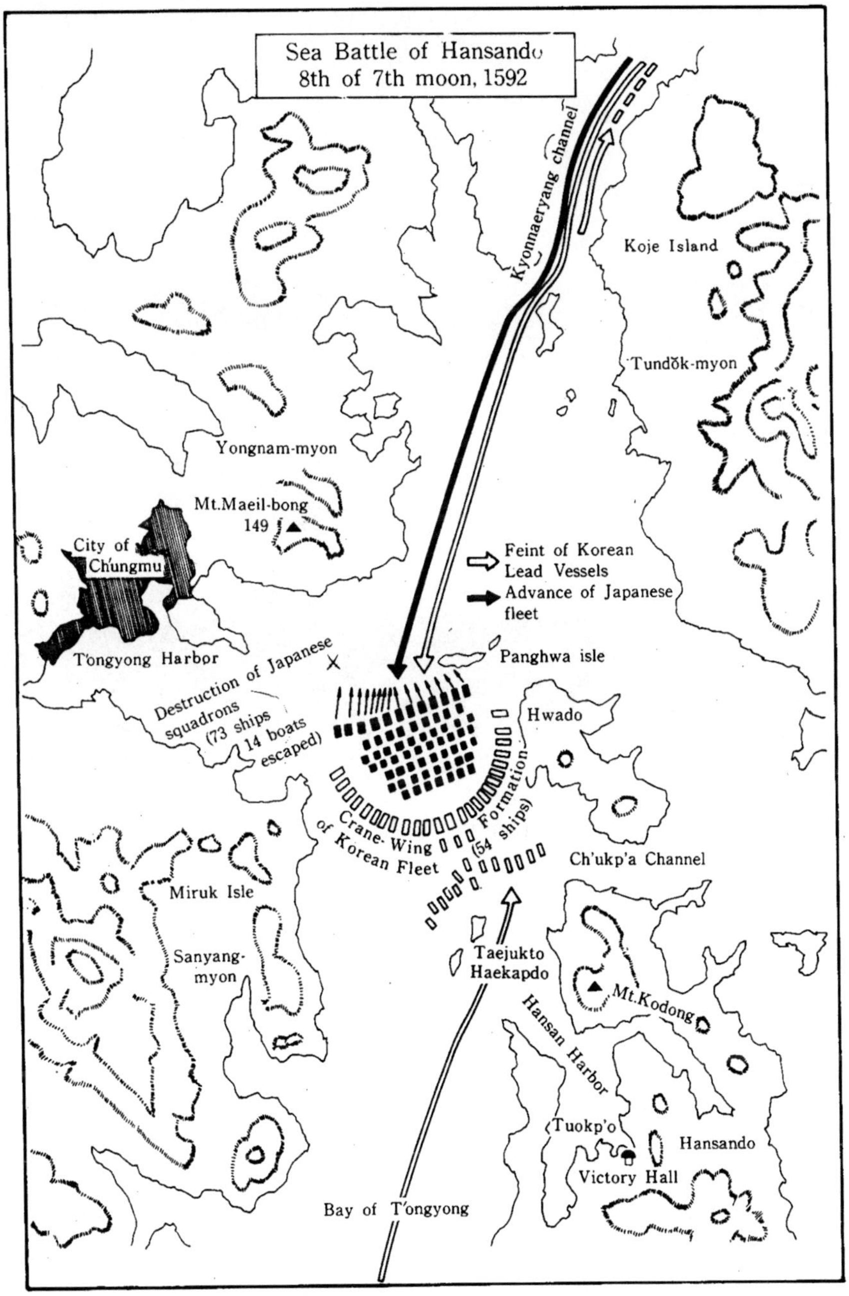

This map shows one of Admiral Yi's famous sea battles.

Third Campaign (The Battle of Hansando): On the 6th day of the 7th moon, after combining his fleet with Yi Ok-ki's reinforcements, Admiral Yi and his 90 ships encountered well over 100 Japanese vessels. The following day, some Korean board-roofed boats entered deep into the narrow channel of Kyonnaeryang between Kosong and Koje Island and, feigning defeat, lured 73 enemy vessels into the open sea near Hansando Island. There the Admiral's fleet ambushed the enemy craft with the famous "Crane Wing Formation," burning and sinking by ramming or capturing 59 enemy vessels in one of the three most famous engagements of the war.

A picture of a full scale floating replica of Admiral Yi's turtle ship taken by the author in Soon-chun.

Japanese Commander-in-Chef Wakinsaka escaped to Kimhae on land, and the remaining vessels fled. Four hundred enemy soldiers and sailors drifted ashore on Hanson Island on rafts where they were to remain for some time, subsisting on grass alone.

On his triumphant return voyage, his fleet tried to lure 42 enemy vessels from anchorage in Angolp'p but they stayed where they were. Therefore, his warships attacked them directly, burning and sinking them all.

The Koreans in this campaign beheaded a total of about 250 Japanese. On the Korean side, 19 were killed and 100 wounded, according to James Murdoch and Isoh Yamagata in their book *A History of Japan* (1903). Their account reads:

The attack straight-away began, and soon the Japanese were put in the same plight as their fellows had been. Many, seeing how impossible it was to make headway against the iron ship, beached their vessels and fled by land, so on that same day, 48 ships more were burned. The few that escaped during the night sped eastward home. So ended, we may well believe, one of the greatest naval battles of the world. It may well be called the Salamis of Korea. It signed the death warrant of the invasion. It frustrated the great motive of the expedition—the humbling of China—and, thenceforth, although the war dragged through many a long year, it was continued on solely with a view to mitigating the disappointment of Hideyoshi.

The battle off Hansando Island was especially celebrated as one of the three great victories of the war against the Japanese. Admiral Yi's success gave complete control of the sea lanes to the Korean forces, with the result that the Japanese plan to move north by sea and link with their land armies was abandoned. Yi's operations imperiled Japanese supply routes and crimped their ability to launch fresh attacks. His victories enabled the grain-rich region of Chulla province to remain safely under Korean control.

Fourth Campaign (The Battle of Pusan): From the 24th of the 8th moon to the 2nd of the 9th moon, 1592, the Admiral's fleet of 74 war ships and 18 auxiliary ships challenged 470 enemy vessels lying at anchor along the eastern waterfront in Pusan harbor. After ramming, then burning and destroying 11 vessels in front of Yongdo Island, the Admiral's ships destroyed four more in the harbor. In a fierce day-long battle, the Koreans burned and destroyed by ramming 100 enemy vessels. Korean casualties totaled six dead and 25 wounded. After this battle, the Japanese sailors became ground troops. Admiral Yi moved his navy headquarters to Hansando as the Supreme Commander of the Naval Forces of Three Provinces.

During the truce talks, in 1594, five enemy vessels were rammed near Chinhae and 21 in the Second Battle of Tanghangp'o (the first occurring as part of the Second Campaign).

During Hideyoshi's second invasion in 1597, following Yi's temporary suspension from command, the inept Korean admiral Won Kyun was defeated with heavy losses, there remaining only 90 ships from the navy headquarters and 200 ships belonging to the three provinces in the south. In 1597 about 1,000 enemy vessels launched attacks from near Tsushima Island and eventually the Korean navy was all but destroyed by the enemy and storms at sea. Only 12 boats survived. King Sonjo received word of the calamitous defeat on July 22, 1597, and by the next day had composed the following incredibly candid, humble apology and plea to Admiral Yi, which read, in part:

To my regret . . . it was my folly to replace you with another person.

There are no words to express my repentance for the wrongs done you in the past. I hope you will answer this call to service with patriotism reborn.

Again, I call on you to save our country.

Yi was reinstated to his command with 12 ships and 120 sailors to salvage his nation's sovereignty with the remnants of a once mighty fleet. The small force was so pitiful that the king himself questioned if it wouldn't be better simply to close down the Korean navy. Yi replied:

A sound navy is the best means to prevent invasion . . . Neither the army nor the navy should be disbanded at any time. I still have 12 ships . . . Though our numbers are small, the enemy will not dare even to look on us as long as I am alive.

***Fifth Campaign** (The Ultolmok or Myongnyang Sea Battle)*: With the 12 vessels given to his command at Ultolmok, Admiral Yi attacked 133 enemy vessels in the Myongnyang Straits in the early morning September 16, 1597. He sank 31 in a fierce fight by taking advantage of the swift current in the narrow sea-channel at Chindo Island without a loss on his side, routing the rest. After this stunning victory, the Admiral moved his headquarters to Kogumdo where the Chinese commodore Chil Lin arrived with his fleet of reinforcements with 5,000 sailors on board. The Japanese invasion force would soon be stymied on land as well as at sea.

***Sixth Campaign** (The Noryang Sea Battle):* On 18-19th of the 11th moon, the Admiral's final battle, he burned and destroyed 200 out of some 500 enemy vessels, taking upwards of 2,000 heads.

In this engagement in which he rushed to aid Chinese Admiral Chil Lin when a fresh Japanese fleet arrived, the usefulness of the *pun-t'ong* or "spraying tube" was well demonstrated. Hurrying to the clash on notice that Admiral Lin and the Japanese were at battle, he determined that he could circumvent any hand-to-hand fighting with this new device of his own manufacture. (Hulbert, 1962) He sent his ships circling around the Japanese fleet, forcing them closer and closer together. When ready, he pulled out his pun-t'ongs which directed incendiary projectiles at the Japanese, setting their boats on fire. A wind came up and fed the flames turning the enemy fleet into a floating inferno. Already his "Invincible Armada" had been feared by the enemy as a death messenger from heaven (although by this time the ratio of its naval strength to theirs was about 1:10). The pun-t'ongs confirmed that fear. Hundreds of boats were consumed with all their occupants, as a brisk wind fanned the flames.

Once he determined his strategy was succeeding, Yi turned his attention to the ships that were trying to escape. Standing at the prow of his boat in an exposed position, he urged on the chase at Noryang off the coast of Namhae Island.

Two nights previously, according to his diary, Admiral Yi had stood alone in prayer on that same deck. Having washed his hands, he knelt and pleaded "I willingly offer my life if I may wreak just vengeance on these invaders!"

Yi's remaining time was too short to fully savor what was one of the major victories of the war. In his exposed position, as he surveyed the rout from his boat, he was hit by a bullet, his men catching him as he fell. Still holding his unsheathed commander's sword in his hands, he called his nephew Wan and his son Hoe to his side, saying "Do not weep, do not announce my death. Beat the drum, blow the trumpet, and wave the flag for advance. We are still fighting. Finish the enemy to the last one."

Thus, like England's Admiral Nelson, he died at age 54, during the hour of his final victory.

Requesting that his body be covered by a shield so the enemy could not see that he had fallen, his last words were, "Do not let the rest know that I am dead, for it will spoil the fight."

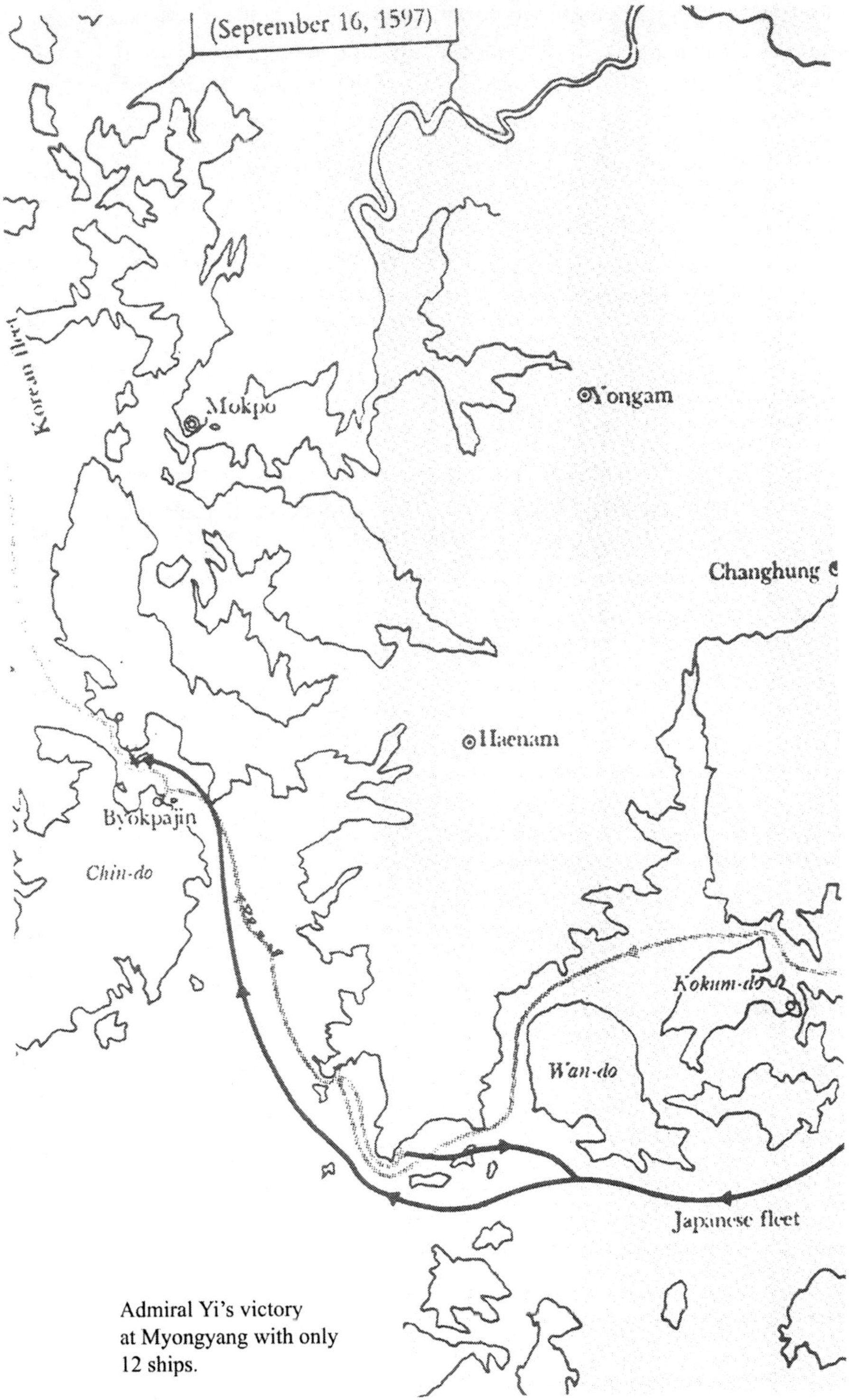

This map shows the route of Admiral Yi's great sea victory at Myongnyang.

Yi Wan, his nephew, quickly assumed command, but his uncle's work had almost been finished. Admiral Chil Lin happened to be in a boat near the fallen admiral's and did not know the Choson commander had breathed his last. However, the moment he noticed sailors on the Admiral's ship quarreling over some war "trophies" (Japanese heads decapitated in the battle), he recognized immediately that such breach of discipline by any sailors under the Admiral could mean only one thing:

"The Admiral must be dead!" he exclaimed.

Boarding the Yi vessel, he found his suspicions confirmed. He immediately prostrated himself three times at full length on the deck.

Celebrated Poems of Admiral Yi

In 16th century Korea, those military leaders inclined to literary interests, as many were, might pause in their contemplation of a day's events to compose poems, including references to their weapons, perhaps some element of nature, and their feelings.

Admiral Yi wrote the following poems at various times in his campaigns, the originals of which survived to this century in the house of one of his descendants. (The reference to "Three Foot" in the third poem, which was an inscription on a pair of his commanding swords, is to the length of the weapons themselves.)

Hansando Serenade

Soft o'er the blue ocean late glows the autumn light,
High in the frosty sky the wild goose honk on wings so cold;
With a grieving heart I roll without sleep the whole night,
The dying moon shines on my bow and sword.

Hansando Song

By moonlight I sit all alone
In my tower on Hansen Isle;
I stroke the long sword at my side,
And breathe a deep sigh toward the tide.
Hark! From whence shrills this tuneful flute
So sharp to pierce my heart?

Inscription Carved on Admiral Yi's Sword:

To Heaven I pledge Three-Foot;
The mountains and rivers tremble;
I whip, I sweep,
Blood dyes hills and streams.

Yi Ch'ungmu-kong Chonso, Vol. I

7

Japanese, Manchurian Invasions Redefine Korean World View

The first invasions of Korea by Japan amounted to a war with no winners among the major participants and three significant losers: Korea, Japan, and the Ming empire. The conflict disrupted all of east Asia and laid the foundations for the cultural disorder requisite for the ultimate Japanese takeover several generations later. The political shifts had notable consequences:

- While Ming was aiding its ally, Korea, the Jurchen people were eagerly building on their power base in Manchuria. The Ming would soon fall to their superior strength.
- Japan was reeling from the cost of the war and the loss of men and prestige. This resulted in the establishment of an entirely new military regime under the Tokugawa house. The country's principal gain from the war was the large number of Korean artisans captured and employed to advance Japan's ceramic arts. Numerous books seized by the Japanese in Korea also contributed to the development of learning on the island, particularly the study of Neo-Confucianism.
- Korea's losses were massive. After a seven year struggle, nearly all of Korea's eight provinces were pillaged and their populations severely reduced by slaughter. Kyong-sang province was the hardest-hit, whole villages being laid to waste. Such was the corresponding extent of famine and disease that the period following the invasion gave rise to revolts throughout the country, the most serious occurring in Ch'ungch'ong province under the leadership of Yi Mong-hak.

The social system of Korea was thoroughly disrupted, beginning with the burning of the registers recording their social status by the slaves, and compounded by the selling of posts and titles of nobility by the government to raise money. The country's treasures reduced to ashes included magnificent wood architecture at Pulguk-sa in Kyongju and Kyongbok Palace, and books stored in three of the four Korean archives. The latter represented a major loss to the documentation of Korean achievement.

Although in 1605, at Japan's request, Korea considered it provident to establish diplomatic relations with the Tokugawa Shogunate, the animosity of the Korean people towards the Japanese had become firmly entrenched. The monk Yu Chung was the envoy in this mission to Japan, and he returned the following year with 3,000 Korean captives released by Japan. While Korean records are not available to indicate the amount of booty the Japanese removed nor the number of Korean artisans taken to instruct the Japanese in their ceramics, Japanese reports assert that immense amounts of treasure were carried off and that the production of the beautiful Satsuma ware was an outcome of the tutoring of the Japanese ceramists by the Koreans. (Hulbert, 1962)

Among the few positive results of the war was the work *The Exemplar of Korean Medicine.* The deteriorating health of the people gave rise to investigations in medicine and the subsequent compilation of great medical treatises such as this.

Also stemming from the wars were weapons developed in self-defense which were now on hand, such as the mobile rocket launcher, and advances in military tactics, including the Chekiang order of battle used by the Ming. As has been noted, at the time of the first Japanese invasion, Korea's Five Commands from the early Yi period existed in name only and there was virtually no national military force. The accelerating war required the Koreans to establish the *Hullyon Togam* or Military Training Command. Within this academy a new garrison was formed, known as the *Samsubyong* or Three Combat Forces, comprised of skilled musketeers *(p'osu),* archers *(sasu)*, and lancers and swordsmen (*salsu).* Their training was based on the book, *New Text of Practical Tactics* (*Chi-hsiao hsin-shu*) by Ch'i Chi-kuang, an authority on the Chekiang order of battle that was developed in China to combat the Japanese marauders. By Sukchong's reign (1674-1720), four more new army garrisons had been created in the capital area: the *Ch'ongyungch'ong* (Command of the Northern Approaches), the *Suoch'ong* (Command of the Southern Approaches), the *Kumwiyong* (Capital Garrison), and the *Oyongch'ong* (Royal Guards Command). From the Japanese wars on, this *Ogunyong* (Five Army Garrisons) composed the core elements of the Yi army.

The Manchu Invasions

During King Sonjo's post-war reign the beleaguered government, in an attempt to offset the economic crisis resulting from the shortage of grain, resorted to selling office titles and ranks in exchange for food. It was the next monarch, King Kwanghaegun (1608-1623), who proceeded to reconstruct the country most effectively, both in domestic and foreign affairs. He rebuilt the history archives, printed many books, and rejected the involvement of Korea with the developing conflicts on the continent.

The rise of the Jurchen Manchu's had put Korea in a precarious situation. Because of its relationship with the Ming empire, Kwanghaegun was compelled to accede to its request for 10,000 troops to strike at the Manchu state of Later Chin. However, he craftily prevented Manchu retaliation by giving secret instructions to his general to carefully assess the likely outcome of the conflict. Should the Manchus begin to emerge as the victors, the general was instructed to surrender immediately to them, which he did. Kwanghaegun's aptitude for military preparedness was then directed zealously toward repairing his nation's defenses, renovating weaponry and instituting training programs. (Lee, 1984)

Just as Kwanghaegun's efforts were stabilizing his nation, the king was deposed by the "Westerners' faction" and their choice for a leader, King Injo (1623-1649) was installed. (So bitter was the struggle between the Northern and the Western Koreans that the Westerners refused to give Kwanghaegun a posthumous title.) Injo rescinded Kwanghaegun's stance on foreign relations with a blatant pro-Ming, anti-Manchu policy, allowing a Ming general, Mao Wen-lung, to build a base for the invasion of the Liaotung Peninsula on the Korean island of Kado, near the mouth of the Yalu River. This move so angered and provoked the Manchu that they were forced to postpone their campaign against the Ming to eliminate this threat.

Return to the Island Refuge

By 1625 the Koreans felt preparations for war would be provident. General Yi So assembled an army of strong, stalwart men, the finest available, forming them into companies and regiments. He drilled them at the Hun-yun-wun, inside the East Gate, and also at Mo-wha-kwan, outside the West Gate.

Meanwhile, a revolt led by Yi Kwal, who felt under-compensated for his services among the western faction, broke out. He succeeded in threatening Seoul and forcing King Injo to flee temporarily, but ultimately he was driven with his supporters out of the country. He took refuge in Manchu territory where he appealed to Emperor Nurhachi to back him in his cause to redress the injustice done to Kwanghae gun. The Manchus seized on this as a further excuse to correct the Koreans' position on allowing the Chinese military at Kado. They sent an army of 30,000 across the Yalu in 1627, took the northern provinces and P'yongyang, and continued south, forcing the court to flee to Kanghwa Island. The situation on both sides was very similar to the Mongol-Korean positions in the earlier wars.

Eventually the two countries agreed that the Manchus would be rather like "big brothers" to the Koreans, framing the relationship just short of a vassal arrangement, but that a large tribute in ships and grain would be required from the peninsula to support the Manchu efforts against China. Various moves on the part of the Koreans were made as attempts to placate the Manchus while not fulfilling the entire debt. These included the presentation of a magnificent sword, 300 pounds of ginseng, and 70 sable skins sent on one occasion with an envoy. It was reported that the Manchus were highly pleased with the sword and its accompaniments and forgave all that had been done to displease them. (Hulbert, 1962)

After the treaty, Injo returned to Seoul, impressed with the need for a better-drilled army. Implementing a renewed training program, he also stationed a general at Kang-wha permanently and instituted the custom of requiring military duty of every citizen between 15 and 40 years of age. Some went to Seoul to drill for three years, the first of which was spent in learning the methods of guarding gates and walls. The second year was devoted to musket practice and the third, to swordsmanship and archery. When training was completed, they were sent to the country as trainers for the militia. In this way, a force of 700,000 men is said to have been made proficient. Also at this time the custom was revived of having the men stand in squads of ten; five in front and five behind. When the front rank had fired, they fell back and the rear line stepped forward while the others reloaded.

When Nurhachi's son Abahai succeeded him and in 1636 demanded that Korea become a true vassal to the Manchu state of Later Chin, war broke out again.

Koreans Score Successful Rallies Against Manchu Invaders

Abahai led a large army across the Yalu, swiftly marching to Seoul and forcing the king to take refuge in the fortress at Namhan while the court fled again to Kanghwa. These refuges were soon identified by Abahai who pursued both the king and the court. At Namhan, where prizes had been offered for Manchu heads, the situation was desperate and the king sent for reinforcements. His intention not to surrender was resolute; a courtier's written plea to capitulate was met with anger and burned. When a Manchu messenger rode to the gate, asking if the king were ready to give up, the answer came in the form of fierce sallies on the south and east sides in which 40 heads were taken, and in which General Yi Chi-wun, with an iron club, killed two mounted generals. The Korean soldiers were so exhilarated by these successes, even though they knew the opposing forces were stronger, that the following day they made simultaneous attacks on several sides, losing only 20 men against much larger losses by the enemy.

A number of heroic acts and decisions were recorded from the Namhan siege despite the desperation of the situation. General Yi Si-bak was twice wounded but did not make it known until the fighting was over. General Sin Kyung-jin was not content with simply driving off one attacking party but pursued them out of the fortress and killed their leader and many of his followers. Envoys of the Korean king received word at the camp of the enemy that the Manchu emperor's anger at their resistance was prompting him to order destruction of the Korean kingdom. King Injo's response was to resist, piling up bags of sand in the breaches caused by the renewed bombardment and pouring water over them which froze to make a hard substitute for the crumbled walls.

Finally, the rank-and-file soldiers, failing in health due to the food shortage, pleaded with King Injo to provide the prominent hostages sought by the Manchu. After the Manchu produced letters from one of the princes at Kangwha, proving that Kangwha had already fallen and members of the court captured, the king decided further resistance was futile. Preliminary to surrender, he ordered that all documents in which the Manchus were spoken of in a derogatory manner be destroyed. (Hulbert, 1962)

Such was the dedication of the Korean soldiers that two of their officers at Namhan tried to end their own lives rather than participate in the surrender. Kim Sang-hon was found trying to hang himself but was cut down. Chong On, after apologizing to his "frosty sword," plunged it into his bowels but the wound did not prove fatal and the king had him treated with care.

On the last day of the first moon of the year 1637, King Injo was taken to the Manchu camp on the banks of the Han and forced to swear fealty to the Ch'ing state, renounce all allegiance to the Ming and to support the Manchus in their attacks on China. The crown prince and his brother were held as hostages by the Manchus, to be sent back to Seoul years later.

The Manchu emperor, in accepting the eleventh-hour surrender of the Koreans, reminded them of his "great kindness and mercy" in determining the terms of the surrender which allowed Korea leeway in commerce with Japan but banned further association with the Ming and prohibited the building of more fortresses. The terms of tribute were the following:

Every year you must send tribute: 100 ounces of gold, 1,000 ounces of silver, 10,000 bags of white rice, 2,000 pieces of silk, 300 pieces of white grass-cloth, 10,000 pieces of colored cotton, 400 pieces of fine linen, 1,000 pieces of coarse linen, 1,000 quires of fine paper, 1,000 quires of common paper, 200 bows made of sea-cow's horns, 26 swords the length of a man's stature, four fine window screens, 40 mats with red flowers, 20 common swords, 200 pounds of dye-wood, ten pecks of black pepper, 1,000 packages of tea, 100 tiger skins, 100 deer skins, 400 otter skins, 200 squirrel skins.

You will commence sending this tribute three years from now. As I have taken one of the king's relatives to wife, I will remit 9,000 bags of rice.

As with similar demands from the Mongols, the Koreans never once attempted to fulfill more than a mere fraction of the tribute since they were so excessive and the country's resources were so diminished by the wars. Fortunately, the Koreans' conquerors were so far distant that enforcement of the terms was difficult.

After the Manchus captured Peking and became the rulers of China, Korea offered no further resistance.

Isolationism Signals Start of Internal Disintegration

The end of conflict with the Manchus also brought about a conviction that Korea's foreign involvements led only to trouble. Those few Chinese who remained in Korea after the peace treaty were segregated and lived as virtual prisoners. Subsequently, great caution was exerted to prevent the Manchus from learning anything of domestic developments, including the implementation of its new exclusion policy. Even the Manchu ambassador was lodged at a ceremonial pavilion outside the capital, where he could not spy or make contacts for intrigues. After 1637, the diplomatic contact Japan initiated in 1615 dwindled until by about 1811 it was discontinued entirely. No Japanese were permitted to live in the country except for a few traders at the southern port of Pusan. It is quite likely that the Roman Catholicism, introduced into Korea in 1686 by unspecified non-European foreigners, died out during this time as it was opposed by some high officials even then.

The ancient system of beacon fires along every coast and the highway to Manchuria was reinstalled with fervor to warn the capital in case of invasion. Against the treaty, new border forts were built and manned, and the standing army was improved, especially the professional skill, morale, and leadership capacities of its officer corps. The coast guard fleet was expanded, with new kinds of vessels developed. Settlements were forbidden in a wide, neutralized area along the Manchurian bank of the Yalu. Chinese were forbidden to cross this belt and it was not to be entered from either side except by official embassies en route to Peking or Seoul and by Chinese and Korean tradesmen who were permitted to hold a joint fair in a specified market town in the area for one week every year. The importation of foreign printed matter and the discussion of ideas foreign to the Korean culture were categorically forbidden.

Past glories became a focal point of nationalism. An assumption grew as the decades passed that freedom from attack had become a permanent condition. No need, once again, was determined for further military development. No entrepreneurial class was developed on a national scale and the country failed to regain the strength of its previous level of economic activity. Agricultural productivity continued to decline, a slide not reversed since the Japanese invasion. The stage was being set for the cultural destruction of two centuries later to take place with relative ease.

Internal Strife Again Subverts Preparedness

The disputes between the Southerners and the Westerners continued over the years, adding refinements and supplanting royal rule. In 1694, the Westerners replaced the Southerners, eliminating them permanently but themselves splitting into the *Noron* (Old Doctrine) and *Soron* (New Doctrine). During the reign of King Yongjo (1724-1776) the Noron faction wiped out their competitors and monopolized power.

The fervor over the doctrines of all these many political groups has had few parallels in history. Their members wore distinctive colors and fashions in clothing design that made them instantly recognizable and erased any hope of post seekers obtaining employment on merit alone. The violent, uncompromising disagreements among them prevented concerted action when the country was threatened from without, yet they were driven not by ideals but by personal greed. (Hulbert, 1962)

The Confucian classics no longer defined the ethics of the country and the nature of politics. Instead the Chinese classics and composition were the ostensible basis of examination for government posts, although the actual appointees were clearly drawn from the power base. The social and economic position of the *yangban* class declined on the national level, and large numbers of these former bureaucrats returned to amassing personal power and wealth in their home provinces (particularly in Kyongsang). The private Soron academies became increasingly vital centers for their activities.

The long rule of the Noron faction brought about the complete collapse of the Confucian system. With much land lying abandoned and fallow, the royal family greatly enlarged its holdings, thereby removing large properties from the tax roles. The Korean tax system came close to being rationalized, and political stability was achieved through breaking of the monopoly of the Noron faction. This occurred by the time of King Chongjo (1776-1800), following the beginning of stabilization with the reign of King Yongjo (1724-1776).

The story of the passing on of power from the latter king to the former was symptomatic of the chaos of succession that would destroy any security upon which Korea could base its steadiness as a nation into the crucial 1800s. The tale is also full of references to the presence of swords on all military men present, including the king, evidence again of the status of the sword in Korea. (Haboush Kim, 1988)

King Yongjo's court was rife with intrigues to succeed the heirless ruler. He himself appointed Prince Changhon, the son of a lady of the court, as crown prince but there were several individuals who disputed this decision. They joined to plot against Changhon by degrees, accusing him of a variety of traitorous acts and planting evidence to support their allegations. The nature of the king was such that his suspicions were incited without reservation and he ultimately demanded the life of his heir for treason, refusing to entertain the sincerity of Changhon's denials.

Requesting that his courtiers execute Changhon in front of him, they refused. The prince protested that, if he had to die, propriety demanded that the execution should not take place in front of his father. The king was too obsessed by rage and the excitement of the moment to care for the dignity of his high station. He drew his own sword to encourage his courtiers to do likewise. When they still resisted shedding what they knew to be innocent royal blood, the prince tried to strangle himself. Prevented by the horrified courtiers who remorsefully pleaded to the king for clemency, he was nevertheless ordered to climb into a wooden box by his crazed father. There he was left to starve to death.

Ironically, none of the plotters attained the throne after Yongjo's death. Instead it was the martyred prince's son, Chongjo who became king, purging all those who had been involved in the scandal of his father's death. He then conferred upon his father the posthumous title of

Changjo, as if he had been a reigning monarch. For this reason, Korean historians have called Changjo the "Coffin King." (Hulbert, 1962) (Han, 1974)

This marked the beginning of the dominance of Korea by the relatives and retainers of royal mothers, several of their sons being only children when they came to the throne. This progressively weakened royal power and encouraged more favoritism and nepotism, discouraging able young men to sit for the examinations prerequisite to appointment to bureaucratic posts.

Shortly before the turn of the fateful 19th century, several significant histories were authored. Notable for coverage of the exploits of Korean troops in battles against foreign invaders was *Biographies of Famed Korean Generals*, written in 1794 by Hong Yang-ho. Historical geographies were popular at that time, including *Kanggye Ko* by Sin Kyong-jun (1712-1781), *Haedong Yoksa Chiri Ko* by Han Chin-so (1777-?), and *Kangyok Ko* by Chong Yag-yong (1762-1836).

All of the writers from the *Sirhak* school of philosophy popular in the 1700s were intensely interested in the Korean historical experience beyond the peninsula, and their writings detailed as vital to national identity that which was known of Korean activity in what is now Manchuria.

King Chongjo, in establishing a research library and institute within the palace, commissioned many works, including the *Revised Illustrated Manual of Military Training and Tactics (Muyedobo T'ongji),* which updated a 15th century prototype.

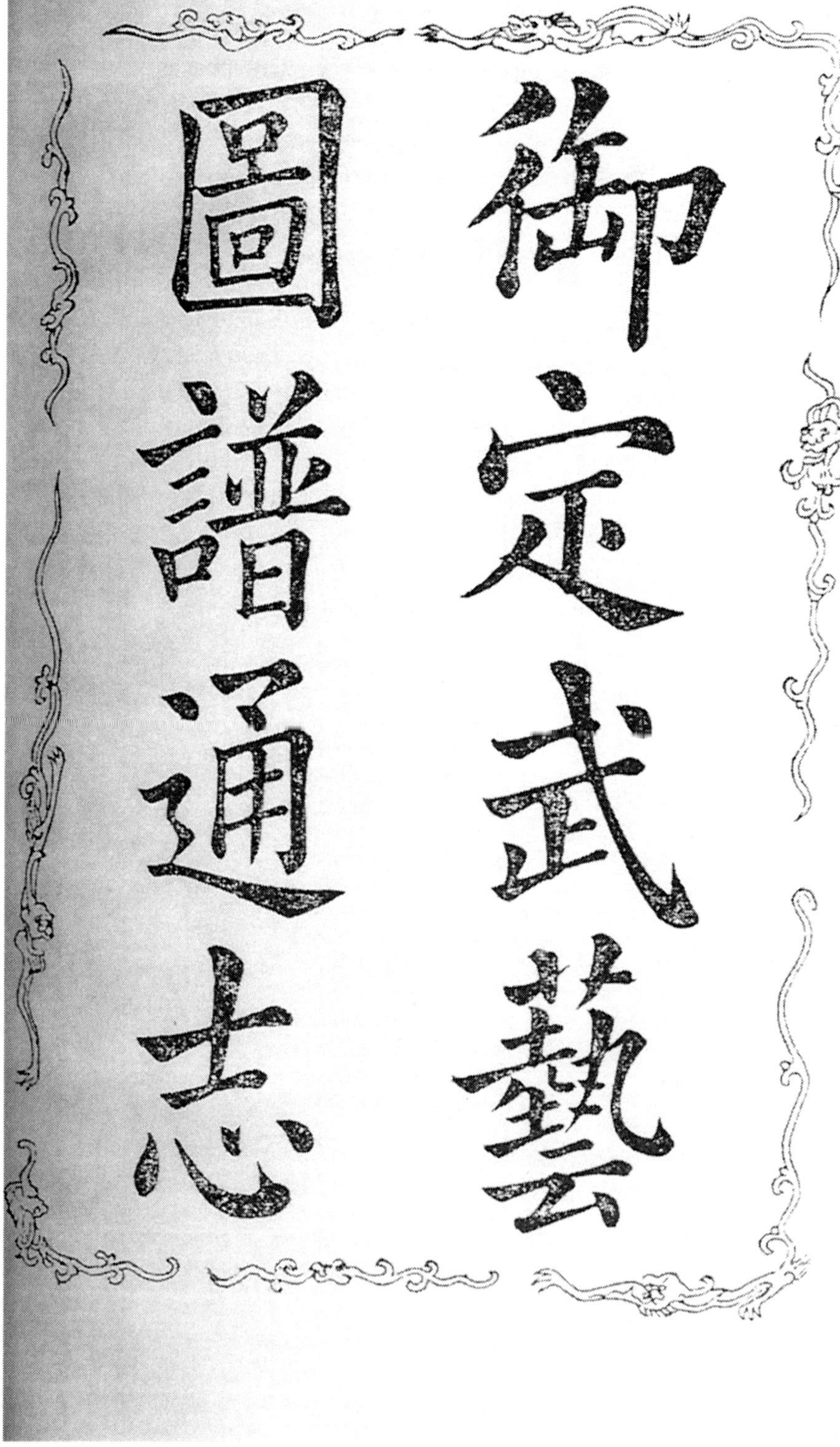

Muyedobo T'ongji
This is the title page of the most famous old martial art book in Korea.

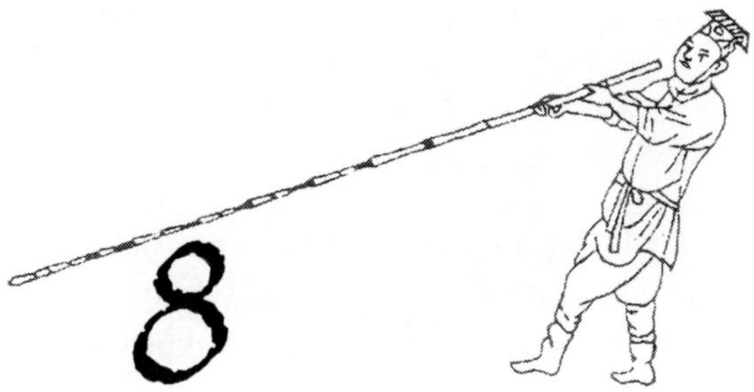

8

Beyond Tolerable Limits: The Rupture of 19th Century Korean Sovereignty

Uprisings, alienation, famine, plague, and foreign economic and political pressure became the crushing issues of the 19th century for a Korea whose traditions were fracturing and losing their central position in the lives of the people. These calamities followed relentlessly, one after the other, on a course that would create ideal conditions for any country to lose its sovereignty, the fate that awaited Korea. The historic capacity of Koreans to muster a capable military became moot as the steamroller of Western industrialism, driven in Asia by its foremost proponents, the Japanese, reached the shores of an insular and unsuspecting Chosen.

The collapsing financial structure of the government had once again estranged its citizens' loyalty. Posters with anti-government slogans appeared and indignation began to build, flaming into the uprising of 1812. Its leader, Hong Kyong-nae, spoke for thousands of discontented officials, merchants, scholars, and farmers who were forced off their land by drought and put to work in gold mines. His rebellion lasted for five months and ended with his death in battle after the fortress of Chongju had withstood a siege of a hundred days. That an entire province had revolted and a government was so weak that the conflict lasted as long as it did is an indication of the level of corruption and lack of commitment to national welfare that pervaded the times. Further aggravating dissatisfaction with the political and social disorder was a series of natural calamities lasting several decades: great floods, uncontrolled fires, epidemic cholera, and famines. Many of these disasters were epic in proportion. One famine continued for nine successive years, each year beginning with a cholera outbreak. The next year, in addition to famine and plague, the palace burned down. The resources of the government became exhausted in trying to help the people who, as a result, lost faith in their leaders. In the early 1860s, more uprisings flared, followed by discussions of effective reforms which came to nothing. Inaction spawned more rebellions.

In the armed conflicts between government troops and various factions of reformers, the use of traditional weaponry and techniques continued to be more prevalent than firearms. Swords, spears, bows, and arrows, as well as empty-hand combat, were also used as a backup to the still rare and more costly newer technology of firearms.

Catholic Missionaries Expand Western Foothold in Korea

The prevailing chaos resulted in the Korean people becoming significantly vulnerable to outside influence and intervention, which appeared initially in the form of Catholic missionaries. The French Foreign Mission Society in Paris considered the entrenched hostility towards Catholicism among the Korean ruling classes as a challenge. To the Koreans, Catholicism was both threateningly foreign and failing to embrace Confucian values. Additionally, letters intercepted from missionaries back to their homelands had carried messages requesting that military expeditions be sent to overthrow the dynasty and to set up another government in sympathy with the

Christian faith. An example of such a letter survives in records, written by a Korean Christian named Whang Sa-yong to European residents in China. (Hulbert, 1962) Korean rulers, always alert to plots by rival factions aided by foreign alliances, knew that the danger from the missionaries was far more than theological corruption of their existing faith. The foundations of their rulership were being threatened and of Korea's sovereignty itself. The religious persecution which followed actually had a strategic dimension of national defense based in valid concerns, considering the zeal of the priests to convert with foreign military support, if possible.

Eventually priests found ways to enter and remain in Korea under disguise. They attracted a considerable following among country people, particularly women, who were dominated and oppressed in practically all aspects of social life.

With the death of King Chongjo in 1800, the new king, called posthumously Sunjo Tawang, took the throne as a boy dominated by his anti-Catholic great-grandmother. Before the end of the year 1800, several prominent Catholics were executed for promoting their faith. One of the Korean converts, Hwang Sa-yong, confirmed the anti-Catholics' greatest fears over the faith's support of French intervention when, shortly after the turn of the century, a message he attempted to send to the French bishop in Peking was intercepted. He had requested help for the Catholics of Korea in the form of a French battleship. At that early date, the French, preoccupied with the Napoleonic Wars, were not prepared to take action even if so inclined.

In the spring of 1839, renewed persecution broke out. Word of beheadings of priests finally reached Peking and French warships approached Korean shores in 1846 to demand an explanation of the deaths of French citizens. They were, however, unsuccessful in intimidating a change of policy and left without orders to act more forcefully. The Catholics were undeterred and continued to send more missionaries to Korea despite renewed attempts by the Korean government to repulse them. An example of the persistence of the Catholic priests in converting Koreans despite the threats to their lives was Bishop Berneux who had been in the country for ten years and, when brought before the tribunal, insisted on his right to rename himself "Chang." He said he had come to save the souls of the Koreans and that he refused to leave the country except by force. He was beheaded, along with other priests.

As the years passed, prejudice against the foreign faith alternately ebbed and flowed as internal problems increased, then grew. When King Ch'olchong came to the throne in 1849, there began an interval of internal foment in which enforcing the anti-Catholic laws was less of a priority. The authorities virtually ceased efforts to suppress the church as the confusion of this reign increased. Messages from higher church officials, including the Pope, were openly printed and distributed. The temporarily diverted influence of the violent anti-Christian party finally erupted into the great persecution of 1866. Death warrants were signed for all the foreign priests in Korea. About 300 of several thousand Catholic converts were initially executed.

Besieged by foreign pressures, the Taewon'gun in 1866 had become enraged at the widely broadcast proposal of a former official named Nam Chong-sam to ask France for help against the Russians who had mounted a military presence on Korea's northern border. Russian warships had appeared off the coast the previous year, but the French-British occupation of Peking in 1860 was still recalled by the king with trepidation. Western vessels continued to demand trading rights and to obtain considerable Korean business without them, encouraging a drain of Korean money and grain. The king was determined to halt the internal and external threats to his policies. "Not to fight back when invaded by the Western barbarians," he said, "is to invite further attacks, and selling out the country in peace negotiations is the greatest danger to be guarded against."

Nine of 12 priests were captured and executed. Many thousands of Korean Catholics lost their lives, and many were jailed. By 1870 when the persecution ended, the French claimed the number killed at 8,000.

The French demanded the handing over of the three Korean ministers directly involved in the killing of the subversive priests, and when no response was forthcoming, in 1867 they sent 160 men to storm the fortress of Chong-jok on Kangwha.

The fortress was defended by far more troops than the French could reasonably expect to overwhelm. Furthermore, their Korean adversaries were mostly hardy mountaineers and tiger hunters from Kang-gye in the far north, the descendants of the same men who, in the ancient days of Koguryo, drove back an army of Chinese 300,000 strong and killed all but 2700 of them. (Hulbert, 1962) The Koreans easily defeated them. As this incident shows, traditional martial art and the skill to use it were not completely forgotten even through all the disorganization of this era.

Western Industrialists Seek Asian Partners in Profit

Elsewhere in Asia, the traditional exclusion of foreigners was crumbling under the onslaught of the Industrial Revolution in Europe. Trade agreements with China and Japan were bringing about a realignment of powers that was watched by the Korean government with increasing concern. English ships reaching Korea's shores were turned away with the warning that it was illegal to allow foreign traders into the country. Regardless, contraband British goods reached port and threatened to further undermine the sinking Korean economy.

Korean Unity Falters as Political, Religious Cohesion Declines

News of the capture of Peking by Britain and France in 1860, the flight of the Chinese emperor and the humiliating treaty forced upon China caused further panic in the Korean court. Added to this insecurity was the continuing collapse of the traditional class structure which had been in progress since the 18th century and the arbitrary rule by the king's in-laws. Static Confucianism was becoming irrelevant to a society in continual flux. Buddhism had become a kind of folk religion, remote from political realities, and Taoist beliefs, emphasizing the ideal of the scholar-hermits, was far removed from political problem solving. Nationalism was no longer supported by a compatible religion.

An incident with the U.S. Navy involving a missing American ship in the 1870s was to lead to the greatest threat to Korea: intervention by a Japan greatly strengthened as a result of its adoption of Western technology, lucrative trade treaties with Western nations, and new, less conservative government. Intent on enhancing its position as an Asian power, Japan chose as one of its first diplomatic actions in that regard to offer to mediate between Korea and the U.S. concerning the missing ship General Sherman. The Korean Taewon'gun government of the time refused to recognize the credentials of the newly formed Japanese government and compelled the Japanese to return home.

Japan Again Targets Korea for Expansionism

In 1873 a Japanese delegation appeared at the southern city of Tongnae dressed in Western-style clothes aboard Western-style ships with another trade petition. Disdainful of the Japanese alliance with the Western "barbarians," the Koreans again said no. Repeated rejection by the Koreans instilled in the Japanese a determination to crack their isolationism. Meanwhile, the Koreans refused to accept the reality of change. They clung to a by-gone era, even to the point of regularly reporting to, and seeking solace from, a now-helpless China.

Korea began to achieve a more realistic view of its changing world with the appearance of the energetic and ambitious Queen Min, wife of King Kojong. Her powerful allies at the palace forced the retirement of the conservative Taewon'gun to his estate at Yongju. King Kojong and Queen Min monitored contemporary world events through the Korean envoys in China. They became well aware of the crisis forming as a result of the contact between the tradition-bound Orient and the powerful and economically dynamic West.

By 1875, tired of Korean rebuffs and aware that the political climate had changed with Taewon-gun's departure, Japan sent a battleship and escort on the pretext of surveying sea routes into Pusan and then north to the Bay of Yiongbung. The captain and twenty men landed on Kanghwa Island, ostensibly to obtain drinking water, and were fired upon. Ships were then sent to Pusan and more clashes occurred. Ultimately, six naval vessels were to convey a Japanese envoy and his party to Kanghwa Island with the news that negotiations must now begin.

Koreans Pressured Into Critical Trade Treaty With Japan

The Koreans very reluctantly sent negotiators to Kanghwa, where a treaty was signed in February, 1876. The Korean rulers, unable to engage militarily in any more wars, tried to convince their people opposed to the compact that it only affected relations between Korea and Japan, and was not an open-door policy to the world.

The nature of the treaty was new to Koreans, not built on the traditional, more sovereign-vassal bounds previously negotiated with China. It was in Japan's interests to extinguish the previous Korean relationships with China and cast Korea adrift, eventually to be made dependent on, and then annexed by, Japan. The treaty provided that diplomatic missions be exchanged and permanently maintained and that Pusan and two other strategic ports open unhindered to Japanese trade. Japanese were to be given the right to lease land and buildings for business purposes and for housing. Most significantly, Japanese nationals in Korea were to have the right of extraterritoriality, placing them outside the jurisdiction of Korean courts. While in Korea they could be tried for crimes only by Japanese consular courts. This feature was widely resented since it not only enabled foreigners to commit crimes with relative impunity but also implied that the nation's criminal system was unjust.

Agents of Japanese firms quickly began acquiring Korean property, leading to the impoverishment of Koreans, as Japanese goods overwhelmed the feeble domestic trade. The drain on Korean wealth began. Japanese currency was allowed to enter Korea, and Japanese were allowed to take Korean currency to Japan. All articles imported from or exported to Japan were to be free of duty for several years, which prevented Korea's economic growth and made Japanese trade dominant.

The first Japanese minister arrived in Korea in 1879. In 1882 the first regular Korean minister to Japan was appointed. It was now considered necessary for Korea to have a flag for representation at official meetings with foreigners. At Chemulpo on board a little Japanese steamer the first Korean national flag was designed.

The Korean Flag: Embodiment of Martial Arts Motifs

In 1948, the Republic of Korea adopted a flag design called the *T'aegukki*. A similar design had been created in 1882 by a team of reformist envoys to Japan. They realized that, unlike other countries, they had no such modern device to represent their previously reclusive country as an equal among nations. Considered as perhaps the most "philosophical" flag in the world, every aspect reflects the Korean outlook and the Korean martial arts view of life.

The white background can be said to stand for both the Confucian concept of purity and the Buddhist concept of "emptiness." In the center is the *T'aeguk*, the Taoist symbol for the balance of, or harmony between, opposites, colored red on top and blue on bottom. The Chinese usually depicted this in black and white and divided the symbol vertically instead of horizontally. The red top half represents *yang* (heaven, day, the masculine, heat, activity, construction, etc.) and the blue lower half, *um (yin)*—earth, night, the feminine, coldness, passivity, destruction, etc. These twin cosmic forces cycle perpetually in perfectly balanced harmony, despite their superficial opposition. Asian spiritual wisdom doesn't see them as fighting each other but as two sides of the same coin.

The three lines at each corner, known as trigrams, come from the ancient Korean book of *Chu Yok* (Chinese counterpart, the *I Ching*). The unbroken bars symbolize Heaven/the Creative, while the opposite three broken bars symbolize Earth/the Receptive. The trigram in the upper right corner is Water/Treacherous Danger, and in the opposite corner lies Fire/Loyal Love.

Traditional martial arts are based on the concepts or *Ki* (universal energy) which divides into *um* and *yang* as represented by the *T'aeguk* symbol on the flag. The white represents the "emptiness" or state of "no mind" often sought in martial art meditation. The trigrams also represent the um and yang, equal but opposites. This philosophy is translated into martial art theory and movement that is still practiced today in martial arts like Kuk Sool Won.

Korean King Moves to Modernize for Survival

The Koreans regularly sent missions to Japan to observe where Japan stood in the adoption of Western technology. It was noted that Japan had advanced weapons, telegraph, new agricultural techniques, and a growing segment of young people educated in the West. While Korean envoy Kim Hong-jip (Koeng-jip) was in Japan, he met with the shrewd Chinese minister to Tokyo, a student of Korean politics, who gave him a book he had written called *Korean Strategy*. The book was presented to the Korean king who circulated copies among his ministers of state. It advocated close ties for Korea with Japan and the United States, and warned about aggression from Russia.

The book's philosophy was rejected by most of the king's advisors, but the court had sound reasons for the course it took in signing its unconventional and inequitable treaty with Japan. Worse evils were anticipated if the treaty had not been made. The only hope for Korea was perceived to be adoption of Western technology in order to make the nation powerful enough to withstand Japanese encroachment. Korean scholars, however, perceived that the ideas in *Korean Strategy* were only unworkable, abstract theories. They demanded that the number of envoys exchanged, the number of ships engaged in trade, and the articles of trade are strictly limited, and that all foreign books in Korea be destroyed.

The Korean monarch rejected their desperate appeal for preservation of the status quo. King Kojong determined survival lay in a judicious updating of Korea's key institutions. A bureau was established to renovate the armaments of the army and navy. The technology of weapon manufacture had to be learned and the men trained to employ them. Modern military tactics had to be studied as well. Kojong set up an elite army unit soon after the Taewon'gun's retirement and this unit supplied the men to be trained in modern methods.

When the Chinese became aware of these developments in Korea, it offered to train Koreans in Chinese weapons technology and military skills. However, before the Koreans could be sent to China, Japan volunteered to supply rifles and train a unit of the Korean army to handle them in a ploy to head off further Chinese influence. Queen Min's faction accepted the Japanese aid but reserved the right also to send trainees to China. Those who remained to be tutored in armaments by the Japanese were placed under a special guard unit established earlier. This unit came increasingly under the control of Queen Min and was given special privileges which aroused envy in the regular military and resentment from the scholars who had opposed the Kanghwa Treaty. Dissatisfaction raged to the point where a plot to overthrow the king and Queen Min's faction was developed, although it was thwarted.

After the government was reorganized by Queen Min, its twelve bureaus were headed mostly by young men who had visited Japan. Dazzled by their experiences there and their privileged involvement with powerful Western technology and cultural overtones, they were decidedly pro-Japanese in favoring modernization. Under their influence, military administration was remodeled, the old Five Camps were abolished, and the army organized in two main divisions. These moves increased the resentment of the conservative scholars and the 3,700 troops called the Tui'lyun To'gam, the former Royal Guard soldiers without the privileges of the 200 new members of the select units. A clear schism developed between them and the queen's faction, which included the Japanese training officer and the Japanese minister in Seoul.

Taewon'gun Makes First Reappearance as Opposition Leader

In 1882 corruption in the distribution of grain rations and anger over the unequal pay scale among the soldiers led to a rebellion backed secretly by the former retired ruler Taewon'gun, who also supported the previous plot to overturn the throne.

The rebel soldiers broke into arsenals to obtain weapons. They attacked police stations to free comrades who had been arrested, destroyed the homes of many of the queen's relations, killed the Japanese training officer, and narrowly missed killing the Japanese minister. He escaped with his staff to Inch'on and returned to Japan. Finally they pushed through the gate of Ch'ang-dok palace and surrounded the private living quarters of the rulers, catching and killing two high-ranking officials in the process. Queen Min, however, escaped in disguise and fled to her relatives' house in Ch'ungju, where she remained in hiding.

There was now no choice but to recall the Taewon'gun to power as he was the only leader with sufficient influence to restore order. The king sent for him and, after nine years in retirement, he was reinstated at the head of the government.

Japan and China were both seriously concerned about the military rebellion. The Japanese minister Hanabuna returned to Korea with three naval vessels and 300 soldiers. With an armed escort he demanded to formally present before the court an order for compensation for Japanese lives and property lost in the rioting. When the government refused to receive him, he delivered an ultimatum: the Japanese forces would attack Inch'on in three days if their demands had not been met.

Chinese Reinstate Queen Min

The Chinese, on the other hand, had already sent a mission to investigate the seriousness of the situation which they soon determined warranted the sending of ships and troops in large numbers. The Japanese, outnumbered, withdrew but only when they were paid an indemnity for their losses. The Chinese leaders subsequently decided that they needed to exert more control over Korea to keep the Japanese at bay. They decided to kidnap the Taewon'gun and take him to China. Queen Min returned to Ch'angdok palace and her faction was once again installed in office. A large unit of Chinese troops was stationed in Seoul.

The Japanese emerged from the conflict with another set of advantages in Korea: a new treaty known as the Treaty of Che-mulp'o (the old name of Inch'on). In addition to the indemnity, Korea now had to agree to allow Japanese merchants to travel within a stated radius of the treaty ports, open another of its ports to trade, and allow the Japanese minister and his staff to travel freely in Korea. The leaders of the riots were to be punished.

King Kojong requested that the Chinese release his father, the Taewon'gun, but his request was refused. Chinese troops were stationed permanently in Seoul under the command of the formidable general Yuan Chih-k'ai. Korean diplomatic relations were now almost completely under the control of China.

U. S. Seeks Korean Involvement

Western nations, particularly the United States, saw these treaties exacted from Korea by Japan as opportunities to introduce its own interests in the long-isolated peninsular country. Commodore Robert W. Shufeldt aboard the U.S.S. *Ticonderoga* sailed into Pusan Harbor in

May of 1880 to seek the help of the Japanese official stationed there in meeting with the Korean government. He was refused help by this official. Sailing to Japan, he attempted to send a letter through the Japanese Minister of Foreign Affairs to the Korean government. The Korean government refused to accept it.

Hearing of the American's difficulties, China offered to try to obtain the treaty sought by the U.S. from Korea. China's leading statesman at the time, Li Hung-chang, discussed the advantages of an American treaty with the Korean representative in Tien-tsin. These included providing a counterbalance to Japanese intervention. The treaty finally was signed, without a clause repeatedly sought by Li implying that China still retained her old suzerainty. The provisions of the treaty included a most-favored-nation clause and clauses that insured American economic activities in Korea would not seriously compete with those of China. Other nations soon moved to secure similar treaties with Korea, but the British terms successfully undermined the Chinese advantage.

The Korean military organization was soon remodeled by the Chinese. Yuan Shih-k'ai created four elite groups of five hundred men, each to be trained by China. Weapons and ammunition were also supplied by China. The government was also restructured by the Chinese according to their more modern institutional models. By 1882, Chinese control becomes firmly established in Korea.

Coup of 1884 Widens Japanese Power Base in Korea

Many Koreans were still of the opinion that modernization would bring subservience to the Westernized powers, but the significant enhancement of Korean daily life by the new flood of imports could hardly be denied. The gradualism of the pro-Chinese Min faction became an increasing irritant among a rising group attracted to the Japanese model, which became seen as the only way to create a more viable nation. This group began organizing and plotting the overthrow of the Min government, its leader visiting Japan for support. His return coincided with a poorly advised move on the government's part to devalue currency, creating inflation. The new Independence Party, oblivious of the power behind the self-serving Japanese interest in Korea, unwittingly helped position its country for the impending disastrous takeover. The Independence Party made secret contacts with the Japanese minister in Seoul to obtain the support of Japanese troops when the time was ripe. This time became apparent as the Chinese, diverted by their own problems with the French in Indochina, lost touch with Korean intrigues.

The momentous coup was triggered at a dinner party on December 4, 1884, in celebration of the opening of the new post office. In attendance were most of the important government officials. The Japanese minister had financed the event and Japanese troops stood in readiness. At an arranged time, a building near the new structure was incinerated with the intention of forcing the officials to leave the banquet and report the event to the king. The plot was only partially effective but meanwhile, Kim Ok-kyun and some of his followers went to Ch'angdok palace. He convinced the king that he must be moved for his own protection. Although he was later returned to the palace, the insurgents notified the diplomatic corps in Seoul that a new government had been established. The coup leaders announced that Chinese dominance was to cease, the old class system was to be abolished, all people were to be treated as equals, and reforms made to the military, police, and taxation.

The rebellion leaders had not counted on the Chinese reaction. With 1,500 soldiers in Seoul as opposed to about 200 Japanese troops, the Chinese quelled the riot, although its instigators escaped to Japan. The Korean government lodged a strong protest with Japan against the interference in its internal affairs by the Japanese minister, but the government claimed he acted on his own. Further, the Japanese again demanded, with force, compensation for the loss of Japanese lives and property.

Economic Warfare Escalates in Korea

After Japanese Foreign Minister Inoue Kaoru landed at Inch'on with two battalions of troops, marching into Seoul, the Koreans had no alternative but to accept the terms he offered. These included the withdrawal of Chinese troops, as well as Japanese, and intensified the rivalry between these two countries for domination of Korea. Japan had managed to gain, in the process, expanded fishing rights, confronting the Chinese already fishing in the treaty areas. Japanese retail stores began to appear in Korean cities in defiance of the treaty and Japanese businessmen accelerated the land grabbing process, buying mines, ginseng fields, and farmland outside their leased territory. Japanese economic penetration spread through every trade and industry. Treaties and trade laws were virtually ignored. The trade war in Korea between the Japanese and the Chinese, with their superior banking and investment schemes, intensified and outright riots took place in 1888 and 1889.

Chinese trade gained steadily on the Japanese. Between 1885 and 1892 the proportion of Korean trade with China increased from 19 to 45 percent while trade with Japan decreased from 81 to 55 percent. The Japanese were highly frustrated. Japan was in serious need for foreign markets in which it could earn hard currency for military expansion and further modernization. Despite the havoc the Japanese tried to create with secret agents infiltrating anti-Japanese or pro-Chinese activities in Korea, changes did not occur in their favor that is, until the Tonghak rebellion in 1894.

The Tonghak Revolt: Prelude to Disaster

The Taewon'gun's isolationism and persecution of Catholics, together with his attempt to reinstitute conservatism, prompted the expansion of the Tonghak sect, an anti-foreign, anti-reformist religion (philosophy). Due to the widening economic catastrophes of the 1890s, many Koreans envisioned this new religion as the only hope for their country. In 1892 there were widespread demonstrations by the also-persecuted Tonghaks in Cholla and Ch'ungch'ong provinces. One of their causes was the posthumous pardons of its executed founder, Ch'oe Che-u. Forty Tonghak leaders went to Seoul in April of 1893, seeking redress from the king himself. Their petition was rejected but they made an impact on foreigners in the capital by posting scores of notices demanding that foreigners leave their country and Catholicism be suppressed. Rumors spread that tens of thousands of Tonghak were converging on Seoul. Foreign warships were ordered to Inch'on to protect their residents in case of violence. An even larger gathering of Tonghak the next month was dispersed by the government with a mixture of force and appeasement, but not full-scale persecution. Tonghak had by now become so prevalent in the south that this would have meant economical ruin to the whole area.

Leaders of this movement were mostly *yangban* whose families had been ruined by the social disarray and political conflicts of the past two centuries. When a corrupt official in Cholla overstepped even the usually liberal bounds of venality, the local Tonghak leader, Chon Pong-jun, realized that further appeals to local officials were futile. In February of 1894 he led about a thousand enraged farmers in an attack on a government office. An inspector sent by the central government to evaluate what happened laid the blame on the Tonghak religion and began arresting believers, destroying their homes. Chon Pong-jun enlisted the help of other Tonghak groups and Cholla was soon on fire with revolution. By May a rebel army had been formed. It turned its attention south, taking every town in its path. By the time its soldiers reached Mujang, they numbered about 10,000. The rebels beat off government troops but both sides were exhausted and ready for negotiations. The radical reforms requested by the Tonghak were partially addressed by the king but the ruler was highly concerned that its unrealistic demand for the immediate abolition of the aristocratic structure of society would bring about further armed conflict.

The Sino-Japanese War and the Fall of Korean Sovereignty

King Kojong sought the help of China, which informed Japan, in compliance with the latest treaty agreement between them, that it was on its way to assist the Korean ruler. The Japanese responded with their own ship which landed troops at Inch'on on June 10, 1894. This provoked a defensive Chinese reaction. Troops of both nations converged on Korea in large numbers. The Korean government protested that the revolt had been squelched. China was willing to withdraw but the Japanese saw an opportunity to drive the Chinese completely out of Korea. They proposed that Japanese troops remain in order to "renovate Korean home affairs," continuing to send in more troops. China opposed Japan's tactics, and the Korean government continued to protest, resisting Japan's demand that it cease trade relations with China. The Japanese then abandoned their paternal pretenses and began openly to prepare for domination of Korea and war with China. At midnight on July 23, 1894, Japanese troops overpowered the guards at Kyongbok palace, occupied it and forced Kojong once again to call back the Taewon'gun. Queen Min and her group were driven out and the pro-Chinese government came to an end. The Korean troops were disarmed, and Japan proceeded into the Sino-Japanese war with a swift series of victories.

In the journal *The Korean Repository* (Vol. III, Jan.-Dec., 1896), Gen. William Dye, the American instructor of the Training Unit in Seoul, responded to a widely broadcast slur on the Korean military that the palace guard failed to execute their duties as protectors of the throne and deserted their posts at the appearance of the Japanese. Dye noted the following:

When the Japanese and pro-Japanese Koreans surrounding His Majesty got possession of the palace in 1894, by treachery, treason and murder, they seized all the arms, ammunition, and artillery in the city. For many, many long months after this, there were the most confused mass of guards in the palace—wheels within wheels—that it was ever my misfortune to encounter. There were no less than six different guards, including Japanese and Korean policemen. And they were all controlled, more or less, by the Japanese. The Tai Wen Kun's grandson, a nephew of the king, was early made a general. Efforts then began to form a guard, under control of H. M. [His Majesty]. *From among our old soldiers, we picked a body, man by man, who, it was thought, would well answer the purpose. Within a very few days, these men began to disappear. When any of them visited their families outside the palace grounds, as they occasionally did, they were seized and sent into the barracks, controlled by the Japanese; and in lieu of them were returned to the palace, recruits, and inferior men. It was not long before nearly our entire picked guard were thus surreptitiously replaced by a body of men, inferior in physique and intelligence, as well as in drill and discipline. This fact, especially, rendered drill an absolute necessity. But, no sooner would drill get fairly started, whether publicly or privately, than the Japanese would learn of it, and cause its discontinuance...*

Besides drill, to render the men serviceable, arms were needed. It was only after the most prolonged and persistent efforts of His Majesty to have some of the arms which had been taken from the men in July 1894, restored to them that he was even listened to. Finally, about four hundred cast-away, rusty arms, mostly without bayonets or rammers, and many without locks or cocks, were resurrected from a go-down [warehouse] *and sent to the palace. These, by cleaning and change of parts, were fitted up as well as could be done, and put into the hands of the men. When it is said that they were better than cornstalks, full justice is done them, for very few of them were fit for firing. This number armed only about half the guard. A very few more worthless arms were found in palace go-downs, and in the lake where they had been thrown when the Japanese assaulted the palace in 1894...*

Another misfortune was that the designing islanders [the Japanese] *would allow the guards no ammunition... From a pond not far from my quarters in the palace grounds, I caused three or four boxes, partially filled, to be fished up from their place of concealment from the looting Japanese. The little ammunition contained therein was dried and quietly distributed to the men. This was all they ever got. Of course, very few of the cartridges could be relied on as serviceable...*

This is not all, for the assaulting procession (may it be called?) was led by the venerable father of the King, willingly or unwillingly, by the feared ex-regent, twice in power, whose presence alone was sufficient to overawe all Korean opposition.

Perhaps, then, you may not be so astounded as I was to learn that the guards had been instructed not to fire upon the assaulting troops, just as if they were out on a picnic. This I only learned afterwards, though presaging, this was the observed fact that the officers generally had doffed their uniforms some minutes before the assault took place.

Clearly, this letter shows that the Korean martial spirit and skills were not deficient on this occasion but that the dismissal of trained guards was part of the political intrigue that once again proved disastrous for Korea.

The Chinese gone, Korea was alone, depleted, and defenseless. It was forced to sign a series of agreements that placed the nation virtually under Japanese rule. The Japanese were given the right to build railroads and telegraph systems. All ports on the Cholla coast were opened to them. A treaty of military alliance turned Korea into an arms manufacturing arsenal for Japan's exclusive use. All Chinese were to be deported.

Meanwhile, the Taewon'gun, who had accepted Japanese help in order to see his enemy Queen Min removed, turned on the Japanese secretly, lending support to the Tonghak leader in hiding, Chon Pong-jun. He, in turn, had already been contacted by Japanese agents pretending to be pro-Tonghak, and had rejected their "help" in fomenting a revolt the agents hoped would lend an excuse for further Japanese repression.

Chon called for revolt once again, attacking Japanese supply bases, but the Japanese retaliated not only with superior weaponry but with orders to exterminate, not just put down, the rioters. Chon was eventually captured, however the slaughter in the provinces continued until the end of January, 1895. Outbreaks continued until Chon and his commanders were executed. In the following treaty, Japan obtained even more concessions than before, including ceding of both the Liaotung peninsula and the island of Taiwan to Japan, the opening of more ports, free passage on all inland rivers, and enormous reparations. A threatening protest by Russia, France, and Germany forced Japan to give up the Liaotung peninsula, but the augmentation of Japan's empire had begun.

Following the Sino-Japanese war, the Korean people were infused with fear and uncertainty. Japanese reforms were not well received. Arrests were being made on the basis of many rumors in circulation.

An assortment of events and modifications occurred to achieve some semblance of stability in Korea. Russia was consulted for help against the Japanese by Queen Min, among others, while King Kojong was immersed in regret over his assent to the reform program. Japan attempted to counterbalance the Russian influence by placing the Royal Guard and the Training Unit directly under Japanese command but both Russian and American ministers objected. Pak Yong-hyo, the newest Korean premier, was dismissed for his opposition to the queen, and his predecessor, Kim Hong-jip, returned to power.

The Death of Queen Min

Backed by the Russians, the Koreans became more open in their disinterest in Japanese domination. Pro-Japanese officials were dismissed and a royal decree demanded that the traditional court dress again be worn. Clashes between soldiers and police occurred as tension between Japan and Russia mounted.

Behind the scenes Japanese Minister Miura presented a conciliatory front to the Korean government, but covertly he was planning to oust the pro-Russian group with violence. The plot to eliminate the queen and her followers was to be disguised as a clash between discontented soldiers of the training unit, who faced disbandment, and palace guards. At 3 a.m. on the morning of October 8, 1895, a party of Japanese escorted the Taewon'gun to the palace. He was destined to preside as a puppet ruler in the service of foreign domination which he had opposed all his life. Blinded by his hatred for the queen and her faction, he agreed. This party was joined on its way by the Training Unit soldiers, Japanese guards, and a group of Japanese thugs. At Kyongbok palace, they opened fire on the royal guards, ransacked the palace and stabbed Queen Min, carrying her into the courtyard where they poured kerosene over her mortally wounded body while she was still alive, and set it aflame. The king was seized in preparation to restoring a pro-Japanese government.

The Japanese had not, however, anticipated being watched during all these proceedings by General Dye and a Russian technician named Sabatine, both residing in the palace. They quickly informed the diplomatic corps which accused Japanese Minister Miura of engineering the murder. He pretended the coup had been only a clash between the Training Unit and the palace guard. Contemporary Japanese records, however, describe the plot in minute detail and give the names of the two Japanese who did the actual killing. They even note how, afterward, the Japanese tried to spread a rumor that the queen had escaped and was in hiding. (Han, 1974)

This act drew international condemnation but the Japanese government continued its subterfuge of ignorance, sending a special envoy to make inquiry into the matter. Miura and about 40 others were arrested and imprisoned at Hiroshima. They went to trial but were shortly freed on grounds of "insufficient evidence."

Resurgence of the Righteous Army Spirit

The Japanese then went back to work at reform in Korea, going so far as to require all Korean men to cut off their topknots and wear their hair short in Western fashion, an insult to Confucianist and those many others who felt their customs and traditions mocked. The 'bobbed hair" order was the final offense for many civilians who rose in armed combat all over the country from January to April of 1896. Their actions were part of a manifestation of the centuries-old Uibyong spirit in the Righteous Army tradition which had been building steadily during the decade. Their fierce spirit of resistance was not adequately supported by military discipline or modern weapons until they were joined by the soldiers unemployed after Japan succeeded in disbanding the Korean army in 1907.

Most of these guerrilla bands were based in mountain redoubts from which they would attack Japanese garrisons and destroy railway and telegraph facilities. They were both supported by the local people and familiar with local terrain which compensated to some extent for their inadequate weaponry. These righteous armies were especially active in Kyongsang, Kangwon, Kyonggi, and Hwanghae provinces, but their presence could be felt throughout Korea. Korean guerrilla units in Kando in southeast Manchuria even crossed the Tumen River to harass Japanese garrisons there. In 1907 Yi In-yong and Ho Wi gathered about 10,000 guerrilla troops from all over the country to attack the Residency-General headquarters. Advance units were able to penetrate to positions within eight miles of Seoul's East Gate. This alone demonstrates how vigorously the Righteous Armies carried out their struggle against the Japanese.

Guerrilla activity reached a peak in 1908 but rapidly declined afterwards. Following annexation the scene of operations shifted to Manchuria and the Russian Maritime Territory where the guerrillas became independence fighters and continued their warfare against Japan. By 1910 more than 17,600 guerrilla fighters had given their lives in the struggle, including Min Kung-ho, Ho Wi, Yi Kang-nyon, and other commanders.

This final revival of the Uibyong was perhaps its most concerted and fiercest. It can be defined between Marquis Ito's imposition of the Japanese Protectorate Treaty on the Korean emperor in November, 1905, and the final annexation of Korea by Japan in August, 1910.

Despite the deepening national crisis and times not conducive to scholarly inquiry, a sense of national pride and self-respect was fostered by the research and writing of such key figures in the study of Korean history as Chang Chi-yon, Pak Un-sik, and Sin Ch'ae-ho. Their accounts of the lives of heroes who fought against foreign invaders included the *Biography of Ulchi Mundok, Biography of Kang Kam-ch'an, Biography of Ch'oe Yong* and *Biography of Yi Sun'sin.*

The Pro-Russian Interlude

Following the assassination of Queen Min and the provocation of the "bobbed hair" order, the Japanese were forced temporarily into more covert activities on the political stage. King Kojong had sought refuge in the Russian legation and for the Japanese to attempt to control the nation's governing without his signature would have amounted to open aggression. For more than two years the Korean pro-Russian faction took control. The Japanese signed an agreement with the Russians endorsing the king's safe return to the palace and the protection of Japanese investments and residents with the presence of Japanese troops. The Korean government then made numerous economic concessions to foreign powers, inviting investments from the European countries and the U.S. These were, however, considerably dwarfed by the Japanese' own enterprises, including 20 banks, one of which was virtually the central bank of Korea, handling customs duties, controlling government loans, managing the treasury, and issuing currency. Japan's influence, despite a temporary political setback, was on the increase in its primary goal, control of both Korea and Manchuria. For the West, Japan's presence served a number of purposes, including as a go-between in the establishment of industry and as a buyer for failed Western projects, of which there were many due to foreigners' unfamiliarity with Korean conditions.

Circumstances were to change as Japan in 1902 concluded an alliance with Britain, the traditional foe of Russia's own expansionist plans. When Russia refused to back down from its interests in Korea, the Japanese opened fire on the Russian fleet at Port Arthur, February 8, 1904. In the aftermath, Japan exacted more concessions from Korea with a treaty laced with dangerous agreements granting virtual control of Korea at Japan's own discretion as protector and adviser. In another protocol soon signed, Korea was compelled to summon home her diplomatic missions whose functions were abrogated by Japanese officials. In everything but name, Korea was a part of the Japanese Empire.

The stream of Korean refugees created by the repression and confiscation of property accelerated not only into adjacent Sikhote Alin on the Siberian Pacific coast and the Kando area of Manchuria (made easier by loosely policed northern borders and large existing populations of Koreans) but to countries overseas, where aggressive resistance organizations and publications were started. Many veterans of the struggle against Japan after the Korean armed forces were disbanded were based in Sikhote Alin and conducted numerous raids into Hamgyong Province until the establishment of a Japanese police network forced them to move their base to the western, then eastern, Kando region.

Subsequently sealing Korea's fate were two agreements made between Japan and the U.S. and Japan and Great Britain. In the first, the United States recognized Japan's interests in Korea in return for a Japanese promise not to interfere or raise objections over American rule in the Philippines. The second was a promise by Japan to support British rule in India. Western colonialism feared the rising power of Japan; Korea was a bargaining tool. Russia faded from the scene after a series of decisive defeats by Japan.

Through several further "agreements" exacted from Korea with no options, the last of its rights were stripped away and the country effectively became a part of the Japanese empire. Freedom of speech, assembly, and other rights were systematically eroded. Ambitious Korean administrators considered pro-Japanese by their dedication in enforcing Japan's interests were recruited and recommended to influential posts at every level.

In 1907, Emperor (a title imposed by the Japanese to underline Korea's parity with, and "independence" from, China) Kojong made one last effort to regain his country's freedom. He decided to send envoys secretly to plead Korea's cause at the second World Peace Conference at the Hague in the Netherlands. The conference chairman, a Russian, said, however, that Korea had no rights to diplomatic representation; additionally, although sympathetic, delegate countries were uniformly opposed to further intervention. The Korean delegation did succeed in making plain the now-stifling exploitation of its homeland, and of prompting considerable criticism of Japan. This resulted in the Japanese forcing the abdication of Kojong on July 19, 1907. The crown prince, posthumously titled Sunjong, was given the crown and was the last monarch to reign in Korea. Officials who opposed the abdication were banished by the Japanese.

From the beginning of Japanese encroachment there was considerable popular resistance to their blatant form of intervention. Much of the antagonism was led by Confucian scholars traditionally opposed to outside influences. Heroes of the popular resistance to Japanese rule included:

- Min Chong-sik, formerly an important official. He organized a force of about 500 men in North Ch'ungch'ong Province and secured 75 old cannons in the spring of 1906 prior to his defeat.
- Ch'oe Ik-hyon, banished for his opposition to the Kanghwa Treaty in 1876. At the age of 70, he organized a rebellion and authored a detailed and widely distributed indictment of the Japanese, calling on his countrymen to rise against them. The revolt spread to Kyongsang and Kangwon provinces.
- Pak Song-hwan, commander of one of the two battalions of the Royal Guard, killed himself in protest over Kojong's abdication and the disbanding of the last remaining Korean military unit. The majority of his fellow soldiers fought a pitched battle with the Japanese in Seoul, escaping after the inevitable defeat to the provinces. There, along with local militia forces, they joined the rebels, bringing their weapons with them. Rebel forces established bases in inaccessible mountain regions and conducted regular raids on Japanese installations, destroying railroad tracks and cutting telegraph lines.

Korean Leaders Refuse to Sign Protectorate Treaty

Even after the Japanese were plotting to fabricate Korean compliance by forcing a signature of their so-called Protectorate Treaty, the Korean ruler and his courageous prime minister, Han Kyu-sol, refused to admit defeat by putting their names to the document. Their pride was well exemplified in their tenacity in stalling the Japanese week after week in order to give the Korean imperial messenger, the missionary-historian H. L. Hulbert, a confidante of Kojong's, enough time to journey to Washington where he would plead the cause of the Koreans. There is no doubt that Japanese authorities were very aware of the nature of his mission before his departure, which hastened their deception. Since neither the Korean ruler nor the prime minister would place his seal on the document himself, the seal of the foreign minister was finally affixed, together with those of four other cabinet members, giving the "treaty" its only authorization. On November 11, 1905, the Tokyo government dispatched to the world powers a proclamation falsely claiming that this agreement, placing Korea's foreign affairs in the hands of a Japanese Resident-General, had been voluntarily accepted by the Korean government.

Hulbert's efforts to see either President Theodore Roosevelt or the Secretary of State were defeated for eight tense days, evidently for the purpose of having the official Japanese notification in hand at the Department of State before any discussion could be held with the Korean ruler's American representative.

It was the precipitating calamity in Korea's decline into protectorate status that the nearest and most capable mentor for its critically needed modernization was an opportunistic foreign power with an initially hidden agenda of expansionism. That Japan was accepted as an authority on the Korean situation by its new Western trading powers seeking fortune in the East further reduced Korea's chances for support when its autonomy became eroded. Additionally, there existed that historical propensity for uncompromising agendas among Korean political factions and opportunistic individuals which had proven fatal in the past to national unity. Coming in an era when isolationism had become economically disastrous, this chasm of divisive interests could not be breached by the patriotism and martial genius that had also been part of the Korean character for centuries.

Korean resistance to colonialism and trusteeship in the 20th century and its eventual evolution in its most representative form as today's Republic of Korea is a turbulent story available in numerous accounts. The systematic suppression by the Japanese of Korean culture drove many teachers and intellectuals to more remote areas where quite a few of them even formed what had to become clandestine educational and cultural organizations. The Korean military arts and spirit went underground, again, periodically surfacing in rebellious demonstrations brutally suppressed. They would only emerge decades later in a new era when their genius, their heroes and the significance of their warriors' ancient lessons in living could take their rightful place among those of the world's other great martial arts.

Korean martial arts came closer to extinction at this time than at any other time in her known history. Most military oriented items were destroyed, including historical writings, traditional weaponry and any material considered to be nationalistic to Koreans.

The Japanese version of Korean history and martial arts was put into place and taught for generations throughout Korea and the world.

9

New Perspectives on Korean Weaponry, Armor, and Fortresses

Despite generations of occupation by invaders intent on destroying its martial arts and discounting its martial heritage, the evidence of an ancient, continuing, and distinctly Korean martial art culture is extensive. This is clear, especially, in the documentation of its weaponry. Without accessing these references, some modern commentators have succumbed to the biased indoctrination of Korea's former oppressors: the most ingenious Korean inventions should be credited to larger or more hawkish nations. The movement of history and new discoveries certainly indicate otherwise.

Before taking a look at material that corroborates the status of Korean weaponry as innovative and traditional, there are a number of historical facts that additionally support Korea's capacity for cultural invention and leadership in East Asia. The trend since the suppression of Korea's martial heritage during the Japanese Occupation has continued to be acceptance of the underestimation of indigenous Korean martial arts and, therefore, a disinterest in investigating them more deeply. Labeling them as derivative has been a great slight to their deserved prestige. When we see the key migration of culture has not been from Japan to Korea, as the Koreans were conditioned to believe for generations, but the reverse, we are not so likely to assume Korea's weaponry and martial techniques were innovated elsewhere. The latter is a notion popular among some Westerners due to their perception of the Japanese as more out-going than the then-isolationist Koreans and quick to embrace technological progress. The tremendous amount of misinformation and obfuscation regarding the origins of Korean martial techniques and weaponry began during the decades when it was especially difficult for Westerners (as well as Koreans) to research matters beyond the then-prejudiced sources of their Japanese allies. Now, with so much corroborative study available, the status of Korean weapons and of the techniques for using them is more than apparent.

Reversing the Propaganda of Attribution

For centuries, Korea was the main channel through which the current of Asiatic culture from China flowed into Japan. Core belief systems such as Buddhism, Confucianism, and Neo-Confucianism, authored by the great Confucian scholar Yi T'oegye, reached Japan through Korea. Relatively few people are aware that, in addition to this channeling of Chinese culture, major features of Korean civilization were also imported to the island. The foundation of Japanese history, including its martial art, is infused with Korean culture. Even some early Japanese myths of origin are retold old Korean stories.

The first intellectuals in Japan were the Korean Wani who migrated as refugees from Korea to Japan in 405 A.D. and began the writers' guild there. These early expatriated Koreans were awarded high rank and noble status for their contributions. For example, the Korean Hata clan brought knowledge of weaving to the early Horserider Court of Japan and kept the court records. Another Korean family, the Soga, was given general supervision over all the storehouses. Even as late as 815 A.D., 30 percent of the nobility in Japan claimed non-Japanese ancestry. An early census shows that many of the nobility had Korean names. The Korean King Syong-myong of Paekche introduced Buddhism to Japan through a laudatory memorial concerning its teachings, sent in 552 A.D., according to the Japanese text *Nihongi*.

The Japanese turned to Korea for guidance in planning and constructing their first great temple, the Hoko-ji. With its three pagodas, the Hoko-ji mirrored Paekche temples such as Miru-sa. Their nature-worshipping Shinto sanctuaries did not need elaborate architecture, thus the Japanese did not possess expertise in this kind of construction. Renowned metalworkers, potters, and carpenters were brought in large numbers from Paekche. Many were listed in records by name and identified as masters in the *Nihongi*. There are still a number of ancient temples in Japan where the influence of Paekche can still be seen. Only when the capital of Japan moved to Nara in 710 A.D., did major Japanese religious edifices begin to borrow architectural features from the Chinese.

The significant influence of Korea on Japanese culture was further underlined when, in October, 1978, Japan's most prestigious private museum, the Yammato Bunka-kan of Nara Prefecture, opened an exhibit of about 70 paintings which they identified as "Koryo Buddhist." Previously, most of these works of art, stolen from Korea by Japanese pirates, had been labeled Chinese or Japanese. Clearly, Korea has long been an innovator in the cultures of Southeast Asia. Logic dictates that the same twists in attribution that have delayed Korea's cultural recognition must have occurred with Korean martial arts and its traditional weaponry.

The Slanted Writing of Korean Refugees in Japan

Many illustrations of the problems in obtaining accurate information about Korea's martial arts past are found in the Silla period. For example, the *Record of Ancient Matters* and the *Chronicles of Japan*, were the products of jealousy and resentment among the Koguryo and Paekche refugees who were driven to Japan by the conquering Sillans. As the intellectuals of the two kingdoms, they rose to high posts in Japan and undercut Silla's military and cultural achievements in both volumes. (Covell, 1984) They made the uncorroborated claim that Silla had been under the control of Japan for more than a century. That they fabricated other information has been shown. For example, since they did not have a clear picture of events during the fourth century, they inserted ancient Korean or Chinese historical role models whenever possible. To fill embarrassing gaps in their knowledge, they fabricated Korean rulers from ancient historical continental leaders. Confucian-style philosophies were credited to some of the early rulers who in fact predated Confucian influence. This clearly demonstrates that these texts were the products of resentful exiles, and were shaped by malicious political motives.

Ancient Korean Cavalry Established Famed Japanese Shrine

The *Records of Ancient Matters* and the *Chronicles of Japan* were commissioned with a political agenda. One goal was to instill in the consciousness of the people of Japan a sense of divine origin for their leaders. For this purpose a Korean historical incident was rewritten with new Japanese heroes. This new legend cast a mythical aura around what was to become one of Japan's most sacred shrines, Iso-no-Kami Jingu, the Shrine of the Puyo Rock Deity. This is located on a wooded slope that is a 20-minute walk from the railroad station in the heart of Asuka.

Less than one percent of today's Japanese are aware of the significance of the unusually shaped iron artifact hidden behind curtains at this shrine. This shamanistic "sacred sword" is not the fabled sword drawn from the tail of a dragon by the Storm God Susa, nor is it the sword allegedly given by the Sun Goddess to her descendants, as told in Japanese legend. It actually authenticates the conquest of Japan's Yamato Plain in 369 A.D. by a cavalry group with iron swords and armor. They were known as "The Horse Riders," and were led by Jingu, a beautiful young princess of the Korean Puyo or "Children of the Rock." Her people were part of a Koguryo valley migration seeking greener pastures in the south and southeast. Their weapon was a double-curved bow, shot from horseback. A small band of these horse-riding nomads, dubbed the "most civilized of the Eastern barbarians," could easily subdue much larger numbers of sedentary farmers.

In reality, the Iso-no-Kami shrine was first established as the Puyo rulers' sanctum. The sword is inscribed with golden characters of an Asian language shared by many peoples of the time and which include a date corresponding to 369 A.D. In that year, few people living on the Japanese islands could read these characters, the only written language common in East Asia. The educated elite of Paekche knew these Asian characters well and would use them for such an inscription. In their attempt at a later date to mask this successful invasion by aliens, the earliest Japanese written histories (eighth century) converted Jingu into a purely Japanese queen and, amazingly, reversed the direction of conquest, claiming she conquered all of Korea. (Kim, 1989)

Jingu's descendants became known as the Puyo-Kaya line. Kaya was a small kingdom, strong in the martial arts. (Kim Yu-shin, who united The Three Kingdoms of Korea was a Kaya man). It lasted 500 years before being absorbed by Silla. These people of Korean origin ruled in Japan for several centuries until another dynasty, half Horse Rider and half tracing its lineage back to Yayoi-period Korean immigrants to Japan, assumed rule. The Paekche kingdom in Korea recognized the new rulers in Japan as suzerain in a remote kind of way but the tributary missions they sent were really a form of international trade and did not necessarily reflect a dominance relationship position between the countries. With the passage of time, Ojin, Japan's first Horse Rider emperor, became merged with the God of War, or Hachiman, in the Shinto pantheon. At important Hachiman shrines even today, the entrance is protected by two large, fierce-looking statues representing Korean dogs. In the northern part of Korea guard dogs were apparently interbred with wolves to make them fiercer.

Hideyoshi Invasion's Failure Downplayed

Although various sources were quick to disparage the performance of Korea in the depleted state of its last dynasty, few remembered the complete military and political failure of Japan's Hideyoshi Invasion (1592-1599). Hideyoshi's fantastic dreams and objectives resulted in the sacrifice of tens of thousands of lives and brought miserable devastation to Korean cities and villages. All this destruction and waste was motivated by an unrealistic and highly grandiose plan to decimate the peninsula and thereafter conquer the Asiatic continent.

The invasion, however, had the peculiar effect of creating a cultural "counter-invasion," as recognized by Japanese historians, during which Korean innovations were discovered and taken home by the Japanese. At the time of the Hideyoshi invasion, according to historian Shidehara Taira, Japanese generals and soldiers obtained Korean copper movable type and blocks, took them to Japan, and dedicated them to Hideyoshi. Although the Koreans had been printing since the early 15th century, the first publication of the Japanese, *Daijo Ichiran*, was published in 1614 with Korean type. The shipment of classical books from Korea to Japan was extensive during this invasion and provided the basis for the revision of laws and philosophy.

Pointing out these historical incidents are not for the purpose of diminishing Japanese accomplishments and culture but to place Korean accomplishments and culture in their proper perspective in relationship to Japanese culture.

A Case of Mistaken Identity

At this point, after having summarized the history of the Korean martial spirit over thousands of years, it is appropriate and interesting to give an example of the kind of unintended misinformation about Korean martial arts which has become so pervasive in the West. Indeed, it was this example, which was the result of well motivated research by Dr. John L. Boots, that stimulated my interest in the pursuit of the truth about the history of Korea's martial arts. As I will detail in the following paragraphs, Boot's research was fatally hampered by the Japanese propaganda machine and the wholesale destruction of Korean historical artifacts.

Dr. Boots was an American dentist and Korean traditional weapons enthusiast who traveled to Korea and joined the Korean branch of the Royal Asiatic Society in Seoul. A collector of Korean traditional weapons, he acquired the contacts he needed among the Japanese. These contacts made him one of the first Westerners journeying to the Far East, as it emerged from thousands of years of seclusion, to have access to Korean, as well as Japanese martial arts history-or rather, the officially approved Japanese version of it. Because Japan's economic progressiveness more closely paralleled the Western approach to development than the point of view of the debilitated and reclusive Koreans, many influential Americans accepted Japan's concept of Korea and the Japanese rationalization for their occupation.

There is no apparent attempt in Boots' research to verify many purported facts that incorrectly relegate Koreans to the status of second-rate warriors. I believe that Boots had no choice but to credit the Japanese or lose the privilege of being there. Nevertheless, his descriptions of weapons and places are an invaluable resource for the study of Korean traditional weaponry. Both the misperceptions he acquired under Japanese influence and the photographs from his superb collection help us understand the impact of Japanese propaganda on both the younger generation of Koreans in his time and later students of Korean martial history.

In his Introduction, Boots begins with an example of the attitude nurtured for decades by the Japanese towards Korean martial fitness. He said that the story of Korean arms was "a tragedy," and their development "a story of a people driven in desperation to a task for which they had no heart." He also noted that Koreans were "forced to learn an art for which they had no natural aptitude. It is the story of a people who repeatedly had to lay down their honored pen and brush to defend their lands and their homes against those who loved the sword."

Boots' experience of the early 20th century Koreans was only as subjugated people. For more than a generation they had been controlled by the Japanese and prior to that, were in a decline prompted to a large extent by the pacifistic Confucian ideals which infused the ruling class. During Boots' time of collecting weapons and information in Korea, the Japanese had done their best to reinforce this perception among both young Koreans and foreigners by blocking access to information that contradicted their propaganda. The erasure of a Korean national identity was the top priority of Japanese occupational forces. It is understandable that his valuable research into what remained of Korean weaponry was colored by intensive and effective propaganda, especially since even the majority of Koreans had come to believe that propaganda. The Japanese viewpoint, however, requires us to accept that the hardy Korean tribesmen and peasants never existed, that its warrior-kings and its great heroes actually found swordplay repugnant, and that 5,000 years of Korean history was focused on calligraphy and poetry readings. A people hardly need to own the appetite for conquest that, for example, the Mongols had, to maintain an avid interest in their own traditions of self-defense. Actually, one needs to research such a discrepancy with reality no further than to observe the large number of modern Korean youth practicing martial arts today.

First, the Korean Confucians, and then the Japanese for their own, but different, interests, wanted to create the impression that the militaristic spirit of the Koreans didn't exist. Westerners eager to trade with Japan were required to accept the deception or subscribe to an inconvenient conflict. Moreover, Westerners during this period did not have any way of learning the facts from a wary and withdrawn population under house arrest.

It is also very telling that Boots chose for the frontpiece photo of his eventually published work on Korean weaponry not one of the scores of indigenous Korean weapons he discussed and owned, but a *Japanese* gun. The frontispiece was photographed in Tokyo during the Korean occupation with the permission of the Kudan Military Museum and was captioned, "All Korean matchlocks were patterned after this gun." Thus, the propagandized fiction of Koreans' disinterest in originating their own means of self-defense was again reinforced and passed on to an unknowing public who had no access to the facts. (Boots could have added, but didn't, to his matchlock photo caption that the Japanese guns were actually copied by the Japanese from the Portuguese firearms introduced to the islands.)

Despite repeating newly minted myths, Boots' Introduction provides verification of the Japanese program to obliterate as much of Korea's martial past as possible. "Museums contain surprisingly few pieces," he said, "to tell the story to posterity." He reported that in the Prince Yi Museum in Seoul, there were only two or three guns, half a dozen swords, and two suits of armor on display. In the Government General Museum at this time there were "some prehistoric stone and bronze relics, and in the storerooms there are some tens of guns, cannon, bows, spears, and swords."

Boots found a notation in a book he had read on Korean weaponry that a large collection of "military antiques" had been taken back to Japan by Hideyoshi's officers in the late 1590s, and were in the possession of the Imperial household. Unfortunately when he made a trip to

Japan, he found that "the entire lot had been destroyed in the great earthquake of 1923." Once again we see the difficulty in gathering information about Korean weapons and armor, even prior to the destruction which took place in the two wars after Boots was forced to flee Korea to escape from the Japanese.

Boots also mentions in his Introduction the great difficulty in obtaining information on Korean arms. "There remain living today only a very few Koreans who have intimate knowledge of the old military things. None of them are writing their memoirs and soon they will be gone." This statement illustrates the circumstances found in Korea at the end of World War II, when Koreans who held onto the knowledge of an indigenous Korean system were few and often secluded, and teachers of Japanese martial arts were the only approved instructors. This situation began the amalgamation of Japanese martial arts with the remaining fragments of the Korean systems still in general circulation.

The Legacy of Korean Weaponry

KOREAN IRON WEAPONS

Boots noted in his book's section on prehistoric weapons that arrowheads of bone and deer horn, together with iron knives having bone or horn handles, were found in tombs near Fusan (Pusan) in the south. They were also found in Yuki in the northeast, far from Chinese influence and dating from the later Stone Age. While the Chinese were developing bronze, Korea was using iron obtained, he was told by a Prof. Torii, from Tungusic sources in eastern Siberia. Actually they didn't have to travel that far. Rich iron ore deposits were known to exist in Korea itself and, as has been previously mentioned, the Kaya people in southern Korea were actively involved in iron technology in the first century B.C.

BOW AND ARROWS

Since ancient times, Koreans have been identified with archery, inventing the compound reflex bow. In the old books of China, the people of Korea were referred to by the use of a character incorporating "great" and the character for "bow." Skill with the great bow was so characteristic of the early Koreans that the Chinese used the word to refer to them and, later, all foreigners or "barbarians" as the word came to be translated.

Boots noted that through the ages, "the Koreans perpetuated the use of the bow and arrow alone, in peace times, as a sport and personal accomplishment, until at the close of the last dynasty it still stood gallantly beside imported muskets, honored and revered. It was the one military practice in which Korean boys longed to become proficient. The one token of martial skill which ever held its own among a people who for thousands of years have preferred silks, pictures, poems and music, the stately crane in the paddy fields, and the gnarled pine on the mountain side."

Since this romantic portrait of an astonishingly serene people was painted for him in Annexed Korea under tight Japanese tutelage and censorship, we can understand why he developed this vision. However, as we can see from the records of prior centuries, the sword, moon knife, and battle ax also were held in high esteem for scores of generations—first in battle, secondarily in competitions, and as the ultimate honorary gift, encrusted with jewels and presented by kings.

The Korean bow was made of mulberry wood, bamboo, water buffalo horn, and cow sinew. Shorter than the Japanese bow, it was about 4' (1.2 m) in height and took greater care to string, to shoot, and to maintain than the simple "self" bows of other nations. However, the result was a bow that could shoot 500 yards (457.2 m), according to an archery book published in the late 1920s by an archery association in Korean and quoted by Boots. It stated that in the records of Silla, armies were named for the bow, and in a ranking of 17 top Silla officials, the bow maker was number eight. When the emperor of the Tang dynasty requested a Korean bow maker to go to China in 669 A.D. and teach the secrets of Korean archery, according to this unnamed book, he would only show them the techniques necessary to achieve a distance of 150' (45.7 m). Although he sent back for different bow materials, he would not demonstrate an arrow carrying more than 300' (91.4 m) and evaded giving any information to China on the secrets of Korean archery. This is a simplified account of a story still told today. Again, it points to the fact that Korean warriors maintained the uniqueness of their martial skills because they were held secret, just like other martial traditions.

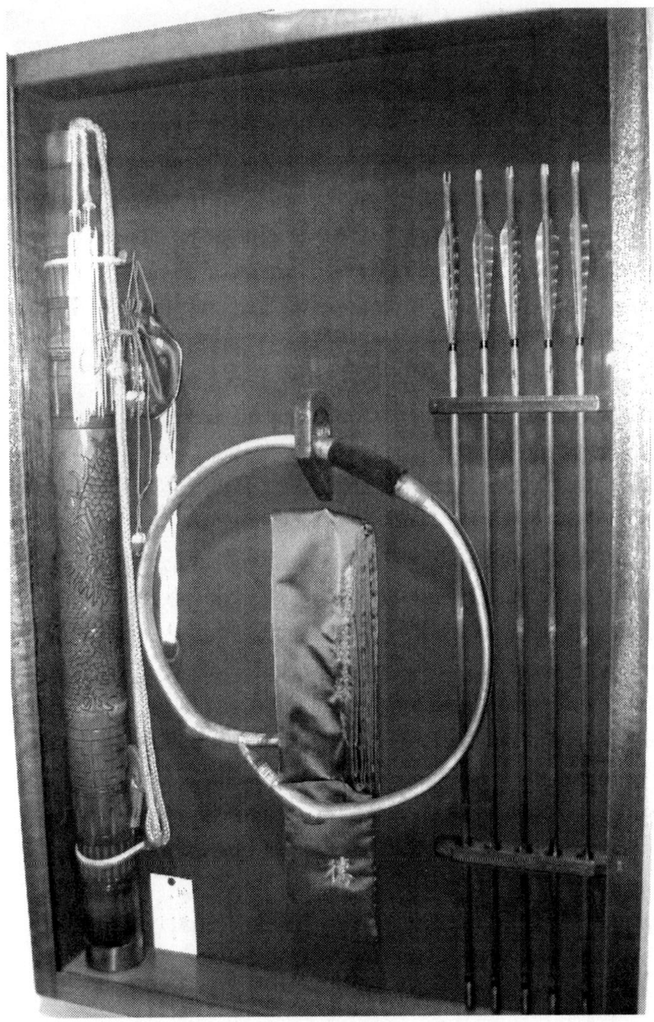

This horn bow was made by one of the "Living National Treasures of Korea" and is in the author's collection. The maker has since passed away. The bow is in the unstrung position. It has five bamboo arrows, a horn thumb ring, a silk bow case and a decorative arrow quiver made of wood.

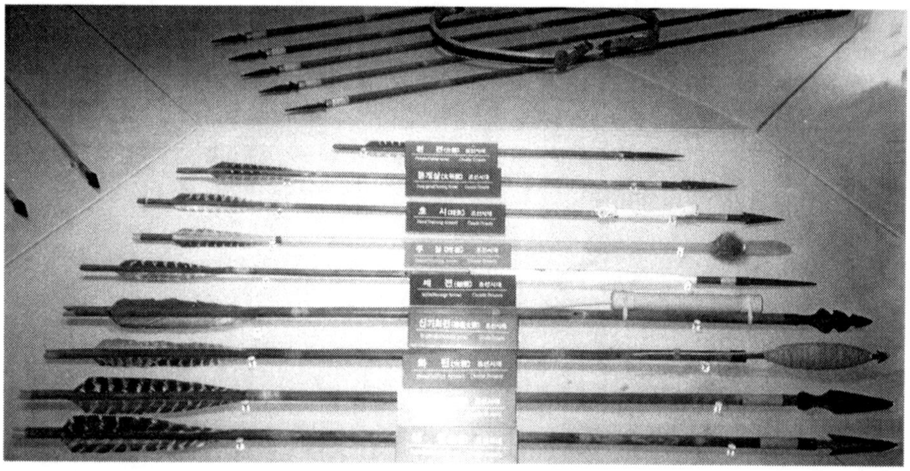

Pictured are battlefield arrows that have different tips including explosive and incendiary tips.

Records also show that the Japanese with their long bows could send an arrow only 350 yards (320 m), as compared with another Korean bow from the time of the Hideyoshi Japanese invasion which carried 500 yards (457.2 m). Said Boots, "I quote this from a Japanese authority and mention it especially as one of the few things [sic] in which the Korean arm was superior to the arm of his adversary." The standard American target distances are from 40-100 yards (36.6-91.4 m); Japanese, 30 yards (27.4 m), and Korean, 173 yards 158.2 m).

The *common short bow* was used in three ways, and shot three different arrows. The cross bow or box bow was held horizontally and shot a short 11x5/16" arrow with a 3/4-inch (.75 m) head, without feathering. Made of mulberry, it was faced with cow sinew and wrapped with sinew thread painted black. Its purpose was not pinpoint accuracy but to lay down a quick barrage against closely advancing troops.

The *ordinary bow,* shot in the standard way, had a long arrow (34x3/8") with a 2" (5.1 cm) flattened iron head and three-bladed 6-1/4" (15.9 cm) feather.

The third type was distinguished by a grooved stick or barrel held by a string tied to the third finger of the hand holding the bow-string. A middle-sized arrow, 18" and slightly over 1/4" thick (45.7x6,35 mm), with a 1-1/3" (33.9 mm) head and 3-bladed, 7" (17.8 cm) feathering was used with this bow and sped out of the grooved stick. The purpose of the grooved stick was to provide a rest for the short, light arrow which is less than half the length of the distance from the bow to the pulled string. An officer of the old Korean army, quoted by Boots, explained that "the grooved stick can be seen by the enemy who thinks that the arrow has not yet been released, so that he continues to watch the bowman when, suddenly, the arrow coming unseen from the sky pierces him." The arrows for the bow were frequently poisoned with sap from a certain tree, taken in the autumn.

Arrows were of similar construction, with a bamboo shaft and an iron head that extended into the hollow of the shaft and was bound with black thread. The butt of the shaft was made from locust wood and was notched to receive the cord. It was set into the bamboo joint and bound with black thread. None of the arrows were varnished or lacquered, as were the Japanese arrows. The three vanes were made from the three end-wing feathers of a pheasant.

The whistling arrow, also known as the "devil arrow," was thought to have originated, according to Boots, in what is now Mongolia. The remains of a devil arrow made of bone were found in a Sillan tomb near Kyung Ju. He noted that a similar arrow came "through Korea" to

This picture show's a man being instructed in the shooting of the bow, another stringing (bracing) and shaping the bow and a man straightening arrows.

Japan. Actually, Mongolia did not exist at the time the Sillan tombs were built. Then, what were to become Mongolia and Manchuria was part of the Korean Koguryo kingdom; however, no definitive information is available concerning this.

Bows were customarily wrapped with willow bark because it is water resistant; the southern countries were always wet. While unstrung, they were bent backward to the full reverse curve of their drawn position, in contrast to the unstrung Japanese bow, which becomes almost straight.

After explaining the differences between the unique way the Japanese and Afghanis held their bows, Boots added, "The Koreans did not copy this nor any other feature of Japanese archery."

Korean quivers were of either open or closed design. The open quivers were made of black lacquered leather with metal mountings and came in two pieces. One piece held the arrows and the other held the bow. Open quivers were used especially in parade. The second or closed form was a long tube of carved bamboo, lacquered wood, or wood covered with sharkskin, with a hinged lid of wood carved into the typical war dog/dragon face. All had well-designed brass mountings, with the lid fastened by a brass lock of turtle design. They were carried by a sash cord held by two loops of dragon or fancy plum blossom design glued to the side of the quiver. They probably weren't used in battle. The arrows carried by Korean soldiers in combat were merely tied by interlacing cords into small bundles. A wild boar's tusk with a brass loop for hanging from the belt was pierced through by two holes and lined with brass eyelets. It was used as an arrow point straightener. The archer thrust the bent point of a used arrow into the hole and, holding the tusk in one hand, by levering the arrow shaft with the other, straightened the point for use again.

In *Muyedobo T'ongji*, the early illustrated martial art manual, a picturesque description is given for the shooting of the bow, indicating the visualization to be applied to facilitate the action:

The front hand goes forward like pushing over a big mountain and the rear hand is like pulling the tiger's tail. Pulling the bow in this way, there is strong power to send the arrow.

SWORDS

Koreans had knives and swords, as discussed earlier, that date back as early as any of China's, and were not a by-product of Chinese invention, as is often believed and advertised. Boots had a fine collection of traditional Korean weapons, perhaps the best in the world. According to his family most were confiscated or destroyed at the onset of World War II when the Japanese drove out or imprisoned all foreigners in Korea. Although his children do not know the whereabouts of his swords, they donated one tasseled sword to Yonsei University in Seoul during the 1990's.

These are the swords from Dr. Boots personal collection.

The best Korean sword seen by Boots, and in his collection, had a large double-edged blade 3'4" (1 m) long and two inches (5.08 cm) wide, weighing 5-3/4 pounds. For comparison an American Civil War saber weighs 1-3/4 pounds. On the 10" (25.43 cm) handle was an elaborate inlaid silver design with Asian characters and a heavy hilt of lotus leaf design, vertically placed. As discussed before, from the Asian inscription we shouldn't infer that there is anything intrinsically Chinese about the Korean sword itself. At that time when anyone wanted to write in a formal manner, an Asian iconography now identified as Chinese was used.

The characters were inlaid with gold on one side of the blade. On the other side, also in gold, was the constellation of the Great Bear with two added stars which, with one in the handle of the dipper, the Koreans call the "Three Tiger Stars." This indicates great good fortune in military things on the day of the lunar calendar when the "Tiger Day" comes on the "Tiger Month" of the "Tiger Year." This sword, Boots was told, was of a design given by the king to a favorite officer of his personal bodyguard and was worn slung across the back by this mounted officer. This particular piece was ordered to be made on this propitious day in the 18th year of 1794. The scabbard was made of wood covered with black lacquer with a copper cap.

The more common Korean swords were curved blades with scabbards of shagreen-covered wood. They had horizontal guards of either iron or brass. Some were quite simple in scabbards covered with coarse cloth or black lacquered leather. There were also short heavy swords for close fighting. Two in Boot's collection were each 23" (58.4 cm) in length, one well-made with grooved blade and lotus-leaf, vertical, brass hilt in a fish-skin scabbard. The second was made of one piece of iron, blade and handle complete, with the characteristic 12-sided knob for a guard. The dress parade swords for officers were 2' (61 cm) long with a hilt and scabbard of bamboo with foliated carvings of the ten emblems of long life. They were mounted with white metal fittings and a horizontal metal bound guard of bamboo. These were similar to the one in the Korean collection in the Smithsonian Institute.

In one source cited by Boots, the author made the preposterous statement that "the sword has been used in Korea since the Japanese came to fight the Chinese." As we have seen, this

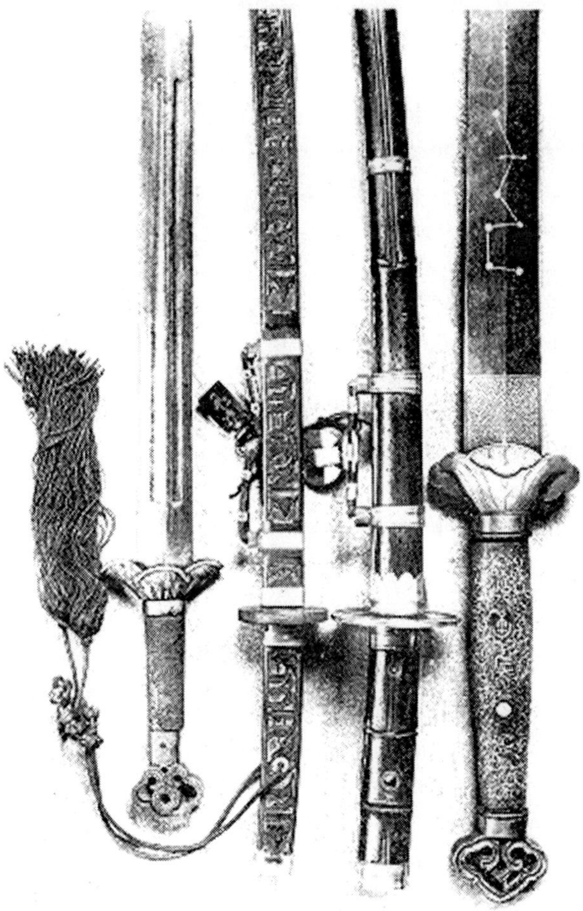

This picture shows four different swords in Dr Boots' collection. It also shows a close up of the "Three Tiger Stars" located on the blade of the big double edge sword.

was far from the case but characteristic of the Japanese propaganda designed to demoralize Koreans and destroy their culture.

One weapon whose history avoided rewriting by the Japanese indoctrination machine was the flail. The flail probably escaped the revisionists because it was not considered as prestigious as other weapons. When Boots reviewed the Korean flails, he not only correctly identified them as Korea's own weapon but found that the Chinese obtained their first flails from Korea, an unusual piece of information to be intact in Boot's era.

Korea's *koong joong mu sool* (royal court martial art) had 24 different weapons. Some gained more popularity and use than others. Among perennial favorites was the sword. Although the sword had roots in *sado mu sool*, (tribal or clan martial arts) military blades were unique in their own right. (Suh and Hallander, 1988)

Koong joong mu sool swords were made in all shapes and sizes but there were basically seven types. Korean Admiral Yi Sun-sin was known for his 2.9 meter sword, which only the strongest could wield. The most common sword was called *san-soo-do*, measuring 129 cm (4.2') in length. The cutting length was 99 cm (3.2 ft) and its handle was 30 cm (11.8 in) long. Many of the contemporary practice swords of the martial art *Kuk Sool Won* are based on it. They had straight or slightly curved single-edged blades and were designed to be held easily with one or two hands.

Double or twin swords were named s*sang gum* in reference to the use of two matched blades. Smaller versions were called *dahn ssang gum* but were larger than daggers. Dahn gum (twin short swords) were popular within Korea's royal palace and court because they could be easily concealed. Some soldiers in ancient Korea preferred the *ah-do* to the *san-soo-do* or s*sang gum*. It had a groove that ran down the length of the blade which could reduce the weight of the sword without sacrificing the strength of the blade. This was a heavy sword with a blade 100 cm (3.3') in length. The blade was sharpened on both sides a few centimeters at the tip, then along the cutting side to the handle which measured 33 cm (13").

Another popular military blade was the *hyup-do,* a heavy, long sword with a curved blade. It was a single edge sword used only by the strongest men. One of the most famous *koong joong mu sool* swords was the *bon kuk gum*. Although it is said to have originated in the Ko Chosun period, it earned its fame during the Silla Kingdom. It was an average sized 80-110 cm (2.6246 – 3.6089 ft), single edged, and slightly curved sword that weighed between 600 and 1,000 grams. It strongly resembles the swords used for training by today's Kuk Sool Won martial artist.

The *yoh-do* had a long, 90 cm (3') handle and a 100 cm (3.3') slightly curved blade. Its long handle gave it the leverage to cut through almost anything.

SPEARS

The "long spear" was a straight, simple blade of steel. It was double edged, sometimes grooved, and sometimes had a decorative lotus leaf guard attached to a long heavy stick with a pointed metal butt. Boots quotes the *Muyedobo T'ongji*'s evocative description of the frame of mind the warrior should employ in using this weapon, along with the nature of each of its moves:

First, visualize [yourself as] a big mountain crushing small eggs. Second, change to an attitude of ease like that of a woman sewing. Third, turn the spear over like an iron fishing pole.

Fourth, pull it back. On all sides, every man will appear to be [submitting]. Fifth, assume the manner of letting it fall into the water. Sixth, with the appearance of the needle that points to the south [compass], with one foot in front of the other, drop it as if to let it fall into the water. Take the second step forward. Seventh, take the position of an iron cow plowing the ground... [etc.]

With these metaphors, the soldier could more easily visualize himself as an extension of his weapon. This flowery language also acted as a code. Those who did not know the exact meaning would not be able to translate it into correct movement. Therefore, martial art secrets were more easily kept because of the difficulty of correctly translating these descriptive movements.

Proceedings XI, Part II, of the Asiatic Society of Japan, describing the North Palace in Seoul in March, 1882, noted that "Chinese-trained Korean soldiers armed with Lafaucheux muzzle-loading rifles" also carried "broad lances," indicating to Boots "that the long spear evidently held its place as a practical weapon to the end of the last dynasty."

TRIDENT

This form of spear was commonly seen in photos and was often used as a symbol in dancing and in parades, as well as in actual fighting. Historical record indicates that its use was pervasive and familiar among Korean weaponry. It had three straight prongs and differed markedly from the Chinese weapon with its outward-curving prongs. However, Boots still indicates that "the weapon itself was without doubt copied from those of the Chinese soldiers." That he uses the phrase *without doubt* in itself indicates that this is supposition. He does not cite any source to indicate that the Chinese originated the trident, a weapon found all over the world, or that the Koreans did not develop their own trident in their ancient insular past. It was the requirement of the Japanese in the Korea of Boots', to attribute everything Korean that was admirable to Japanese or Chinese precedent.

Warriors were advised by the *Muyedobo T'ongji* to visualize the following in regard to the trident:

First, point to the heavens. Second, put it level and thrust it forward as you take a step. Third, take one step forward and assume the manner of riding a dragon. Thrust it forward, then step backward and make the appearance of a crouching tiger. Repeat that four times, then take the attitude of riding the dragon again.

Fourth, with one step forward, pull the spear tightly. Fifth, make the appearance of marching, hold the spear level and thrust, then advance one step... [etc.]

RECLINING MOON SPEAR (MOON KNIFE)

As Boots noted, this is probably the most unique and typical of all Korean cutting arms. It was often seen in Korean military and hunting pictures, and frequently was used as an emblem in military parade. We have shown evidence that this weapon was carried in the 11th-12th centuries by generals. It was considered a general's weapon and was presented by kings in ceremonial form to distinguished generals. Yet Boots was given the information that it was only used in parades, and that "the Korean soldier apparently did not like the battle ax," as the Japanese called it. Even more curious is his repetition of an unidentified person's observation that "these reclining moon knives in Korea are thin like the leaf of a tree, but in China they are heavy and fearful things." This contradicts a previous statement that the Koreans made them in various thickness and weights, and used them "as a beheading knife for the execution of criminals until after the opening of the country to Westerners."

Even when faced with the fact that Korea's deep involvement in the martial arts extended over centuries, we find a number of students of martial history more inclined to accept the status quo than rethink 20th century Japanese propaganda. Boots was greatly influenced by both the Japanese and their indoctrinated Korean captives. For example he said, "There is little mention of [the moon knife] in Korean writings," most likely because so many wars had destroyed so many books. However, those that do exist point clearly to the efficacy and status of the moon knife in Korean history.

The *chun yong whule-do* (heavenly dragon moon knife) was a thick-bladed weapon with a staff-like handle believed to be originally designed for use from horseback. It was from the Ko Chosun period (233-108 B.C.) and first became popular in Koguryo. A legend tells that its name was chosen when a Ko Chosun general was looking into a lake meditating and saw the reflection of a shooting star and the moon. The shooting star is thought to be a heavenly dragon. The general interpreted the shooting star as a sign of good luck in the construction of a special weapon. The shape of the half moon reflected in the lake became an omen that dictated the shape of the blade. This is the Korean legend about the creation of the heavenly dragon moon knife and how it was a noble weapon from its creation.

As its staff was well over 6' (1.8 m), it was an ideal mounted warrior's weapon that kept enemy soldiers at a safe distance from the mounted general and his horse. Excellent balance was obtained from a heavy staff end that offset an equally heavy blade. With such a well-balanced weapon, a mounted soldier could ride full-speed through enemy ranks, cutting with his moon knife from side to side in a figure-eight pattern without falling.

Eventually the moon knife left the ranks of exclusive use by generals and became a weapon of the average soldier. Some latter-day Korean armies utilized the long-handled weapon to bring down enemy cavalry by cutting its horses' legs. As a foot soldier's weapon, it was excellent for wading through cavalry. As with most weapons the weight and length could be varied according to usage.

Artist depiction of the Korean legend concerning the founding of the moon knife.

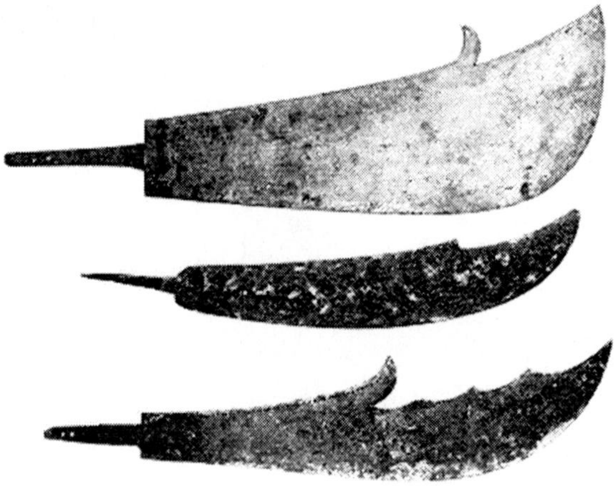

Plate 19->

<- Plate 18

These are pictures of Korean moon knife blades and cross spear heads that were in Dr. Boots' private collection.

CROSS SPEAR

The cross-bladed spear was used to dismount a man on the pull stroke, in addition to serving as a thrusting weapon. Boots said this spear was the favorite weapon of the Japanese general Kato, sent by Hideyoshi to conquer Korea in the late 1500s. Boots comments that the Korean pieces were "shorter than the Japanese and the steel of much poorer quality," copied, he heard, although without documentation, from the weapons carried by Kato's men. As Korea was overwhelmingly the victor in this war with the Japanese, it does not seem likely that they would adopt a weapon that obviously did not serve their opponent well, whereas their own famous head-severing swords were more than adequate for sending home what remained of the Japanese forces. Regardless, we know by Boots' statement, that very few Korean weapons from centuries past survived even to his day. Drawing conclusions from these specimens which favored the prevailing teachings of the occupying Japanese might be a mistake. We may even speculate that poor villagers created from available material the surviving specimen he cites as poor quality, or that it was made in the capital during a time of economic duress.

As we've noted from cited references, Korea probably influenced China and Japan particularly during the centuries its kingdoms spread over what is now Manchuria and Mongolia as much as the other way around. There can be little doubt that Korea, Japan, and China influenced and were influenced by one another. The whole of human history is replete with examples of cultural exchange between countries at war and at peace. I am simply pointing out that Korea influenced both China and Japan throughout her history.

ARMOR

Archaeological evidence suggests that iron technology was developed in southern Korea by the first century B.C. "at the latest." (Pak, 1995) The Kaya people were famous for what Harvard scholar Yangjin Pak called their high technology and the manufacture of iron products which they exported not only to neighboring societies in the Korean peninsula and the Japanese islands, but also to China.

Armor found in a burial mound that dates from the kingdom of Kaya.

Iron armor has been found in the burial mounds of political and military leaders of Kaya, dated between 450 A.D. and 550 A.D. One of the earliest sets of iron armor found in southern Korea is from a tomb in Kyongju, which was Silla's capital. Sometimes called a cuirass, it was designed to cover the torso and is made of rectangular vertical iron strips bound together with leather thongs. It is dated to the late third century or early fourth century.

In the mid-fourth century, a new method was adopted to assemble iron plates for body armor. This armor used iron rivets to bind together long, vertical iron strips. It was also during this period that another type of body armor, lamellar armor, appeared among the Kaya elite. It was more flexible than the cuirass and usually consisted of hundreds of small iron plates with about a dozen holes around the edges and bound together without any backing. Cuirasses made of vertical iron strips were continuously used in the fifth century. Some of these were made of triangular iron pieces that were riveted together. Others were constructed of horizontal iron strips bound with rivets. This horizontal plate body armor was popular during the fifth and sixth centuries.

In addition to body armor, iron helmets, cheek guards, neck guards, and arm guards have been found in many tombs of Kaya, together with horse armor. "The recent discovery of this archaeological evidence," says Yangjin Pak, "clearly presents a new picture of the Kaya elite: a warrior mounted on a horse, both clad in shining silvery iron armor."

Other burial goods included many different types of weapons: swords, battle axes, spearheads, arrowheads, and quivers. "These weapons," Pak notes, "once again demonstrate the importance of warfare among the Kaya nobility."

In the development of iron armor in Kaya, the influence of the northern states, and especially of Koguryo, is obvious. Although actual examples of Koguryo armor are almost nonexistent, the wall paintings of Koguryo tombs clearly provide the evidence of their contribution to the development of cavalry armor in Kaya society.

Pak says the iron riveting technique as a binding method was introduced along with the lamellar armor from the Korean peninsula to Japan during the mid-fifth century, and together with other items of Korean origin such as horse trappings and Sueki stoneware pottery. Japanese tombs of the Kofun period (310-710) A.D. have produced iron body armor and helmets, some of which might have been imported from Korea.

Due to a shortage of surviving evidence, it is very difficult to corroborate or dispute some of the statements made regarding Korean armor by pro-Japanese sources, who themselves did not cite references. However, considering the tremendous influence Korea had on the development of earlier Japanese culture, it is at least equally reasonable to assume imitation happened on the part of the Japanese who imported many Korean ideas and artisans to their shores. In the mid-seventh century, the Korean fortress of Liao-tung likely fell only because of the exceptional armor of its Korean enemies of Paekche who had allied themselves with the Chinese. Said historian Hulbert: "In this battle, the Chinese were materially aided by armor which Pak-je (che) had sent as a gift to the Chinese emperor." (Hulbert, 1962) It is likely that over time the armor from Pak-je came to be known as Chinese helping to propagate the idea that all armor came from China or Japan.

As mentioned previously, the *Samguk Yusa* does indicate the Korean use of steel armor came quite early. In a legend from King Hyegong's reign (765-780) steel armor is clearly identified as being worn by the honor guard of a famous general.

Boots does say the more flexible type of metal armor plates mutually lashed together in regular rows was continually undergoing development in Korea. He notes that the Koreans never copied the elaborate and intricate armor of the Japanese at Hideyoshi's time nor did they follow the typical Chinese design of separate upper and lower garments. The only armor known by him was one model: a square-cut, knee-length tunic with short sleeves opening in front and on the sides and fastened with buttons of bone and loops of leather, edge to edge. There were three separate types of this design, all simple. He says they remained in use "without change up until the end of the last dynasty."

Examples, he says, of that very early leather cuirass, and of that "strange and interesting suit of 15 to 20 thickness of paper sewn together, unfortunately do not remain." He notes that Korean paper was highly prized by the Chinese for use in making armor and says that the records of Silla state clearly that Korean armor was the same as Chinese. Or, perhaps, more correctly, Chinese armor was the same as Korean. He quotes a turn-of-the-century author of books on Korea, William Rlliot Griffis, as saying that this paper armor was capable of resisting a musket ball, but not a rifle bullet.

In Boots' own collection he had a suit of coarse hemp cloth lined with blue cotton and covered on the outside with a formal flower design printed with wood blocks. On the inside of the front and the back there were *cuir bouilli* plates 2-3/4x 3-3/4" (2.6x3.8 cm). Each plate was the same size in eight even rows, fastened by two iron rivets. The rounded heads of the rivets served as a decoration on the outside. On the inside, the rivets were hammered over a rough hand-cut washer. The plates overlapped from above, downward, and from right to left. The rivets pierced the center of the plates, one at the top and one about halfway down, except those of the rows where the garment opens, which are riveted only at the edge. On the outside was an *epauliere* of heavy iron, hinged in three sections, below was a group of ten half-sized plates in two rows protecting the front of the shoulder. The open round neck was finished with white leather sewn with coarse thread.

The casque accompanying this coat was of conical shape, of two iron plates riveted together and banded on the outside. A visor of iron decorated with silver inlay was riveted on, and below it was another piece of iron to protect the forehead. Ear protectors and *couvrenuque* of the same material as the coat and filled with smaller leather plates were riveted to the bottom of the helmet. They hung loose, to be tied with strings of the hemp cloth. The helmet was surmounted by an iron cap, which held an iron trident and a tuft of red horsehair.

Boots described two other kinds of armor, one with padded cotton and without plate, "no doubt worn in cold weather, the pseudo-armor of an officer," and a vest of flexible mail made of a combination of small iron plates and iron rings. Griffis said this was worn by the foot soldiers, but, according to Boots, "Korean authorities" said that all armor was worn by officers and mounted troops and none by foot soldiers. He quotes the historian Laufer as saying the elegant metal plate mail of the Tang era "was preceded by those of coarser and cruder workmanship, as we see, for instance, in the Korean specimen." However, he says, modern Korean historians of his time insisted that this type of armor was designed during the early years of the Yi dynasty under Yunsankun, "100 years before Hideyoshi." (It should be noted that, symptomatic of the circumstances of the times, Boots consistently used Japanese historical dates as focal points for identifying Korean events.) In the book *The Five Ceremonies*, he says there are good descriptions of Korean armor of this period:

Mercury armor. Made of iron plates woven together with leather thongs and painted silver white with mercury.

Willow leaf armor. Made of raw pig skin pieces in place of iron plates, painted black.

Paper armor. Made of twisted paper strings painted black.

Iron ring armor. Of small iron rings linked together.

Mirror flag armor. Made of iron plates and rings woven in alternating series.

Iron studded armor. With iron plates, studded like stars on a blue cloth, or on a red cloth. The red suit had separate sleeves tied with a cord. The sleeves were copper studded. The coat was lined with deer skin and had a wide red belt.

Boots reported one reference has been found in "some old unofficial writing" concerning a bamboo armor used by Korean soldiers.

There is an interesting note in Boots' presentation regarding the Chinese opinion of Korean armor when they came to assist the Koreans against Hideyoshi's men in 1594. They complained about its clumsiness and inefficiency. Yet the Koreans, supposedly always eager, according to their detractors, to copy anything and everything foreign, resolutely held to the same design for 400 years, "on down to the end of the era, giving us some idea of the qualities which made for their independence and their ability to adapt only whatever they thought best for the style of fighting which they had found efficacious for themselves." There were also two kinds of iron helmets: one with a brim, one without.

According to Boots, nothing is known of Korean shields prior to the Yi dynasty, but those used were "probably of Chinese type." Two distinct shapes are illustrated in *The Five Ceremonies.* At Boots' time, there were a few specimens preserved in collections. One was round and made of reeds. "The only one of this type I can find is in the Prince Yi Museum in Seoul."

The other type was rectangular, of heavy horse hide, fastened with large iron rivets to a willow board. On the front surface is an elaborate war dog (sometimes called "lion") design, painted in bright colors. The shield was held from the back by the soldier's hand passing through a rope loop and grasping an iron handle. "I think there are only four of these remaining," said Boots, "and all are exactly alike." Many years later, Boots' son auctioned his father's shield of this type at the New York auction house of Sotheby's.

A variety of information and misinformation is available on what constituted Korean armor during various periods. One of the more impossible examples is taken from a book of foreigners' reminiscences published in the 1940s. (Keith and Scott, 1947) Even though it first describes what a soldier wore to a portrait sitting for one of the artist-authors, as "the uniform of a soldier" in the late 1880s, it immediately corrects this observation to read "The dress was actually worn at Court." It then goes on to describe what was obviously ceremonial garb, including a hat of blue plush decorated with peacock feathers and amber beads, and "clumsy soft boots." Yet the writer finishes the commentary on the inappropriate note that when the obviously venerable veteran tied a blue sash around his waist, "he was ready for battle!" This type of commentary can only be credited to a bad habit among Westerners to follow the lead of the dominant Japanese in denigrating Korean culture. (See front cover picture).

Painted hide military processional shield
19th century plate 78. Sotheby's

This shield was in the Boots collection and was sold by the auction house of Sotheby's.

CALTROP

The caltrop is a small defensive weapon that was also used in medieval European warfare. It is an iron spike with four prongs, simply made and shaped in such a way that, however thrown, the piece would land with three prongs as a base and the fourth pointing upward. It was small, about 2" (5.1 cm) from point to point, and large quantities of them were thrown on the roadways to slow cavalry attacks, protect retreats or help defend the walls of fortresses from attack.

It may or may not have been imported from China where "it is thought to have been invented." The historian Werner traced its use back as far as the Han Emperor Wen Ti (B.C. 179-156). It is just as possible that this weapon could have been in use or invented in Old Cho-son. It was not so complicated that a creative mind anywhere with the materials and skill for its manufacture at hand, could not have originated a version of this simple roadway booby-trap. However, credit even for this small object has been given, by some, exclusively to the Chinese or Japanese Ninja.

The name used by Boots is Caltrops.
This picture of Caltrops is from Boots' collection.

The Muyedobo T'ongji: Manual of Ancient Korean Martial Arts

The *Muyedobo T'ongji* is a highly treasured artifact for students of Korean martial arts. It was compiled at the request of King Chongjo (or Yong Jo, r. 1776-1800), beginning in 1789, the 13th year of his reign, and completed in four volumes by the summer of 1790. Authors of the *Muyedobo T'ongji* or *Illustrated Overview of the Martial Arts* were Yi Tok-mu (1741-1793), former bioliographical official of the royal library and archives (the Kyujanggak); Pak Che-ga (1750-1805), military officer and bibliographical official at Kyujanggak; and Paek Tong-su, garrison officer. Yi's assignment was to survey esoteric books of ancient times. Pak was ordered to edit and compile the findings of the research, and Paek was in charge of experimenting with the findings. Paek arranged performances and demonstrations by officers and soldiers of the garrison to verify practical accuracy and resolve any discrepancies. Later, during the reign of Chongjo, a book of captions for illustrations of the martial arts was published.

The idea for this book began in 1592 with a Ming military manual, the *Jixiao Xinshu* (also *Ki Hyo Shin So*) or *Complete Martial Arts Manual* by General Qi Ji-guang (also Chok Kye-Kwang). This book was discovered by King Songjo when he asked Ming Army Commander Li Ru-song how he engineered the defeat of the Japanese army at P'yongyang. Li replied that this manual guided his victory. But when King Songjo asked to look at the book, Li declined on the grounds of military secrecy. King Songjo responded with a covert mission to the Ming camp to purchase the manual. He selected a committee to compile the volume in Han'gul. He appointed Regional Army Captain Han Kyo and a soldier, Yu Song-nyong, to study the book and revisit the camp of the Ming to clarify puzzling points with the officers who had participated in the war against the Hideyoshi invasions of 1592. Han Kyo edited the result of their study of the six techniques (weapons) called the *Muyejebo (Various Annotations on Martial Arts),* after analyzing with General Xu Guo-wei the use of the spearheaded cudgel, wisteria shield, thorny spear, long spear, three-pronged spear, and two-handed long sword.

During King Hyo Jong's reign, all the previous martial techniques were reviewed and revised. The most effective techniques for striking and stabbing were clarified and agreed upon and the scope of group training was widened. However, the specific weapons techniques were not expanded from those six listed above.

In Chongjo's reign, another illustrated manual was published with 12 more techniques (weapons) added, including the long bamboo spear. Combining these twelve with the original six weapons, a course was given in which all of these were taught.

The term *Ship Pal Ki,* used for 18 specific techniques, originated at this time in accordance with the wishes of Chongjo's minister, Hyon Ruyung Won. Following this, the six styles of equestrian technique began to flourish again. This included using various weapons from horseback and special riding skills. These six techniques were added to the previous 18 techniques and now totaled 24 techniques. They now became known as *E Ship Pal Ki* (24 techniques). Before receiving the order to train in these martial arts there were only two or three men who had mastered all 24 techniques. Gathering together all the scattered martial art manuals, they quickly corrected the mistakes in meaning, examples, and terminology. Having found the original source of all these martial traditions and refined their systems, they created a special product and in doing so they revived the excellent function of this art. They bound all of it together in one book, and that book is called *Muyedobo T'ongji.* It is not only that the methods of striking and stabbing were more accurately supplemented, but also the true explanation of the training of the royal court troops came out at this time. (Frankel, 1989)

Despite the tremendously weak military and lack of national support for martial arts during the Yi dynasty, publication of the *Muyedobo T'ongji* is strong evidence that the martial arts were still thriving during this period. It also suggests that both hand and weapons techniques were alive and well. Contemporary Han'gul translator John Frankel notes that of the 24 techniques covered in this work, only six came from the *Jixiao Xinshu*. Therefore, the other 18, in view of their lack of specific title and author, must have started not as official texts but, instead, as Korean family and religious traditions that were passed down orally and in unofficial works. Reinforcing this likelihood is the parallel in Korean art and literature in which all official works done by the nobles are titled and the writer credited. Similarly, printed traditional Korean songs, poems, plays, stories, games, art, sports, and, of course, martial arts have come from not single individuals but from families, villages, and even regions of the country.

Frankel translates King Chong-cho's introduction to the work as follows:

As for our country's military training system, the Three Brigades were in charge of the outlying areas, while the Guardian Corps were in charge of the royal courts. The most effective period of military training in the royal court began with the reign of Prince Kwang Hae [r. 1608-1623]. *However, it only covered archery and failed to consider other skills such as the spear or sword.*

The honorable King Son Cho [r. 1567-1608], having suppressed the invasion by the Japanese marauders, obtained and read a copy of Chok Kye-Kwang's Ki Hyo Shin So. *He then* sent [Regional Army Captain] *Han Kyo to the Chinese officers who had participated in the war against the Hideyoshi invasions of 1592, and having inquired completely concerning their techniques, Han Kyo made a comprehensive illustrated manual covering six techniques, including the staff. During Hyo Jong's reign, they took all the previous martial achievements, and frequently carried out revisions* [to improve them] *Therefore, as soon as the methods for striking and stabbing became better understood, the scope of group training widened somewhat. However, the specific details* [of martial technique] *did not grow from these mere six techniques. In the 25th year of King Yong Jo [1749], while Minister Sa Do Se Ja was tending to general affairs, he made another illustrated manual with an additional 12 techniques, including the long bamboo spear. Combing them with the original six techniques, he gave a course teaching all of them.*

The name Ship Pal Ki began at this time in accordance with the wishes of Sa Do Se Ja, otherwise known as Hyon Ryung Won. Following this, a formal style of martial ceremony arose. Also, because the six styles of horse-riding technique began to flourish again, the martial arts were now called 24 techniques. Before, having received the order [to train in martial arts] *there were only two or three men who had mastered all 24 techniques. Gathering together all the scattered martial arts manuals, they quickly corrected mistakes in meaning, examples, and terminology. Having found the original source of all these martial traditions and refined their systems, they created a special product, and in doing so they revived the excellent function of this art. They bound all of it together in one book, and that book is called* Muyedobo T'onji.

It is not only that the methods of striking and stabbing were more accurately supplemented but also the true explanation of the training of the royal court troops came out at this time. When the soldiers are trained in the outlying areas using the book Illustrated Explanation of the Five Outstanding Battle Arrays of Generals, *it becomes a magnet pulling together both the seeds and the cutting edge, and it is very beautiful to see these taught together. However, I've already spoken of the positioning and movements of soldiers and, after that, of horsemanship. Why is it then that in the famous* Five Teachings of the Military Families *horsemanship is taught second and troop positioning third?*

Generally, ascertaining the movements of the sun, moon and stars, they examined them for formations of a strange [i.e., particular] number. [This makes reference to the common Asian practice of divining the heavens for auspicious signs to guide actions.] *The outstanding point of their positioning technique was that they combined the end result of their astronomical investigations with the conditions of the rain and wind. However, as for colliding on the inside and attacking on the outside, out of sheer necessity the hands, feet, and weapons techniques were established as most important. For troop positioning could only be accomplished when the enemy was not present. Therefore, it would be impossible for any book on military operations not to have as its specialty close quarters striking and stabbing techniques. In all truth, as for the various techniques outlined in this book, if the soldiers guarding Seoul and the skillful martial officials practice daily the fighting strategies of the dragon and tiger, and draw their bows long, they will become skilled warriors just like the Bi Hyu* [presumed to be a group of legendary warriors]. *They will also become the faithful warriors that defend the nation. Furthermore, my original intention in expanding and publishing this book is that it will continue for one trillion years to aid in the instruction* [of martial arts] *and I truly command that it be this way.*

Summer of the Fourteenth Year of My Reign,
King Chong Cho

(Frankel, 1989)

A detailed explanation of the training of the royal court troops can be found in the book *Illustrated Explanation of the Five Outstanding Battle Arrays of Generals*. When soldiers in outlying areas applied these methods along with the recorded moves of striking and stabbing, the scope and precision of the men were impressive to watch, according to the *Muyedobo T'ongji*. The book also noted that the movements of the sun, moon, and stars, plus the weather conditions were significant in military strategy. In his *Introduction,* King Chongjo reminded his men not to forget the fighting strategies "of the dragon and the tiger," and expressed the hope that his original intention in expanding and publishing the book was that it would continue "for one trillion years" to aid in the instruction of martial arts. "...And I truly command that it be this way," he encouraged in closing.

Among the other surviving ancient Choson military classics were, *Chinsol* (*Discourse on Troop Formation*) by Ha Yun in the reign of T'aejong; *Chinsol* by Ha Kyong-bok in the reign of Sejong (1433); *Tongguk Pyonggam* (*Military Manual of Korea*) and *Kijongdobo* (*Illustrated Annotations on Novel Skills*) by Prince Suyang in the reign of Munjong; *Yoktae Pyongyo* (*Soldiers' Manuals in Succeeding Periods*) in the reign of Tanjong (1454); *Pyongjangdosol Yujang-p'yon* (*Illustrated Explanations for Soldiers and Generals*) and *Pyonggyong* (*Soldiers' Mirror*) in the reign of Sejo (1460); *Pyong-gasamsol Chuhae* (*Annotations on Three Military Theories*) by Shin Suk-chu; *Wujing Qishu Chuhae (Annotations on* Wujing Qishu) in 1462 by Shin Suk-chu; *Pyongbop Taeji* (*General Outline of Military Maneuvers*) in 1464; *Kukcho Mujongbogam*

(*Manual of National Military Rules*) in the reign of Yejong (1469); *Sok Pyongjangdosol* (*Follow-up to the Illustrated Explanations for Soldiers and Generals*) in 1749; *Changp'illam Hunyong-damnok* (*Manual for Garrison Officers*) in 1754; and *Muyeshinbo* (1759) in the reign on Yongjo. As mentioned, the later was an expansion of a book called *Muyejebo* (*Various Annotations on Martial Arts*), compiled by Han Kyo who added to the new work more skills: long bamboo spear, flag spear, sharp sword, Japanese sword, crescent sword, long handled sword, paired swords, commander's sword, native sword, fist-fighting technique, lash cudgel, etc. In the reign of Chongjo, the book was finalized with the addition of six more skills, making a total of 14. Most of these were theoretical books with no illustrations, explaining the connecting movements of battle skills.

Muyedobo T'ongji's contents included information on various types of spears in Vol. 1, various swords and daggers and the wisteria shield in Vol. 2 and 3, and fist-fighting techniques, cudgel, lash, Korean polo, equestrian skills, illustrations of military costumes, and a list of references in Vol. 4. The chapter "General Outline of Military Skills" presents a chronological history and covers changes in military organization, training in military skills, compilation of military manuals, and drills in troop formation among other topics.

The *Muyedobo T'ongji* also mentions heroes associated with the weapons and techniques it covers, including several Hwarang. Hwang Ch'ang Rang was a young citizen of Shilla noted for his precocious use of the sword. According to legend, at the age of seven he traveled to Paekje and demonstrated his sword form in the village square. The villagers felt he was amazingly bold and confident. The king of Paekje, upon hearing of his daring skill, summoned him to court and commanded the boy to display his prowess with the sword. Ch'ang Rang took advantage of this opportunity and while jumping and lunging, stabbed the king. The Paekje soldiers killed him. The people of Shilla, grieving for the fearless child, made masks to resemble his face and wore them in a sword dance to commemorate his patriotism which was reenacted for subsequent generations. The sword dance is still preformed today in Korean traditional dancing.

Hwang Ch'ang was one of the legendary Hwarang of Shilla mentioned in the text to have great competence with the Korean sword, along with other great Hwarang swordsmen it cited, such as Sool Rang, Nam Rang and Young Rang. There can be no doubt about the character of the Shilla military officers who "gathered together like clouds" and practiced "extreme loyalty and trust" among themselves, the text affirms. After their appointment based on their talents and physical attributes, it was ascertained "whether or not they were wicked or true-hearted," and they were chosen or rejected on that basis. The Original National Sword was said to have been developed due to the sacrifice of Hwang Ch'ang Rang.

It was thought, according to the authority Mo Won Ui, that an instructional manual for this sword was *found* in Korea. But, compared to statements from Tung Un of the Western region, it becomes clear that the instructional manual for the Original National Sword was *created* in Korea. A Japanese text, Sang So, says the technique came to Korea in a Chinese text.

KOREAN WEAPONS FROM THE MUYEDOBO T'ONGJI

Also referred to as the "New Sword," the ORIGINAL NATIONAL SWORD, as it was called, is a "back sword" in function, as is the so-called "Sharp Sword."

Mention of the LONG HANDLED SWORD (*hyopto*) includes interesting information as to the difference of this weapon from country to country. Its length varies slightly from Korea to China and Japan. In Korea, the tip of the sword is slightly curved upward. It has a tassel attached to its crest, a round tin plate, and the finish on the handle is in iron-work. In China, the tip of the sword is curved more upward. The tin plate is octagonal shaped with one more round-shaped tin plate beneath. A hold is made between the two tin plates and a string is put through. The ironwork at the end of the handle is round and the end was pointed with the addition of a small iron plate. The Japanese version has its tip further curved upward than the Chinese type, with no tin plate and the ironwork at the end of the handle is more slender but with a heavier finish at the end. (Kim, 1986)

The WISTERIA SHIELD (*tungp'ae*) was used with a throwing spear (javelin) and a waist-sword, and was noted as a little smaller than the Chinese version. It was made by binding thumb-size bamboo bark and wisteria, with the middle part of the shield protruding and a carving of a human face on the hand grip. The hand grip behind was made of mulberry, unlike the Chinese version.

This is a picture taken by Boots of a Korean wisteria shield that was in the Prince Yi museum during his time.

The LASH CUDGEL FOR HORSEMEN, a small lash, was made from strips of bamboo bark bound together and painted red or black. The Korean lash is relatively short and slender, with a ribbon attached at the end connecting an auxiliary lash to the main with an iron ring. The auxiliary lash is pointed with square iron leaves and nails attached, making it an effective arm for striking. The Chinese lash is long and thick, with spiral patterns on both ends, the auxiliary lash being connected with an iron chain and rings at either end. The flail was square-shaped.

Black Powder

The first black powder in Korea was made by Ch'oe Mu-son in 1377, and the General Bureau of Gunpowder Artillery was first established in that year. The creation of this agency was initiated by a Korean, Ch'oe Mu-son, who learned the procedure for preparing gunpowder from Li Yuan, a Chinese known for supplying saltpeter to the Yuan (China) army. (Chae, 1990)

Ch'oe Mu-son manufactured many kinds of firearms and gunpowder, according to *Koryosa* (*History of Koryo*) and *Choson Wangjo Shillok*. The "running fire" and "fire arrow" are among the firearms that were made by Ch'oe Mu-son between 1377 and 1391. Some types of Chinese fire arrows were rocket propelled but Ch'oe's was an incendiary arrow for shooting from a bow.

Ancient Rockets

The oldest book on Korean firearms, and perhaps the oldest description of rockets in the world, is the *Kukcho Orye Sorye*, published in 1474 and containing figures and detailed descriptions of 23 kinds of firearms that were developed between 1448 and 1452.

Even in the 15th century, Korean rockets were manufactured with considerable precision, as evidenced by the use of a unit of measurement known as the "ri" (0.31 mm). The first Korean rocket was called *Chuhwa*, which literally means "running fire" and was manufactured between 1377 and 1389, near the end of the Koryo dynasty by Ch'oe Mu-son. Detailed descriptions are not available but indirect information indicates that it was a rocket-propelled arrow.

The great King Sejon said to an official in November, 1447:

Running Fire is incomparable and very efficient because it can be fired easily by a mounted soldier using a quiver. It is detrimental to the enemy. Its loud noise and shape instill fear and incite surrender. When used at night, its exhaust flame lightens the fields and shakes the enemy's spirit...

When used where the enemy is lying in ambush, its flame and smoke cause the enemy to disclose themselves for fear. Running Fire does not fly straight. It spends more powder and requires more precautions than cannon.

From these comments we can deduce that Running Fire was a rocket-propelled arrow. Only such a weapon with a rocket motor could be fired from a simple tube like a quiver, make a loud noise as it ejected gases, produce exhaust flames and smoke during flight unlike a rifle or cannon, not generally fly straight due to their stabilizing sticks, and would use more powder than a gun or cannon.

Many types of new Korean style firearms were developed during King Sejong's reign, which was a turning point in the art of making firearms. His rule marked the time when the Choson dynasty stopped imitating the Chinese models and created distinctive Korean style firearms. (Chae, 1990).

Running Fire was developed into three sizes of rocket propelled arrows: small, medium and large. Many were used until 1448, at which time the "Magical Machine Arrows," *shin'gi-jon,* began to appear.

According to the *Hwap'oshik unhae*, the powder tube of Running Fire was the same as that of the "Medium Magical Machine Arrows," which were made from paper. The length of the powder case was 100 mm (4"); the weight of the black powder in a power tube was 44 g.

The "Large Magical Machine Arrow" was 695 mm (2.3') long and 17.8 mm (.7") thick with an internal diameter of 63.1 mm (2-1/2"). The propellant case was charged with black powder and the top was sealed with paper several times. On top of this a large explosive tube was attached, with a fuse that connected the powder of the propellant case to the explosive tube. This cylindrical paper tube was filled with black powder with both ends capped and was divided into four compartments.

Fire Cart

This device had wheels 874.7 mm (2.9') in diameter with a wood hub and 15 spokes. The axle tree was made in three parts: a middle square pillar and two end columns which were inserted into two wheels. Two wide posts were set up at both ends of the top side of the middle square pillar. A small post with a square bottom pillar and a round upper pillar was set up at the center of the square pillar. Thin wooden boards were attached between each wide post and small two-part post. A lower center crossbar with a hole in the center for the small post was placed on two wide posts, and two yokes were set up at both ends. Further boards and crossbars were constructed to hide a wooden box containing some arms.

Four U-shaped nails were driven into the front and middle of the column part of the yokes to insert rods used to pull the fire cart. It could be drawn by two men on level ground but it would require another man pushing from behind when going uphill, and two more men had to push the cart when it was going up a steep hill. This device carried a multiple rocket launcher or a box installed with 50 four arrow guns which could shoot 200 thin arrows at the same time.

This picture of the machine arrow was taken by the author
in the military museum in Seoul S. Korea

Magical Machine Arrow Launcher

This cart had 100 cylindrical holes in a shallow rectangle box that held the explosives in banks. The cart body was raised above the axle by short pillars that regulated the angle from zero to 43 degrees, so that the rocket launch angle could be varied through that range. Capacity was 100 medium or small "Magical Machine Arrows." They were launched 15 at a time in quick succession. In peace time, the fire cart, without its launcher, was used as a simple cart. Seven hundred of these were built in Korea in 1451, according to the *Munjong Shillok.*

Students of ancient Korean firearms can see reproductions of all the firearms used from 1448 to 1451, 4 types of rockets, 13 versions of guns or cannon, six models of bombs, 13 different projectiles, a rocket launcher cart, and an armed cart on permanent display at the Haengju Castle Memorial Museum near Seoul. All were built from descriptions and drawings in the *Kukcho Orye Sorye* by Yeon-Seok Chae who published new plans for these antiques in his book *Early Firearms in Korea 1377-1600* (Ilchi-sa Publishing Co., Seoul, 1981).

WALLS

It is difficult to imagine any sensible nation that would ignore its own natural defenses in planning battle strategies. Why would Korea's generals abandon high rocky bluffs and craggy headlands to meet their enemies on the open plains, if given the option? Yet for this they have been faulted. Furthermore, their numerous victories far from their forts have been ignored by a number of Japanese-influenced Western writers, and their courage and competence at sea downplayed. When fate brought conflict to Korea during times when its people were in a position to adequately equip their soldiers and provide experienced leadership, Koreans distinguished themselves on the open battlefield again and again—against one another during the forming of their kingdoms, against the Mongols for decades, against the Chinese and the Japanese. Even the relatively meager collection of historical records extant plainly displays their competence and bravery. Nevertheless, Boots echoed Korea's detractors when he paid them this backhanded "compliment":

Since the Koreans were geographically and psychologically always on the defense in warfare, the wall naturally came to be their most respected and efficient weapon. Several historians have made special mention of the remarkable bravery, bold courage, and skillful daring which characterized the Korean soldier when he was fighting behind his wall, though attacked by superior forces bound to win.

Also caught up in the disparaging mode of the Japanese was one of Boots' primary sources, a historical commentator identified by him only as Griffis, whom he quotes, in part:

The Koreans are poor soldiers in the open field and exhibit slight proof of personal valor...but put the same men behind walls...they are more than brave, their courage is sublime, they fight to the last man and fling themselves on the bare steel when the foe clears the parapet. The Japanese of 1592 looked upon the Korean in the field as a kitten, but in the castle as a tiger. The French in 1866 never found a force that could face rifles, but behind walls the same men were invincible.

Griffis did not add what the Japanese thought about the Koreans at sea where the Japanese were seriously and consistently battered, outmaneuvered, and defeated. Boots does add afterwards that Admiral Yi had "remarkable skill in naval strategy," a widely known fact the Japanese could not conceal. Looking further back in history, we find Hulbert in his *Korean History* praising the Korean foot soldier: "China was willing to do anything but meet the hardy soldiers of Koguryo in the field."

We can safely assume that Griffis never observed Korean soldiers in open combat during the iron rule of the Japanese Occupation, the time of his writing. We have no way of knowing, then, which was the period of history his source referred to for such a derogatory portrait of the Korean soldier. It can only be assumed that pro-Japanese authorities he sought for information on Koreans gave him a point of view compatible with their goals.

FORTRESSES

There were three main types of Korean walled refuges: walled cities, large fortresses to be used as places of sanctuary for the king in case of invasion, and smaller mountain fortresses. The latter probably were used for a variety of purposes: as dwelling places during the tribal and Three Kingdoms periods when attacks by neighboring tribes and countries were frequent; for the stationing of frontier garrisons; and as bases for waging guerrilla warfare during invasions. There were three walled cities; Seoul, Suwon, and Kanghwa, and three places of refuge for the king; Kanghwa-do, Namhansan-song, and Pukhan-sansong.

Wilbur D. Bacon in his survey, "Fortresses of Kyonggido," an article which appeared in a journal of the Korean Branch of the Royal Asiatic Society, noted that the weapons used to defend these fortresses were arrows and swords until the Yi Dynasty (1392). We know this date is not accurate as documentation exists that catapults were used by Koryo commander Pak So at Kuju prior to this date and undoubtedly before, since Koreans warred against Koreans and Chinese in their forts prior to the arrival of the Mongols and siege machines were bound to have been used.

Needless to say, Korea spent only a small fraction of its long history in the debilitated condition in which the Japanese found it at the end of the 19th century. In more prosperous times, Koreans defeated the Japanese repeatedly, including the rout in 404 A.D. when the Koguryo navy defeated a Japanese fleet sent to aid Paekche and seized temporary control of the Han basin. An obvious example of the Koreans' capacity for enterprising warfare was the period in 392 A.D. when King Kwanggaet'o of Koguryo attacked and captured a number of Paekche fortresses along their border. It is unlikely that this could have been achieved without catapults, even though no records have survived substantiating the precise methods used.

A prime example of Korean fortress-building was T'aejo's capital, Hanson, meaning "Fortress on the Han" at Seoul. Construction began in 1394, and was confined to 49 days in the early spring and 49 days in the late fall in order not to interfere with farming. Conscript labor was extensively used. Workers from each province were required to complete a designated portion of the wall. Records state that 118,000 people worked on it in the spring and 17,400 in autumn. Following the construction of this wall, there was a long period during which no fortresses were built. It was exactly 200 years following the accession of T'aejo to the throne that another invasion, Hideyoshi's, took place and fortresses again became important.

One of the many strategies of fortress-holding was subterfuges. An example which survives concerns General Kwon Yul, commander of Cholla, and the fortress he built called Tok-san-song. From this point, it commands a magnificent view of the main route from Seoul to the southwest. His soldiers attacked Japanese stragglers in the area. During a Japanese siege, the Korean defenders ran out of water. To fool the enemy, General Kwon had a horse washed with rice, which sparkled in the sunshine. Deciding that a garrison which had sufficient water to wash horses could hold out indefinitely, the Japanese withdrew.

In 1629, records show that King Injo, preparing to go to war with the Manchus, began training a large army and establishing new forts in the north. Garrisons on Kanghwa and in Hamhan-sanson were created. The training focused on four areas: guarding gates and walls, musket practice, swordsmanship, and archery. That guarding fortresses was first on the list indicates the importance of this strategy to a nation prepared to be substantially outnumbered, not just dependent on walls to wage war successfully. Crop destruction by the enemy did more to defeat the Koreans than the might of enemy arms.

Except for repair of the Seoul wall during the reign of King Hyojong, no work was done on fortresses subsequently until Sukchong came to the throne in 1657. During his long reign of 45 years there was extensive fortress building and repair. In 1677 the Kanghwa city wall was rebuilt, and in 1710 enlarged to a circumference of almost four miles. In 1693, while on a trip to visit Hunung, the tomb of Chongjong south of Kaesong, the king saw in the distance Munsu-san, the mountain on the mainland opposite Kanghwa. He sent one of his party there to draw a map of the area, and the next year ordered the construction of a fortress leading from the strait between Kanghwa and the mainland, up the mountain and down to the strait again, almost four miles in length. The fortifications of Kanghwa were strengthened and many of the smaller forts on the island were built at the same time. In 1686, 1693 and 1705, additions were made to Nahan-sansong. Sukchong's most outstanding building project, however, was the construction of Pukhan-sansong in 1711, and in 1715 the wall connecting Pukhan-san with the Seoul wall. Pukhan-sansong is over five miles in circumference, the most spectacular of all the fortresses in Kyonggi-do Province south of the Imkjin River where the capitals of three countries have been located and where there were probably more than 50 fortresses.

During the even longer reign of Yongjo, no new fortresses were built, although repairs continued. Bricks and a better grade of concrete began to be used extensively. The last major fortification to be built in Kyonggido was the city wall of Suwon, which has been called, the "crowning glory of Korean fortress building." A palace was built upon the eastern part of the wall, but before the Korean capital could be moved there, the king died in 1800. His successor decided to remain in Seoul.

In the last years of the Yi Dynasty, the fortifications on Kanghwa again played an important part in Korean history. Korea was under siege by the French, irate over the persecution of their priests, and by Americans investigating the burning of their ship, the *General Sherman*, which was on a mission to obtain a trade treaty with the Korean government. The Americans captured five forts on Kanghwa before deciding their mission was both costly and futile and, like the French, they returned home. These successes prompted the Koreans to overestimate their position and underestimate the resources of those seeking economic entree to Korean resources. So, when a Japanese ship passed the north side of the island on September 19, 1875, the fateful decision was made to fire upon it. As previously detailed, this led to Japanese retaliation and the subsequent events signaling the decline of Korean self-government as China, Russia, and Japan vied for supremacy in the Far East. Korean fortresses fell into ruin.

Since the Yi Dynasty, no fortresses in the old style were built. However, most of the fortresses in Kyonggido Province were used during the Korean War, as indicated by the large number of foxholes and trenches dug along their walls. Pukhan-sansong played a particularly important role since it was inside this fortress that the Communist spring offensive of 1952 was stopped and Seoul was saved from a third occupation. Some fortresses have been repaired and are tourist attractions today.

This is one example of a fortress wall that was typical throughout Korean history.

Composition of the Fortresses

The Three Kingdoms fortresses have been difficult to assess as to style of parapets, whether there were any embrasures or what their heights were. With those of stone, the facing was frequently of relatively small shaped stone, backed with unshaped stone mixed with earth. With only a few exceptions, the side of this type of wall was not elevated above ground level. This was accomplished by filling in the space behind the wall up to the point where the natural elevation of the hills on which they rested was the same as the top of the wall. Outside the stone wall, there was frequently an outer wall of earth, at least in those places where attack was most likely. No gates remain. The fortresses may have been entered by means of wooden ramps or ladders, filled with stones or closed with a wooden gate at times of attack, or the gates may have been functionally simple and subject to deterioration. Evidently, from the large amount of tile and broken pottery found inside these fortresses, they contained many buildings which probably were residences for long periods of time. None survive.

It is not possible, said Bacon, to reach any general conclusions concerning Koryo fortresses from those in the area of Kyonggido south of the Imjin River since several are of earth and the existing walls on Kanghwa were built during the Yi Dynasty. It is evident from the stone fortress at Chuksan, however, that a major improvement in fortress architecture had occurred. The outer face of the wall is made from larger stones, much thicker and thus more substantial with square-arch gates still partially standing.

The Yi Dynasty fortresses have stood in fairly good repair. Like the earlier forts, the walls are faced with shaped stone backed with unshaped rock mixed with earth. Many of these facing stones, relatively large and sometimes polished, are shaped like elongated pyramids in order to allow them to be pushed into the backing stone and earth. The gates are two types: large and round-arched, topped with wooden pavilions, and small with round or square arches. The latter probably was used to send out messengers or small parties of soldiers since they were somewhat hidden.

The parapets consisted of crenellated battlements with quite narrow crenels, or open spaces, between the merlons (the tooth-like verticals of the battlements) which were usually 3-4' (91.4-121.9 cm) in height and made from stone or gray brick held in place with concrete. Each merlon had from one to three embrasures or openings for the firing of projectiles.

Inside the fortresses were a number of buildings: soldiers' barracks (all fallen into complete ruin), warehouses, living quarters for the king, Buddhist temples, pavilions, etc. There are also the foundation stones of command posts where the fortress commanders directed battles. As these buildings were usually on high ground on or near the walls, they must have been well protected or the generals could have been killed relatively easily.

Some Fortresses of Interest Surviving To Modern Times

A number of fortresses remaining from Korea's tribal period may still be seen. One of the most deteriorated but beautifully situated is Hamwang-song, located on the western edge of Yongmun-san in Yongch'on-ni, Okch'on-myon, Yang-p'yong-gun. According to legend, about 3,000 years ago, a man named Ham arose from his mother who was a pool in the bed of a stream flowing south from the fortress. He became ruler of the people in the area and attempted to establish a kingdom with its capital inside the fortress he built alongside the stream. He was eventually defeated by the Samhan, an event caused, according to the story, by the fact that he left his mother, the river spring, outside of the fortress walls, thereby showing a lack of filial piety. At Sanha-sa, a small temple in the valley of the fortress, prayers are still recited for the spirit of King Ham. The site of this fortress is quite spectacular: a ring of heavily wooded peaks as high as 1,031 meters (3,383 feet), surrounding a valley through which flows a stream filled with deep pools and beautiful waterfalls. All that remains of the fortress, however, is a pile of stones at the entrance to the valley.

The largest of the Paekche fortresses left in Kyonggido Province is P'ungnam-ni T'osong, located in P'ungnam-ni, Kuch'on-myon, Kwangju'gun, near the bank of the Han River south of the road leading to Inch'on. There are many opposing points of view concerning its origin.

One is that it was the original Hanam Wirye-song of Onjo, first king of Paekche. Other authorities claim it was built during the reign of King Kaero, or that it was the original Snake Fortress built in 286 A.D., or that it was built by the Manchus in 1637. None of these points of view account for the massive size of this earth fortress, almost two miles in circumference. It had no natural protection except for the river and was flooded during the rainy season, so much so that almost all the western part of the wall has been washed away by the river. It seems much too large for a protective fortress, according to Bacon, unless it was the main camp for the army during an invasion. A tablet erected by the Manchus to commemorate the surrender of King Injo is located near the southwest corner of the walls.

Located on Ach'a-san beside the Han River on the eastern edge of Seoul is the fort known as Ahan-song or Changhan-song in Silla times and popularly known as Kwangjin-sansong today. It was probably built in 286 A.D. to protect the Paekche capital. One of the best known Silla songs concerned its recapture. It consists of two parts, a medium-sized fortress on the southern slope of Ahc'a-san and a wall running along the top of the mountain for several miles, only remnants of which survive. The former is quite well preserved with the distinctive feature of the wall rising about ground level on both sides. The fortress was used to protect a small summer house belonging to the former Korean President Syngman Rhee.

One of the most impressive of the Three Kingdoms fortresses in Kyonggido is Kye-yang-sansong, located on Annam-san, southeast of Kyeyang-san in Pup'yong-ni. This fortress was built in such a way that it is a protection against attack from the south rather than the north. It may have been built by Koguryo in the fourth or fifth century. It commands a spectacular view of the Seoul-Inch'on area and has a circumference of perhaps over half a mile.

Another of the most interesting forts in the province is Chukchu Koson, located on a peak east of Pibong-san, just north of Chuksan in Ansong-gun. It was built in 1226 under the direction of General Song Mun-ju. When the Mongols invaded Korea for the second time in 1235, they surrounded this fortress and demanded that the garrison surrender. Instead, the Koreans attacked the invaders. The Mongols then constructed catapults and flung stones into the fortress. The defenders also built catapults and forced the Mongols to withdraw further from the walls. The Mongols then set fire to straw and flung it into the fortress but the Korean soldiers rushed out of the gates and killed many of them. General Song seemed to anticipate all the Mongols' tactics and earned the reputation among his soldiers, according to Bacon, of having clairvoyance. The Mongols finally gave up the siege and withdrew. The fortress has a number of structural peculiarities, including its division in two by a large thick wall.

Kanghwa Island is, of course, a mammoth museum of fort remnants. Sixty to 70 square stone individual forts, alone, according to Bishop Trollope who surveyed them, were built under the direction of General Kim Ki-hwan in 1746. Most were made to hold cannon, 12 being garrisoned continually. Most of these forts surround the entire island but the wall is confined to the eastern shore. They are the only forts of this type in the province. The magnitude of the fortifications and the beauty of the natural scenery make Kanghwa-do one of the most interesting fortresses to visit.

Samnan-song (also Chongjok-sansong), located on Ch'ondung-san in the southeastern corner of Kanghwa-do, was constructed by a son of Tan-gun (Samnang), probably while the Koryo capital was at Kanghwa. The present walls, 1-1/4 miles (2.01168 km) in circumference, the three arched gates, and 705 merlons date from 1738. The fortress was defended by monk soldiers stationed there until the 1890s. Its glory day was October 17, 1866, when a detachment of French soldiers who had been sent there from Kanghwa City, attacked the fortress and were driven away by the Korean defenders who had been reinforced by a group of fierce tiger hunters. This defeat precipitated the French retreat from the island and gave the Korean government a sense of military competence and security that convinced it of the practicality of isolationism. This led to its fatal complacency and the subsequent takeover by the far more ready Japanese.

The Seoul city wall, over 10 miles in circumference, connects four mountains: Nam-san, Tarak-san, Pugak-san, and Inwang-san. It is said the course of the fortress wall follows a line of snow seen by the king one winter morning. The wall had eight gates, two for each of the cardinal directions. Speed was required at the time of their building and, as a result, unshaped stone and even clay were used. The first extensive rebuilding took place in 1422 when 322,400 laborers were mobilized to replace dilapidated sections.

An interesting story concerning the South Gate of the Seoul wall focuses on its sign board and its calligraphy, supposedly that of Prince Yangyong, the oldest brother of King Sejong. This prince preferred scholarly pursuits to politics and was happy to see his younger brother made king. The signboard disappeared following the Japanese invasion and was later found buried in a ditch during the reign of Kwanghae. According to legend, it was located by digging where strange light rays pointed at night. Portions of the wall leading from the gate were destroyed in 1907-08 in order to facilitate the flow of traffic. Only remnants remain of the Seoul City Wall, which rarely provided significant protection from any enemy in history. Its most recent breach was from within as the vastly expanding city grew and industrialized.

One of the larger forts in Kyonggido near Seoul was P'asa-song, located on P'asa-san Mountain in Ch'onso-ri, Taesin-myon, Yoju-gun. It was built in 1592 under the direction of a monk-warrior named Uiam. The location was chosen because it commands an excellent view of the Han River at a ferry crossing from which the Japanese would likely approach.

Like Boots' book, the book *Fortresses of Kyonggido* contains invaluable research into its subject as well as misinformation and negative views of the Korean martial spirit and history. For example, in the introduction it states; "As Korea has always been a small nation surrounded by large powers, it has eschewed any attempt to attain physical security by maintaining a large army trained to defeat invaders on the field of battle or carry the war to the enemy's country, and has instead depended on numerous fortifications."

We are now well aware that for centuries longer than its modern boundaries existed, Korea was a vast country, extending far north through Manchuria and present-day China. Under several leaders it maintained large armies which did indeed defeat invaders on the field of battle. The Korean people's political complexion was far more significant in limiting its readiness at all times than any other factor. We find the slighting of Korean ability in open combat an attitude easy to imagine as having originated with invading forces who found the Korean use of fortresses such a constant source of frustration and humiliation.

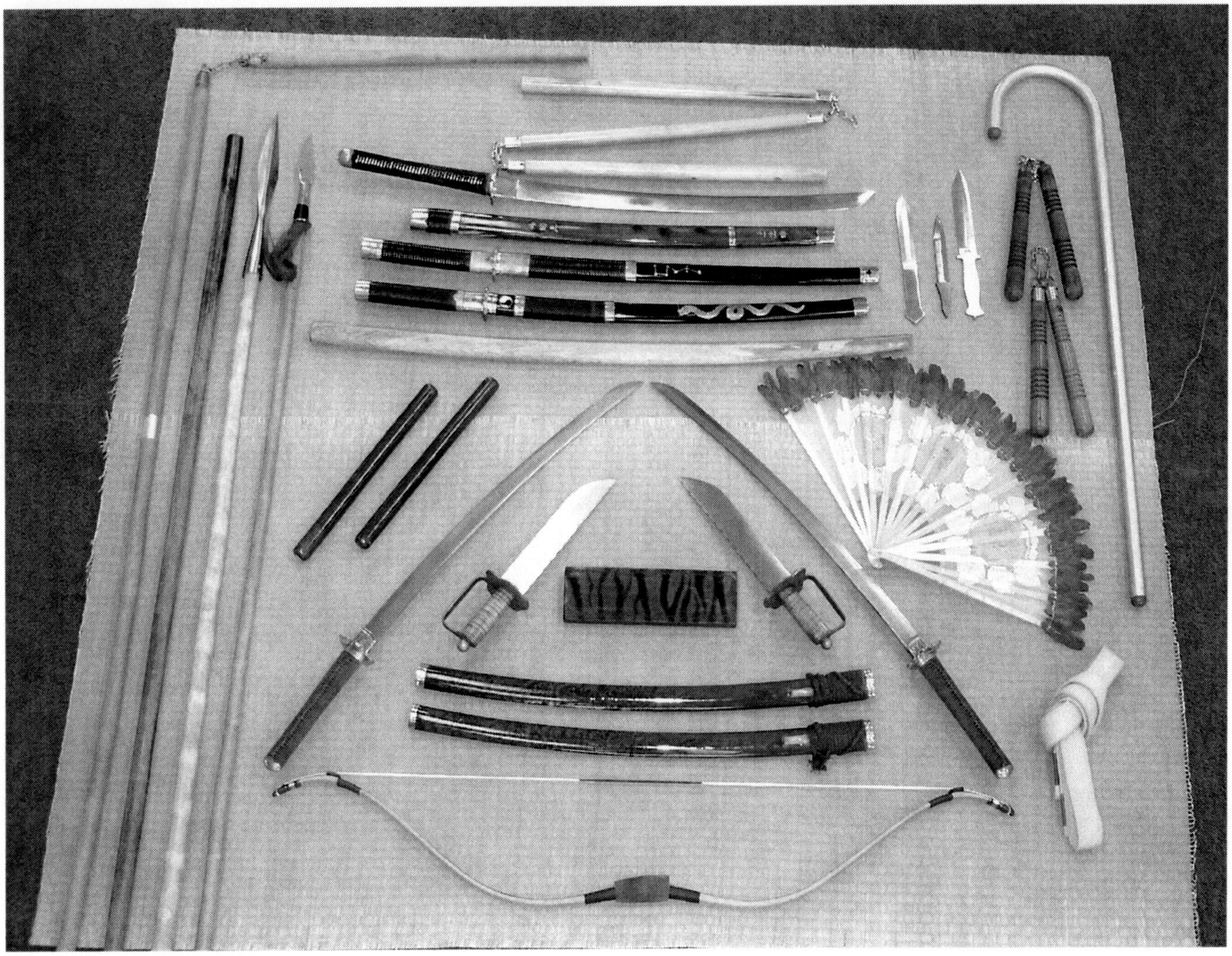

This picture contains some of the author's weapons that are used today in the modern Korean martial art of Kuk Sool Won.

Admiral Yi Sun-sin eloquently stated in his diary (1597) what I believe makes a true martial art master even today.

[undated] *"Warriors who embody culture and martial training are invincible.*

Those skilled in empty-handed combat and the use of arms must first develop their own abilities before requiring it of others.

They must be intelligent and mature before they can teach.

They must first become invincible before they can achieve total victory."

BIBLIOGRAPHY

Bacon, Wilbur D., "Fortresses of Kyongi-do," *Journal of the Royal Asiatic Society*; read before the Society February 13, 1931 (?).

Boots, John L., D.D.S., *Korean Weapons and Armor,* transactions of the Royal Asiatic Society Korea Branch. Vol. XXIV, December, 1934, Part II.

Chae, Yeon-Seok, "Ancient Korean Rockets," *Korea Journal*, July, 1990.

Choy, Bong Youn, *Korea: A History,* Charles E. Tuttle Co., Rutland, Vermont, 1971.

Covell, Jon Carter, Dr. & Alan, *Korean Impact on Japanese Culture: Japan's Hidden History,* Hollym International Corp., Elizabeth, New Jersey, 1984.

Frankl, John; translation in manuscript of *Muye Tobo Tonji (Illustrated Martial Arts Textbook)* by Yi Tok-Mu, Pak Che-Ga, and Paek Tong-Su, by order of King Yong Jo (Chongjo),1790; Berkeley, California, 1989.

Gale, James Scarth, *History of the Korean People,* Tae-won Publishing Co. Seoul, Korea, 1972.

Grant, Bruce K., *Korean Proverbs* ("Dragon Head," "Snake Tail," and "A Frog in a Well"), Moth House, Salt Lake City, Utah, 1982.

Ha, Tae-Hung & Mintz, Grafton K., translators, *Samguk* Yusa *(Legends and History of the Three Kingdoms of Ancient Korea)*, Yonsei University Press, Seoul, 1972.

Ha, Tae-Hung, translator, *Imjin Chang Ch'o (Admiral Yi, Sun-Sin's Memorials to Court),* Yonsei University Press, Seoul, 1979.

Ha, Tae-Hung, translator, *Nanjung Ilgi (War Diary of Admiral Yi, Sun-Sin),* Yonsei University Press, Seoul, 1977.

Ha, Tae-Hung, *Behind the Scenes of Royal Palaces in Korea (Yi Dynasty),* Yonsei University Press, Seoul,1983.

Ha, Tae-Hung, *Tales from the Three Kingdoms,* Yonsei University Press, Seoul, 1969.

Haboush Kim, Ja Hyun, *A Heritage of Kings: One Man's Monarchy in the Confucian World),* Columbia University Press, New York, 1988.

Hong, Won Tack, *Relationship Between Korea and Japan in Early Period: Paekche and Yamato Wa,* published by Il Sim Sa, Seoul, 1988.

Henthorn, W. E., *Korea: The Mongol Invasions,* E. J. Brill, Leiden, The Netherlands, 1963.

Henthorn, William E., "Some Notes on Parhae (P'ohai)," *Journal of the Royal Asiatic Society Korea Branch*; read before the Society February 13, 1931(?).

Hulbert, Homer B., *History of Korea (2 vols.),* Seoul, 1905, reprinted by Hillary House, New York, 1962.

Hulbert, Homer B., *The Passing of Korea,* Yonsei University Press, Seoul, 1969.

Han, Woo-Keun, *The History of Korea,* translator Kyung-Sik Lee, Eul-Yoo Publishing Co., Seoul, 1970.

Jamieson, John Charles, translator, *The Samguk Sagi and the Unification Wars,* Ph.D. dissertation (Language and Literature) in manuscript, University of California, Berkeley, 1969.

Keith, Elizabeth and Scott, Elspet Keith Robertson, *Old Korea: Land of the Morning Calm*, Philosophical Library, New York, 1947.

Kim, Jeong-Hak, *The Prehistory of Korea,* first published by Kawade Shobo, Japan, 1972; translated and edited by Richard J. and Kazue Pearson, University of Hawaii Press, Honolulu, 1978.

Kim, Samuel Dukhae, *"The Korean Monk Soldiers in the Imjin Wars: An Analysis of Buddhist Resistance to the Hideyoshi Invasion, 1592-1598,* Ph.D. dissertation (Philosophy) in manuscript, Columbia University, 1978.

Kim, Won-Yong, "Problems in Korean Cultural Research," *Korea Journal*, September, 1990.

Kim, Hyun Koo, "A Study of Korea-Japan Relations in Ancient Times: Centering on the Taika Reforms and Formation of Cooperation Among Shilla, Japan and Tang, China," *Korea Journal*, October, 1989.

Korea, Government of, Office of Public Information, *Korea: Her History and Culture,* Seoul, (undated).

Korea, Government of, Korean Overseas Information Services, *Korean History: Focus on Korea,* Seoul International Publishing House, Seoul, 1986.

Kim, Zae Geun, "An Outline of Korean Shipbuilding History", *Korea Journal*, October, 1989.

Kim, J. Jaihiun, translator, *Poems By Zen Masters,* Hanshin Publishing. Co., Seoul, 1988.

Kim, Yung Chung, editor, translator *Women of Korea; A History from* Ancient *Times to 1945,* Ewha Women's University Press, Seoul, 1976.

Lee, Ki-Baik, *A New History of Korea,* translator Edward W. Wagner with Edward J. Shultz, Ilchokak Publishing Co., Seoul, 1984.

Lee, Peter H., ed., *Sourcebook of Korean Civilization* (2 vols), Columbia University Press, 1996.

Lee, Yoon Ki, "The Sonbi Spirit and its Manifestation in the Political Domain," *Korea Journal*, April, 1989.

Okamoto, Shumpei, *Impressions Of The Front (Woodcuts of the Sino-Japanese War, 1894-95),* Introduction by Donald Keene, Philadelphia Museum of Art/Eastern Press, 1983.

Pak, Yangjin, "The Armored Warriors of Kaya,", *JOM* Journal of The Minerals, Metals & Materials Society, January, 1995.

Park, Yune-Hee, *Admiral Yi Sun-Shin and His Turtleboat Armada,* Hanjin Publishing Co., Seoul, 1978.

Sato, Kanzan, *The Japanese Sword,* translated & adapted by Joe Earl, Kandansha International/USA Ltd., with Harper & Row Publishers Inc., New York, 1983.

Storey, Robert, *Korea,* Lonely Planet Publications, Hawthorn, Australia, 4th edition, 1997.

Sugaware, Makoto, *Lives of Master Swordsmen,* East Publications, Inc., Tokyo, Japan, 1988.

Suh, In Hyuk, *Kuk Sool: Traditional Korean Martial Art,* Pusan, Korea, 1984.

Suh, In Hyuk, ed., Barry Harmon and Jay Lee, contributing writers, *A Brief History of the Korean Martial Arts,* Houston, Texas, 1991.

Suh, In Hyuk and Jane Hallander, *The Fighting Weapons of Korean Martial Art,* Unique Publications, Burbank, Ca. 1988.

Winchester, Simon, *Korea: A Walk Through the Land of Miracles,* Grafton Books, London, 1988.

Yumoto, John M., *The Samurai Sword: A Handbook,* Charles E. Tuttle, Tokyo and Rutland, 1958.

Yun, C. K., *Third Millennium of Korean History,* Youl Hwa Dang, Seoul, 1989.

CPSIA information can be obtained at www.ICGtesting.com
Printed in the USA
BVOW051307150113

310675BV00004B/494/P

9 781598 585636